Boosey & Hawkes

The publishing story

Boosey & Hawkes

The publishing story

Helen Wallace

BOOSEY & HAWKES

First published in 2007
by Boosey & Hawkes Music Publishers Ltd
Aldwych House, 71-91 Aldwych, London WC2B 4HN

www.boosey.com

British Library Cataloguing in Publication Data
A catalogue record for this publication can be obtained from the British Library

ISBN 978-0-85162-514-0

Managing Editor: David Allenby
Picture Research: Jo Dawson/David Allenby
Designed and typeset by David Plumb ARCA PPSTD
Printed and bound in Germany by WEGA Verlag GmbH, Mainz

Contents

Introduction

The invitation to delve into the history of Boosey & Hawkes as a
publishing company was irresistible: from Bartók to Britten, Copland to
Kodály, Shostakovich and Strauss to Stravinsky, who of any importance
had not come under its imprint? Today B&H has contracts with Adams,
Birtwistle, Górecki, Lindberg, MacMillan and Reich. Then there was the
light music: not a day goes by when we are not reminded of the firm's
success in that area by *The Archers'* theme tune. In educational music B&H
first published Bartók's *Mikrokosmos*, Kodály's *Choral Method* and went
on with the innovative violin tutors of Sheila Nelson, Christopher Norton's
Microjazz and many other best-sellers.

But this is to scratch the surface of nearly eighty years' worth of activity,
and indeed it would take another, much more thorough-going academic
study to uncover all the complex workings of this company and its
composers. That was never my remit: I was asked to write a brief,
20,000-word summary of the main events in the publishing company's
history. The idea was that this should not be a mere vanity project, but a
lively account of the triumphs, trials and tribulations of a company as seen
through the eyes and ears of those involved. The living presence of many
of these protagonists and the availability of correspondence led me to
adopt a journalistic style, in which events could be described in the often
colourful language of witnesses, rather than as a monochrome report.
What soon became clear was the impossibility of isolating the business of
B&H from the cultural and economic events of the time: the Depression,
the Second World War and the aesthetic revolutions that followed it all
played their part in the story of an international music publisher.

20,000 words soon grew to 150,000 as I unravelled the relationships with
important composers from the often hair-raising internal politics of the
company. (The story of Benjamin Britten's interaction with B&H staff has
not been aired in detail before, and is particularly significant.) In order to
keep the project from sprawling out of control, I was compelled to focus
on the 'serious music' side of the business as it was run from the London
headquarters. I am all too aware that there is more to be written about the
light music department, and the work of the New York office, and the hubs
in Germany and France, not to mention the original offices in Australia
and South Africa. Moreover, the history of Boosey & Hawkes as an
instrument manufacturer is a fascinating story in its own right and
deserves to be told. A clear decision was made to deal with it in this
volume only when it directly affected the publishing business.

Another constraint on the writing of the book was time: 295 Regent Street, the London headquarters of Boosey & Hawkes for 75 years, was being vacated in 2005. There were just four months to go through the entire archive housed in the basement of the building. Thousands upon thousands of files of business affairs and composer correspondence needed to be investigated: a daunting task for one person armed with only the bare facts of the history. Knee-deep in dust and papers I was at once aware of the privilege and the futility of the task. On opening a box, a letter from Vaughan Williams, Walton, Copland or Britten was as likely to appear as an order for three copies of *God Save the Queen*. I shall never forget coming upon Box file 72, which contained a complete record of almost daily war-time correspondence between Ralph Hawkes in London and Hans Heinsheimer in New York for the years 1941–43; Box 73, 74 and thereafter unaccountably contained permissions slips and some rights correspondence. Such random finds became commonplace: it was a question of picking out the gems and moving on.

Some readers may be surprised that there is not more interview material here with living composers. Perhaps the answer lies in German composer Detlev Glanert's comment: 'The relationship between a composer and his publisher is like a marriage.' Trust and discretion are paramount: this was not a publication for kiss-and-tell revelations. While information on contracts and fees was occasionally available for deceased composers, naturally all such information on living composers is confidential.

As you will discover, Boosey & Hawkes has survived any number of commercial environments: it has been a public limited company and is now once again a private company, operating successfully today in a streamlined form where rights management and promotion are paramount, printing and manufacturing a thing of the past. My research was full of surprises: boardroom battles, family feuds, fraud and plain good fortune all play their part. Above all, I have glimpsed a largely unseen, backstage world, peopled by extraordinary characters whose influence on music in the 20th century has been greater than they could ever know.

Helen Wallace
London, 2007

Publisher's note

Our gratitude to Helen Wallace extends well beyond her agreement to undertake this history. What started as a modest booklet to mark the 75th anniversary of the company grew inexorably as her researches revealed an unexpected wealth of detail. The enlarged form of the book, coupled with the stringent time pressures we put on her, would have daunted a lesser spirit. Faced with a basement archive resembling an obstacle course, with box locations changing mysteriously from day to day as materials were packed up for remote storage, Helen battled the odds against an impossible deadline.

After this frantic rush, the timescales reversed and the schedule for production stretched ever longer as we settled into new offices, weathered a corporate sale process and undertook the necessary fact-checking and legal clearances. To say that we tested Helen's patience through this period would be an understatement.

The resulting history is much more than a company chronology. We are indebted to Helen for bringing our professional forbears to life and shining a light on hidden corners of our past. Our hope is that this book will provide the impetus for future research into the history of twentieth-century music publishing.

David Allenby
Boosey & Hawkes Music Publishers
London, 2007

Acknowledgements xi

My thanks to all the people who gave so generously of their time and knowledge:
David Allenby, Nona Ampenoff, Louis Andriessen, Paul Banks, Nigel Boosey, Simon Boosey, Michael Boxford, David Bray, Arnold Broido, Sally Cavender, Nicholas Clark at the Britten-Pears Library, Robert Cowan, Sally Cox, Jo Dawson, David Drew, Colin Dunn, Tony Fell, Katherine Gale, Detlev Glanert, HK Gruber, Martin Hall, Ian Julier, Jim Kendrick, Calum MacDonald, Simon Maguire at Sotheby's, Nicholas Maw, John Minch, Donald Mitchell, Tony Pool, Steve Reich, Stephen Richards, Janis Susskind and Marion Thorpe.

I had access to recorded archive interviews with: Roger Brison, Sylvia Goldstein, Muriel James, Richard Mackie, James MacMillan, Kenneth Pool and Stuart Pope.

Helen Wallace

Credits

It was never a love match: Leslie Boosey, the very model of a Victorian
gentleman, dignified, inscrutable, with a strong sense of family duty, the
heir to a rich and venerable music business that owned half of upper
Regent Street; and the dashing Ralph Hawkes, 11 years his junior, an
ocean-racing yachtsman, a champion of the Cresta Run, an instinctive
entrepreneur of vast ambition and steely determination, a man who
belonged to the future. Legend has it that Ralph Hawkes assisted with
the evacuation of Dunkirk. For Leslie Boosey a game of chess was 'too
exciting'. For Hawkes, though he laughed to admit it, after the blitz he
missed 'the howling banshee and sweet symphony of gunfire'. And while
he was throwing lavish parties in his Knightsbridge penthouse, Boosey,
famously frugal, reportedly brought apples from his Hertfordshire
orchard to sell to the staff. Ralph lived at large and at break-neck speed,
burning out suddenly in his early fifties, mourned by an international
coterie of admirers. Boosey was the survivor, nursing the company
through painful transition, living to see his family ousted from the
business he had built up, and dying at 92 without even a *Times* obituary.
More significantly, Boosey had four children, while Hawkes had two
wives but no heirs, a fact that would one day bring the company to the
brink of destruction. And yet, despite all their differences, the twenty-
year partnership of Boosey and Hawkes created one of the world's great
music companies, whose legacy shines with artistic vision and
commercial acumen 75 years on.

Leslie Boosey (1887-1979)
Ralph Hawkes (1898-1950)

So how did they work together? 'He was the engine, I was the brakes,' recalled Boosey of Ralph Hawkes. This was typically self-effacing: there is evidence that both men had an inexhaustible energy for building the business: hundreds upon hundreds of letters reveal a downpour of bold decisions, deals and contracts formulated in meticulous detail and at great speed, an international network of influential contacts nurtured with charm and diplomacy. They also had important life experiences in common: both had served, and suffered, in the First World War. Ralph was wounded, and Leslie watched his brother die at Ypres and was then interned in a prisoner of war camp. Both lost their fathers in 1919/20, immediately inheriting large businesses, Ralph when he was only in his early twenties. Both were cosmopolitan in outlook: Hawkes attended the Handelhochschule in St Gallen and Boosey learnt his trade at Debussy's publisher, Durand et Fils in Paris, where he also studied singing. Both had travelled in the States; Boosey had even attended the New York premiere of Puccini's *La Fanciulla del West* in 1910. Neither could be accused of artistic snobbery: both of their companies had dealt with music on every level, from ballads to Beethoven, from film tracks to military marches.

Crucially, neither had musical pretensions: although Boosey had a fine discernment for voices, having studied with Jean de Reske, his comments on music are strictly personal, modest and always defer to authority. He had in a smaller way what Hawkes had been exceptionally blessed with, a *nose* rather than an ear for music, 'an instinctive reaction to the slightest jerk of the inborn divining rod, the only reliable guide in the arid desert of music publishing, where so many, equipped with a doctorate in music from the University of Oregon lose their way and are never heard of again'. So wrote the one-time employee, publisher and author Hans Heinsheimer. He goes on, in praise of Hawkes, 'He was not led astray by personal taste, misguided by prejudice, cockily opinionated, burdened by tradition, blinded by jealousy, allergic to open fifths ... he had never heard of parallel octaves nor did he know what Josquin des Près had done for this world. He was a born music publisher.'

Though both men were more personally allied with the music publishing side of their businesses, both also manufactured instruments. In Hawkes's case, this side of the firm was run by his wheeler-dealer elder brother Geoffrey, an equally flamboyant but erratic and rather unreliable character. In Boosey's case there was a host of family members and associates caretaking the instrument workshops, including his cousin Evelyn, who was head of the factory's military department. And it was the competition in that market which eventually persuaded both that a merger was mutually advantageous: 'We can work together or cut each other's throats discounting instruments,' Leslie Boosey is said to have declared.

The two companies

Thomas Boosey, founder of Boosey & Co in 1816

Boosey & Sons was set up by John Boosey as a London lending library in the late 18th century. His grandson Thomas expanded the musical side of the library and imported scores from abroad, including works by Rossini and Hummel, Donizetti and Verdi. His own company, founded in 1816, controlled the British rights to popular Italian operas including *La Traviata* and *Rigoletto*, or rather he had hoped he did, but a celebrated lawsuit (*Boosey v Jeffreys*) deprived him of these and numerous other works. As a result of this blow, around 1850, Thomas's son John began issuing cheap editions of the classics, for parlour consumption, and later the Royal Edition of Operas. He specialised in opera buffa and this time the uncontestable English rights were obtained for Lecocq's *La Fille de Madame Angot*, and Edmond Audran's *La Mascotte*. He also ventured into wind and brass instrument manufacture, which was destined to become a significant part of the business.

More important still was the launch in 1867 of the London Ballad Concerts. For seventy years these events proved the most successful musical formula on the market, presenting an irresistible mix of star singers, sentimental ballads, orchestral lollipops and exotic virtuosi. Boosey both presented the artists and published the music they were singing, and for several decades this near-monopoly over both proved highly lucrative. Tenor Sims Reeve sang *Come into the garden, Maud* – Michael Balfe's setting was made at the suggestion of John Boosey himself – in 1870; Dame Clara Butt launched *Land of Hope and Glory* at a 1902 concert and John McCormack's appearances singing *Bless this House* and *I hear you calling me* paved the way to his international career. The concerts, held at first in St James's Hall in Regent Street, and then the Queen's Hall and Royal Albert Hall, also built the foundations of a serious music catalogue at a time when divisons between serious and popular were unselfconsciously blurred. Alongside Sullivan's *The Lost Chord*, Adams's *The Holy City*, *Danny Boy* and Liddle's *Abide with me* came premieres of Elgar's *Pomp and Circumstance Marches*, *Sea Pictures* and Delius's *Sea Drift*. It is important to remember that Leslie Boosey was

St James's Hall in Regent
Street, venue for the Boosey
Ballad Concerts between
1867 and 1894
(Image from the Illustrated News of
the World, 1858)

familiar with the world's top flight musicians: artists appearing at Boosey concerts included cellists Piatti, Madame Suggia and Leo Stern, who premiered the Dvořák Concerto, violinists Mischa Elman, Henri Vieuxtemps and Jan Kubelík, the double bassist Bottesini, the Dolmetsch family (who gave a concert of early music in 1897), Percy Grainger and Rachmaninoff himself, who appeared as pianists. The celebrity allure of the Boosey events gave the best promotion to their sheet music, and sales in the peak year of 1919 exceeded two million copies.

In 1874 John Boosey had moved the firm to 295 Regent Street, where Boosey & Hawkes would eventually be based, and was there assisted by his nephews William and Arthur. William played an influential part in the rival publishing house Chappell & Co from about 1894 (his flamboyant life story of boom and bust is told in *Fifty Years of Music*), but Arthur directed the firm throughout the ballad boom, dying in 1920 at which point his son Leslie took over (and remained as Chairman of the company, apart from one or two years, until 1964).

William Hawkes, founder of Hawkes & Son in 1865

That same year Geoffrey and Ralph Hawkes inherited the firm of Hawkes & Son from their father, and split responsibilities between the music publishing – Ralph – and instrument manufacturing – Geoffrey. They were grandsons of William Henry Hawkes, a member of the Scots Fusilier Guards and the State trumpeter to Queen Victoria, known as the 'Little Corporal'. Upon his retirement in 1865, William joined forces with the French bandmaster Jules Rivière. They had both had an interest in providing printed music for reed and brass bands, which extended to the manufacture of instruments, fittings and reeds when William's son Oliver had become involved. The Empire provided a large market for the latter: no maharajah worth his salt would be without an entire military band, equipped with every instrument including clarinets and flutes. After Oliver Hawkes took over, he launched the *Military Band Journal*, which published pieces for bands, educational tutors for every type of instrument and great quantities of orchestral arrangements. Hawkes's commercial hits included *The Glow Worm, Venus on Earth, Valse September* and *In the Shadow*, which sold over a million copies. In 1913 came the biggest hit of all, *Colonel Bogey*, by the army major F J Ricketts (aka Kenneth Alford), who had stumbled on the tune while playing golf. It was one of seventeen 'quick marches' published by Hawkes, and forty years later achieved another wave of success when it was chosen as the song whistled by servicemen in the film *Bridge on the River Kwai*.

The merger

By the late twenties, Hawkes & Sons had become a prosperous company without representing a single significant composer. Based in Denman Street off Piccadilly Circus, and involved in a minor way with music for film, it was viewed as a relatively junior company from 'tin pan alley'. This was to overlook Ralph Hawkes's pioneering work during the twenties. In 1925 he bought the catalogue of Winthrop Rogers, a discerning editor of vocal and piano music, whose list included works of John Ireland, Frank Bridge, Armstrong Gibbs, Julius Harrison and Peter Warlock. And throughout the twenties he travelled to the Continent, seeking to acquire the British agency of the Viennese publishing giant Universal Edition and its Wiener Philharmonischer Verlag, something he would eventually achieve ten years on. He also made the acquaintance of Éditions Belaieff of Leipzig and Édition Russe de Musique and Gutheil of Paris, both owned by Serge and Natalie Koussevitzky. Thus Hawkes forged the necessary links that would enable him, with Boosey's capital and the fortunes of war, to construct a catalogue that reads like a roll-call of the twentieth century's greatest composers.

The Hawkes & Son office in Denman Street, which continued to be used after the merger (c1900)

Leslie Boosey, too, had shown foresight and independence during the twenties in the critical matter of performing rights. The Performing Right Society (PRS) had been formed in 1914 in an attempt to create a system of obtaining performance revenue for composers, songwriters and their publishers. Yet as ballad sales were still riding high at the end of the First World War, many publishers objected to the principle of charging for performances. When LAB (as he was known in the business, and from henceforth will be titled) first took over the reins of the company, he was torn between two worlds. Despite the fact that his cousin William Boosey was one of the founding fathers of the Society, he was not convinced. LAB's son Simon recalls, 'It just did not make sense to him to charge for playing Boosey's music. He felt it would just discourage use of the songs they were promoting, thus harming sales of sheet.'

Yet LAB was all too aware of the sudden and seismic upheaval in the economics of the music trade in the twenties. Figures from six publishers, including Boosey's, show that between 1921 and 1929, sales of sheet music fell from £537,000 to £318,000. In 1924 cinemas were employing over half of the membership of the Musicians Union, all playing live from sheet music. After the arrival in Britain in 1929 of *The Jazz Singer*, cinemas adopted mechanically-produced music within months and an entire slice of the music market disappeared. Hawkes had the resources and resourcefulness to find another, long-term solution to this collapse in film music: in 1937 he founded his own Recorded Music Library, Cavendish Music Company. It provided the entertainment industry with an affordable supply of light music which could be simply licensed through one source. Decca was awarded the contract to make the first 78s, and Hawkes gathered his own scratch band, the Regent Concert Orchestra, to play mood music by such as Armstrong Gibbs and Arthur Wood, whose *Barwick Green* proved a record-breaking success, and is still heard 24 times a week on BBC Radio 4 – *The Archers'* theme tune.

But that is to leap ahead. The craze for American 'hot' dance music swept over Britain, gradually edging out the ballads and their appeal to the

Staff of Hawkes & Son (c1900)

THE · STAFF · OF

·HAWKES· AND ·SON·

DENMAN STREET, · PICCADILLY CIRCUS, LONDON, W.

sentiments, with jazz and its appeal to the body. In economic terms, this meant a reduction in the number of concerts, and a drastic decline in amateur music-making as, by 1926, two million homes already enjoyed the London Radio Dance Band twice a week from the BBC. Nevertheless, as head of one of the biggest and most influential publishers, LAB showed considerable pluck and imagination when, in that same year, he decided to cross the floor and join the PRS board.

Almost immediately he made his mark in a series of legal battles. In 1926 he successfully fought off the BBC's decision to combat 'plugging' by preventing announcements of the names of works or their composers. By 'plugging' the Corporation meant, in effect, the bribing of performers by publishers to ensure their music was prominently and frequently played. Boosey 'deplored the practice' (though of course he was able, quite legally, to do the same thing on a grander scale at his own ballad concerts) but rightly insisted that no composer should ever go unacknowledged. More famously, in 1929, he helped defeat the Tuppence Bill through Parliament, a crazy proposal which would have meant two pennies would be the largest amount ever paid for the performance of a piece of music.

The Simplicity Tutor, first published by Hawkes & Son in 1903

It was on the board of the PRS that Ralph Hawkes and LAB had the opportunity of assessing each other's strengths. Hawkes must have seen an experienced and skilful negotiator in LAB, and a man of quiet confidence and steely determination. LAB saw a charismatic rival, with serious ambitions in the music field. As he recalled in a tribute to his colleague: 'Anyone meeting him was quickly impressed with his powerful personality and tremendously vital and active mind. He gave everything he had to everything he undertook.' Boosey recognised that no one in his immediate family could match Hawkes's flair and drive for music publishing. Great savings would also be made if they could combine their instrument manufacturing businesses. After six months of negotiations, the merger was completed in October 1930.

The home front

At the initial joint board meeting of Boosey & Hawkes two decisions were made of enduring consequence. The first was that the company would actively develop its serious music catalogue. At first this meant building on Boosey's current list of works by Elgar, Delius, Ireland and Holst, rather than pursuing younger composers. The second decision was to develop 295 Regent Street as the headquarters of the new firm, a psychological boost coming as it did as the Depression hit. Hawkes's Denman Street premises were retained as were the factories in Edgware, built in 1924. In the first Directors' report, in February 1931, the Chairman notes that the accounts had been skewed by the 'active and intensive competition' that existed between the two companies up until the point of amalgamation. The first share certificate was issued in October 1930. Astonishingly, not a year went by without a dividend being paid until 1982.

Though Hawkes and LAB sat in next-door offices with their own secretaries on the third floor of Regent Street, it is clear that in the early years LAB still had one foot in his former life. He continued to use his Boosey notepaper and to correspond with singers and musicians appearing in his concerts (the final London Ballad Concert did not take place until 1933). He was clearly regarded as the nation's Mr Music, and the smallest queries came his way from the highest places: in 1931 the Marchioness of Londonderry asked if he knew an old song 'about an Arbutus tree' and could he please post a copy to the Prime Minister with all due haste. Sir Adrian Boult at the BBC was on familiar terms, as were

The Regent Street premises in 1820, 1870 and 1936.
(The Boosey & Hawkes Gazette 1937)

The Pile 1820

1936

Rebuilt 1870

John McCormack, Vaughan Williams and Roger Quilter, who, like many composers, was indignant at LAB's request to make the piano part of a song easier: 'I'm afraid I cannot make a different ending to "I arise from dreams of thee". It would entirely spoil the shape of the song. I'm sure you will see my point.' That same year he sent a new 'school song book' to the Head of Schools, Sir Percy Buck, in the hope it could be distributed throughout the land, and pestered a sceptical Sir Hugh Allen at the Royal College of Organists to give his new Hammond organ a decent trial (a major contract was signed with Hammond Organs in 1935 and soon after in America: it was to become one of the firm's best-selling brands).

New directions: all paths lead to Vienna

This period of busy, local, low-key activity was not to last long, as Ralph Hawkes recalls in an essay on Béla Bartók. He had first heard his music in 1931: 'I am bound to admit that I had little interest in it at the time – the merger of Boosey & Company and Hawkes & Sons had just been effected and found us so steeped in ballads, popular orchestra and band music that the "newfangled" musical ideas passed us by. However, in 1933, our policy changed. Realising the force of what was being done in Central Europe by Universal Edition in the direction of contemporary publications, I interested myself in this development and shortly afterwards we became the sole agents for Universal. This brought about direct contact with the music of Bartók and his great friend and compatriot Zoltán Kodály... At that time ... [Bartók's] music was heard only at gatherings of "believers" ... the great orchestras, radio and concert artists, except in rare cases, eschewed performances of such "Chinese Chord Music".'

Béla Bartók (c1936)
(Photo: Kalman Kata)

Though it was several years before Hawkes would have Bartók and Kodály on his own books, by 1933 he had embarked on a mission to find new composers in earnest.

Another visitor to the Universal Edition (UE) offices in 1934 was a young English composer. He went there to experience the excellence and

The Universal Edition offices in Vienna, with Erwin Stein (seated, left) (c1930)
(Photo: Universal Edition A.G., Wien)

professionalism of the Viennese orchestras, and to have lessons from Alban Berg, but was bold enough to hand a bundle of his scores to a certain Hans Heinsheimer, who passed them to an editor named Erwin Stein – who was 'very nice indeed'. Stein, in turn, was impressed by what he saw. Their paths were to cross again. But no one could have then predicted that the Jewish Viennese staff of Universal Edition – Stein, Heinsheimer and Ernst Roth – would end up as editor, agent and publisher to the greatest British composer of his generation: Benjamin Britten.

'Let Booseys waste some money on him'

The key, of course, was Ralph Hawkes. Like Britten, he looked to Central Europe for inspiration, and had the foresight, after the 1938 Anschluss, to look out for the most talented executives from UE. But back in 1934, he was becoming more and more intrigued by the works of the 22-year-old Britten, then published by Herbert Foss at Oxford University Press (OUP). His *Phantasy* for oboe quartet was chosen to be performed at the International Society for Contemporary Music festival in Florence, and OUP had several other works in their catalogue already, including the Simple Symphony. Foss was dithering, reluctant to commit to the young composer, despite his opinion of *A Boy was Born*, which he named 'one of the most remarkable choral works I have ever heard'. He still felt Britten was mostly writing 'uncommercial' pieces and saw no danger in allowing Hawkes to publish the *Sinfonietta* and *Phantasy* oboe quartet, writing in an internal memo: 'it may be worth while to let Boosey waste some money on him so long as we can keep his more remunerative efforts'.

Foss would rue the day he allowed Hawkes to become involved with Britten. His rival publisher had all but insisted that Britten join the PRS when he agreed to publish the *Sinfonietta* and oboe quartet, while Foss was set against joining the collecting society, believing, as many still did at that time, that membership would discourage performances. But this difference of opinion quickly became critical: when it was clear an agreement could not be reached, Britten withdrew the *Friday Afternoons* songs from Foss. By January 1935 the composer had had enough of the 'bother and hold-up' with publications at OUP, and decided to throw in his lot with Boosey & Hawkes. Immediately, Hawkes proved a more dynamic and forward-thinking collaborator: he published *Friday Afternoons* and immediately commissioned a piano suite, *Holiday Tales* (later called *Holiday Diary*) which was performed by Betty Humby at the Wigmore Hall in November to kinder reviews

Benjamin Britten, c.1938
(Photo: Enid Slater. Courtesy of the Britten-Pears Library, Aldeburgh)

than Britten had been used to. Ralph Hawkes's approach was also more holistic: he offered the young composer work vetting scores, introductions to foreign publishers and was willing to act as his ad hoc agent in the commercial music world. It was with Hawkes's encouragement and contacts that Britten gained valuable work in film and theatre between 1935 and 1939.

If the signing of Britten was a red letter day in the history of the company, it took a while for some staff to realise it. Hawkes, who immediately became, and remained, friendly with Britten, had to champion his cause time and again on the Board during the next decade. Hawkes recalled that the first time he was able to face the Board and the shareholders and *not* have to account for the loss made on Britten was in 1946, when the international success of *Peter Grimes* was plain for all to see (in the year of its premiere over 700 vocal scores of the opera were sold in Britain). Yet hire library records show that in the thirties, Britten's newest scores enjoyed considerable interest. After its initial run at the Mercury Theatre, *The Ascent of F6* received seventeen performances over the next two years.

And before war broke out the company had already published the perennially popular *Variations on a theme of Frank Bridge* (1937), as well the ambitious Auden collaboration, *Our Hunting Fathers*. This work was dedicated to Hawkes, who failed utterly to detect its underlying political and symbolic messages, unless this was written tongue-in-cheek: 'It is very nice of you and I feel a little awkward in this respect, for I know nothing at all about hunting, neither am I a father but I will try to live up to it by learning more about monkeys and other hunting animals.' Britten wrote several overtly left-wing political pieces in his early years with B&H, to which Hawkes, a conservative capitalist to the marrow, never objected. However, from 1937 onwards, he did begin to steer Britten towards more conventional musical forms, brokering the BBC commission for the Piano Concerto, pushing for the Violin Concerto, suggesting a work for children rather like Prokofieff's *Peter and the Wolf* and encouraging Britten to think about opera: he gave him a score of *Rigoletto* for a Christmas present in 1938.

Ralph began to treat the young Britten to expensive dinners and motor trips – they shared a passion for powerful cars and played fiercely competitive games of squash. For the rest of his life, he was something of a godfather to Britten. He expected – and demanded – the earth from his protégé, but would go to extraordinary lengths to ensure his every material need was met, especially during the war years. He was both mentor and manager, nurturer and counsellor. Britten's respect and affection for Ralph never wavered despite the various crises and differences of opinion that were to follow. 'You could tell him *anything*,' Britten recalled near the end of his life to Managing Director Tony Fell. The implication was that Hawkes was utterly relaxed about Britten's homosexuality, at a time when few others were.

Almost immediately after joining Boosey & Hawkes, Britten took an active interest in the running of the firm, a quality that marks him out from almost all the other major composers, and one which was often not welcomed by certain members of staff. As early as 1936, when Aaron Copland had just written *El Sálon México*, he was urging Hawkes to 'cash in on Copland', then published by a tiny imprint called Arrow Press. Hawkes met up with Copland in 1938 when he was in Paris writing his ballet *Billy the Kid*, and grappling with his capabilities as a 'cowboy composer'. An exclusive contract was signed there and then, and *El Sálon México* chosen as his first piece to go out under the B&H imprint.

'Dear Willie'

Another composer Hawkes was pursuing at the time, ultimately without success, was William Walton. Letters show them to be on frank and friendly terms. After lunching Walton in December 1936, Hawkes even sent a draft contract to the young composer, who amended it and then got cold feet. He signed a five-year contract with OUP, and then again in 1941 Hawkes made a definite offer which Walton mulled over and finally rejected out of loyalty to Herbert Foss. There must also have been a desire on Walton's part to separate himself from the *wunderkind* Britten. When, in 1942, Hawkes blithely invited him to supper with Britten, enthusing over the latter's new works which he intended they 'play through' at the piano after dinner, Walton's rejection was polite but cold. A scribbled postcard later that year begs Ralph 'not to let BB have the *Christopher Columbus* radio play music [a BBC commission] – on second thoughts I want it!' Walton did oblige Hawkes on a couple of occasions by writing military band pieces, including an arrangement of *Façade* (1942) and a commission for Hawkes's 1946 *Military Band Journal* Centenary edition, about which Walton wrote: 'I've got an idea for the military band piece – a cake-walk entitled *295 Regent Street* in my so-called comic vein.'

Gerald Finzi
(Drawing by Joy Finzi, 1940)

Reading a 1937 company gazette which sets out the stall of composers, one would think the Boosey & Hawkes catalogue was essentially British. Editor Herbert Hughes writes rather apologetically of them: 'They do not lack genius or talent, but they are a shy breed; they require confidence and encouragement as much as tough criticism. While John Ireland and Roger Quilter, Arthur Somervell and Armstrong Gibbs continue to write good songs and the first-named to add a "London" overture to the orchestral repertory; while E J Moeran has been finishing his first symphony in the mountains of Kerry, we have younger men like Benjamin

Magazine published from
the Denman Street office

Britten, Christian Darnton and Gerald Finzi contributing their quota.' The grouping of these three seems odd now, but one was the clear favourite. In 1939 when LAB was blowing hot and cold over the publication of his Three Choirs commission *Dies Natalis* – one of his masterpieces, as it happened – Finzi was infuriated that they had agreed to publish Britten's *Our Hunting Fathers.* Another young composer on the B&H books, Howard Ferguson, was warmly supportive of his friend Finzi: 'For heaven's sake, don't compare *Dies Natalis* with it. *Dies* is at least attractive music, written for string orchestra, whereas the other work is unattractive and requires xylophones, bedpans and the Lord knows what.' Both Finzi and Ferguson had works published on a piece-by-piece basis, and suffered rather in the shadow of Britten, who so obviously represented a new, more exciting aesthetic in Hawkes's eyes.

Despite the presence of these composers, 1937 was the last year that British composers would dominate. In 1938 LAB sent a letter of rejection to Michael Tippett after receiving *Robin Hood*, his school operetta, and by the time his star was in the ascendent, he was already signed by rival publisher Schott. No further significant British signing would take place until the 1960s: Hawkes was determined from the start to make Boosey & Hawkes an international enterprise – in today's speak, a global brand – and LAB, with his long experience of trading with the former colonies, was happy to concur.

Binville

At the time of the merger, both Boosey & Co and Hawkes & Sons shared an agency in New York (Boosey, Hawkes, Belwin), and a presence in Paris (Éditions Hawkes). An office in Toronto was quickly established and in 1933 an Australian office was set up in Sydney on the premises of a large music retailer. Soon after the Second World War offices were established in Germany and South Africa, and later Sweden. Physical and commercial conditions were generally tougher in the outpost offices, and none more so than in the dingy, lamp-lit warehouse on 23rd Street, home to Boosey, Hawkes, Belwin.

Max Winkler, the wiry, fast-moving and indefatigable high priest of the outfit, was focused on one thing only: sales of sheet. Described by Heinsheimer, who came to work there in 1938, as 'king of the school bands, emperor of the xylophone solo', the determinedly low-brow Winkler inhabited a 'labyrinth of steel bins packed with music.

The narrow passages between the bins were lit by countless 25-watt bulbs swinging from the ceiling and every time the boss had finished with bin 68d he pulled a little chain to extinguish the light, pulling another chain at bin 147 to show him, dimly, the way to Octavo 2024, where lay *Bless this house.*'

Winkler, author of the *Encyclopedia of Music for Pictures*, listing twenty thousand titles, had made a fortune in compiling and selling scores of 'mood' music for film, but when the industry collapsed overnight as Talkies came on stream, he turned to the American church and school market with equal zest. Easy arrangements, tutors and marching band music were his stock in trade; his editors were scissors and glue. The Hawkes band music catalogue and the Boosey ballads provided him with a wealth of material to plunder for his high school bands and glee clubs.

Max Winkler

The clash of cultures between Winkler and the London bosses comes out in a series of colourful letters during the 1930s. Winkler loved to refer to LAB as 'my old pal Leslie' and even dared to suggest to him that the so-called 'prestige' of the old Boosey firm was nothing but 'high hat policy and bad service', which he was, of course, busy rectifying. (LAB in his turn regularly questions Max's sketchy understanding of copyright laws and suggests that the 'New York lot' are 'rather coarse'.) Winkler is forever boasting to Hawkes about his sales: 'you have nothing on me when it comes to hard work' (Hawkes admired Winkler's work ethic but confessed to composer Arthur Benjamin he was a 'bit rough around the edges').

The great theme to which Winkler returns again and again is the laziness of his bad-tempered colleague Michael Keane, who was responsible for song sales. 'Mike' is always 'getting in my hair' and sending his blood

Advertisement from the Boosey & Hawkes Gazette, 1937

MUSIC IN FILMS

Composers represented in the catalogues controlled by Boosey and Hawkes contribute their quota to the thrills and the humours and the pathos of the Talkies. Here is a little list taken from recent releases. (News films are, of course, excluded).

Capitol Productions. "Love from a Stranger," with Ann Harding. *Music by Benjamin Britten.*
Strand Film Co. "The Way to the Sea." Commentary by W. H. Auden. *Music by Benjamin Britten.*
Fox British Pictures. "The End of the Road," with Sir Harry Lauder. *Music by Kennedy-Fraser.*
Herbert Wilcox Productions. "Millions." *Music by Stephen Adams.*
Publicity Films. "Plantation People." *Music by Woodforde-Finden.*
Gaumont British Instructional. "Kamalam." *Music by Coleridge-Taylor, Woodforde-Finden, Haydn Wood and others.*
Publicity Films. "Fascinating Facts." *Music by Rimsky-Korsakov.*
Paramount Pictures. "Musical Charmers." *Music by Rimsky-Korsakov.*

Strand Film Co. "People in the Parks." *Music by Maurice Besly.*
London Film Productions. "Men are not Gods." *Music by Rimsky-Korsakov (arrd. Lotter).*
Herbert Wilcox Productions. "The Three Maxims." *Music by Offenbach (arrd. Middleton).*
Warner Bros., First National Productions. "Irish for Luck." *Music by Battison Haynes, Herbert Hughes and D. Macmurragh.*
Metro-Goldwyn-Mayer. "Pup's Picnic." *Music by Offenbach (arrd. Myddleton).*
Mentone Productions. "Riders to the Sea." *Music by Stanford and Hamilton Harty (arrd. Haydn Wood).*
Gainsborough Pictures. "Windbag the Sailor." *Music by Stephen Adams (arrd. Kappey).*

pressure soaring. At the centre of their dispute were the abysmal song sales: 'By heavens!' explodes Max, 'how will I ever convince Mike that he should make it his business to go out and contact the popular type of singer ... Morton Downey, Bing Crosby – but will he degrade himself to see such punks?' Keane did seem reluctant to leave his desk, but he was right in predicting that it was the *hiring* not selling of parts that would secure their future business: 'I am convinced there is a big future in this business if we ever get into the Rental business. With Musical Societies generally, money is always scarce, and the inducement of being able to perform comparatively new works for a modest outlay would appeal strongly to every one of them. It would also put Rental Libraries – our greatest menace – out of business.'

Aaron Copland with
Leonard Bernstein, 1940
(Photo: Viktor Kraft)

The bickering rose to fever pitch in 1934/5, becoming highly personal, with Keane accusing Max of looking 'after his own race' when it came to employing staff, and at one point LAB was well-nigh summoned over to Manhattan to sort out internal relations. Ever conciliatory, LAB thought he had ironed out the problem, only to receive a barrage of blustering letters on his return. He appealed to the naturally more autocratic Hawkes, who resorted to literary yelling: 'Please understand, Michael, that when I send you gratis copies and expect something to be done, it has just got to be done.'

It was into the merry hell of 'Binville' that the distinguished publisher Hans Heinsheimer came looking for work in 1938, forced out of Austria after the Anschluss. From the hallowed rooms of Universal Edition, where he had dealt with Janáček, Kurt Weill, Paul Hindemith and Béla Bartók, he now sat staring through 'a yellowish, unopenable wire mesh onto the roof of a factory on Twenty-fourth Street' placing orders for '*Dapper Donkey* (Grade 1) by Brunt for B♭ clarinet'.

He stuck it out in the Stygian gloom for a few months, until he was hailed one day in 57th Street by 'a very well-dressed, ruddy man with sparkling, restless eyes and a little black moustache'. It was Ralph Hawkes, briefly in Manhattan visiting Max, who recognised Heinsheimer from his Viennese visits. Hawkes went with Heinsheimer back to the office in 23rd Street and promptly appointed him Head of Serious Music, a subject in which Winkler had no interest. At first he dusted down copies of Delius's *Irmelin* and Elgar's *Pomp and Circumstance Marches*, but within weeks Hawkes wrote to say that a young American composer named Copland was in London, and that he had just signed him. 'A gangling, bespectacled, broadly smiling man' soon arrived at the 23rd Street offices and perched on the desk. The first work Hans was to promote was the young Copland's *El Sálon México*, which Hawkes had heard in London. It went down a storm. A little later Hawkes commissioned a piano arrangement of the piece and Copland offered the work to a young friend of his in need of money: the man was Leonard Bernstein. The American branch of Boosey & Hawkes was truly in business.

Three men on the run

While Heinsheimer gave new gravitas to the New York operation and by 1939 had already set up the American edition of *Tempo* (he was 'a gift from the gods', according to Britten, and for more than a decade advised all the European émigré conductors and musicians on repertoire for the American market), a clutch of other talented figures arrived in London from UE. Although it was Hawkes who had initially established contact with Ernst Roth, Erwin Stein and Alfred Kalmus, they were also known to LAB, and it was he who went to Vienna to sort out their release and re-employment. Some say this was because Hawkes may have had Jewish family connections through his mother, and there was concern for his welfare in Vienna at that time, but it may just be one of several examples where LAB's brilliant diplomacy went uncredited.

Alfred Kalmus
(Photo: Universal Edition A.G.Wien)

There is no doubt, however, that it was Hawkes who established close personal friendships with the refugees, as Erwin Stein's daughter Marion recalls. She was a girl of eleven when she came to London with her father and mother, Sophie. 'Ralph was always very generous. He even offered to pay my school fees when we first came over. He made sure we were all right, that we found somewhere to live. My father was just glad to be back

The Regent Street boardroom in 1935, used as an office by Ralph Hawkes

in his proper milieu again, meeting musicians and composers. He was never homesick.' Erwin Stein – the eminent musicologist, conductor, music editor and pupil of Schoenberg – was an enormous asset to the company, revered by composers, Bartók, particularly Britten and later Stravinsky. Behind the scenes, he became the musical authority of the firm's London headquarters, a role inherited in the fifties by his colleague Leopold Spinner, another Viennese refugee and a pupil of Webern, an enigmatic individual whose own music would emerge from the shadows decades later.

Boosey & Hawkes also benefited from the Nazi dismissal of the genial and experienced publisher Alfred Kalmus, already in London to manage UE's British outpost. B&H bought up all the shares in UE's London subsidiary, and retained Kalmus as director. Kalmus established himself independently after the war, becoming a much-loved figure on the London musical scene and remaining on good terms with the men who had helped him.

These newcomers gave Boosey & Hawkes a new status and a credibility it had hitherto lacked in the international contemporary music world. There was resentment in some quarters, but few could argue that such professionals raised the tone. And they were not alone. During this period Jewish refugees were establishing some of Britain's most important cultural institutions: the publishing houses Gollancz, Weidenfeld & Nicolson, Phaidon, André Deutsch and, thanks to Carl Ebert and Fritz Busch, Glyndebourne Opera itself.

It was the third man, Czech-born Ernst Roth, who was to be most influential in the history of Boosey & Hawkes and who eventually became Managing Director and Deputy Chairman. Legally- and musically-trained to a high level, fluent in several languages and a talented literary translator, Roth was ruthlessly commercial, had a razor sharp mind and the old-world charm to bring the grandest composers to heel. He was perhaps the most consummate publishing professional the company ever employed. Without him, two of the greatest composers might never have sworn loyalty to this British firm. But, as we shall see, musical conservatism and a Machiavellian streak overshadowed his legacy.

The eve of war: two important signings

When Hawkes heard that Bartók was refusing to allow German radio permission to broadcast his works, he grasped his opportunity. He realised that both he and Kodály were effectively marooned in Budapest, and despite being 'Aryan' would not want to be part of the nazified publishing company. In the spring of 1938 he flew over to Hungary to discuss their future and found both eager to work with him (Bartók made his decision

January
2nd.,
1 9 3 9.

RH/EJ.

Mr. Bela Bartok,
Csalan-Utca 29,
BUDAPEST 11

My Dear Mr. Bartok,

⠀⠀⠀⠀Many thanks for your letter of December 28th.,which reached me this morning.

⠀⠀⠀⠀I hasten to advise you that we have already approached Universal Edition with a suggestion that we should buy the rights in all your works for all territories outside Greater Germany and in so doing,acquire the copyright for the world but leave them the exploitation in that particular territory.

⠀⠀⠀⠀We have also suggested that we might take over your Contract with them and thus relieve them of their obligation. Under these circumstances,therefore,it would appear to be a satisfactory move for you to make to advise Mr. Schlee when he calls upon you that you would feel happier if they did such a deal,for it is obviously of no use to them to have any arrangement with you whereby you are not willing to publish with them. The answer to the question contained in your letter, therefore,is that you may certainly mention our name as a possible Publisher. If such an arrangement were made with Universal Edition,you would then be able to look upon us as the owners of your copyrights for the world and you would do all your business with us. Since you are a member of the P.R.S., the situation would be much improved for you and I must say that,speaking personally,I should be more than happy to have this association with you.

⠀⠀⠀⠀With my best regards to Madame Bartok and yourself.

Yours sincerely,

Ralph Hawkes

Letter from Ralph Hawkes to Béla Bartók, January 1939

with characteristic directness; Kodály, a shrewder, harder businessman negotiated for the next three years).

He invited Bartók and his wife to come to London and play his *Sonata for Two Pianos and Percussion* at the ISCM festival that year. 'It was then, I think,' wrote Hawkes later, 'that I realised what was the tremendous force of this man. The intensity in his music was only a reflection of the man himself and as one knew him better, this became more and more apparent.' He later said Bartók's 'sincerity inspired me in a way that has only been matched by one other composer.' (One assumes he was referring to Britten.) Discussions began early in 1939 about the publication of his important pedagogical *Mikrokosmos*, which Bartók had started in the twenties – at the suggestion of none other than Ernst Roth, who was intimately involved in its genesis – and completed in 1937.

Then, late in 1939, Bartók wrote to Hawkes in some distress, 'perplexed' about what exactly he needed to do to release himself from UE, who had written to him to ask about his intentions. 'It seems I can no longer put off the settling of this business. Now, what shall I say to him?! My plan is: 1. To release me from the obligations of our contract, expiring in Sept. 1941 immediately and without condition. 2. To sell all my works already published by UE to an editor of England or France or USA. The question is: may I mention Boosey and Hawkes as an editor who would buy these works or not?'

Zoltán Kodály (c1930)
(Photo: Universal Edition A.G., Wien)

Hawkes was there before him: 'I hasten to advise you that we have already approached UE with a suggestion that we should buy the rights in all your works for the territories outside Greater Germany and in so doing, acquire the copyright for the world but leave them the exploitation in that particular territory. We have also suggested that we take over your contract with them and thus relieve them of their obligation.' He says that the situation would be much improved for Bartók, and 'speaking personally I should be more than happy to have this assocation with you'.

Just after Hawkes's Hungarian visit, Kodály was in Vienna, assessing the situation at UE. He advised that LAB should not come over to settle any deals until the 'Commissar' arrived who would decide everything. Kodály realised that all non-Aryan composers would be suppressed and that 'nationalism and anti-semitism' would drive all policies.

Hawkes immediately commissioned him to write some brass fanfares and fell upon a work for strings on which Kodály was then engaged, suggesting a British premiere by the Boyd Neel String Orchestra in the summer of 1940, and requested rights. This turned into Kodály's 'Peacock' Variations. They also discussed a translation of his *Hymn to St Stephen* to be sung by the Fleet Street Singers in 1939, the first work Kodály had published by Boosey & Hawkes. Ralph was less 'sanguine' about the commercial value of Kodály's school songs series *Bicinia Hungarica*. Kodály was prickly: 'If you are in doubt about the vendibility of *Bicinia* you are free not to publish them. Some of a dozen school songs I have with OUP reached 10,000 copies sold in ten years … perhaps I would do better to publish them in America.' The songs were eventually translated and published by Boosey & Hawkes and remain in print to this day.

Another casualty of the nazification of UE were the works of Gustav Mahler. His wife Alma put her trust in the men from Regent Street, as her appeal to LAB reveals. Writing from Paris in 1938 she authorises him to negotiate with UE officials to dissolve all contracts: 'I trust you will find some way suitable to safeguard the interests of Gustav's works, thanking you for all your endeavours…'. After the war, the rights in Mahler's works were returned, but the temporary ownership would prove significant in the promotion of Mahler's works in Britain and America.

Ralph Hawkes intended to win over UE's Mrs Hertzka, the widow of its formidable director Emil, by employing her as a director of the UE London branch. The plan did not work out, and, after the war, staff at UE in London and Vienna engaged in bitter legal recriminations over the robbery of rights they felt the British company had committed while they were powerless to fight back. By the time war broke out, however, the exploitation of UE was complete and a host of new opportunities were about to present themselves to Boosey & Hawkes.

Grounded

When war broke out in September 1939, Hawkes was grounded in London. Writing in November to Britten, who had left for the States that spring, he remarks: 'I had of course intended to spend a considerable time there this winter had the War not broken out and it would have been my intention to take over the Department.' Even at this stage, Hawkes was privately planning to move the music publishing side of the business (which he judged to be 'in the doldrums') to New York, leaving the instruments back in London, and thereby giving himself more independence from the Booseys.

Britten in exile: with Eugene Goossens in Maine (1940)

Characteristically, his main gripe was a lack of drama in the war: 'Boredom is probably worse than bombardment.' He had taken a house in Haslemere, Surrey in order to get out of London and was enjoying riding horses again. As a former soldier he had signed up with his old company, though was not forced to serve for reasons of his business, and on several occasions during the war earned an Atlantic passage by volunteering on a naval vessel. Neither he nor LAB was impressed by Britten's pacifist stance: Hawkes wrote to Walton in 1940 that Britten was 'in bad odour here', and to the composer himself that his remaining in America was having 'an unfortunate effect' on his reputation: 'We are going to have difficulty in getting performances of your works.'

He was wrong. While concert life was temporarily on hold in Britain, this proved a period of intense activity in America. That year alone Britten completed *Les Illuminations* ('I am very pleased with it … definitely my Opus 1' he told Hawkes) and started work on the Violin Concerto. He also began two works which he later withdrew, the 'School operetta for Max Winkler', *Paul Bunyan*, and his 'fanfare' for piano and orchestra *Young Apollo* which he wrote while holidaying with Copland in idyllic Woodstock, 'inspired by such sunshine as I've never seen before'. (These were subsequently published by Faber Music.) Copland encouraged Britten to stay on in America, writing to him: 'Anyone can shoot a gun – but how many can write music like you?'

The older composer's own *Quiet City* was premiered and published in this year, as were several other important B&H works: in the spring Bartók's Violin Concerto (known as No. 2 since the posthumous exhumation of the first), was given its first performance by violinist Zoltán Székely. Bartók could not get to Holland for the premiere and had to allow publication before he had heard it played. He spent the summer in Switzerland as a guest of Paul Sacher, busy at work on the latter's commission: the lithe, spritely *Divertimento*, completed in fifteen days. (Marion Thorpe remembers the day the score arrived on her father Erwin Stein's desk: 'He was tremendously excited and brought it home, sat down at the piano and played it to me there and then'.) He also began work on his sixth string quartet while there. Later that year, in Amsterdam, where both Bartók and Kodály's stock was high, Mengelberg gave the premiere of the latter's politically outspoken 'Peacock' Variations, initially the result of a commission to celebrate 50 years of the Royal Concertgebouw. Hawkes cabled him: 'All of us deeply moved by your beautiful Variations – undoubtedly one of your finest works. BBC wish to perform as soon as possible.'

Bartók and Szigeti in New York (1940)

In 1938 Benny Goodman had commissioned Bartók to write a piece for violin, clarinet and piano in the style of his violin rhapsodies, and *Contrasts* was the outcome. It was incomplete at its first performance – the slow movement was missing – but in 1940 it was finally recorded complete by Columbia with Goodman, Bartók and Szigeti. Throughout 1939–40 Heinsheimer was still sweating over its publication in New York: 'This is certainly a great headache. Everything, even to find points where to turn the pages, is extremely complicated. My greatest problem has been to find a man who can cope with the layout, inserting of keynotes, etc etc. I am not in the fortunate position of having Stein, and you know yourself that there is nobody around to deal with such complicated matters.' The main rival publisher, G Schirmer, had forbidden its only freelancer to work for B&H, so Heinsheimer cast about the city for others. Hawkes replies that an editor is the 'hardest post to fill in any part of the world', and wishes he could send one of his own over: 'The tragedy is that I cannot send Roth to New York – not only on account of shipping difficulties, but the fact that his wife and various mothers-in-law have to accompany him.' (Roth loathed New York, and would have come up with any excuse not to go there; and Hawkes would have missed him in London as he was already single-handedly launching the Hawkes Pocket Scores.) Hawkes's acknowledgement that good editors are thin on the ground and of supreme importance is significant: B&H early on acquired a reputation for the quality of its editors that remains as strong today.

'Life in the old dog yet'

But at this point Hawkes, too, was struggling with a lack of specialist editors: no sooner had he recruited his star cast from Vienna than, in the summer of 1940, all three were interned on the Isle of Man as 'enemy aliens'. As Hawkes had finally got permission to cross the Atlantic in February, it was left to LAB to sort out their release, a tortuous process that required all his gifts of diplomacy and persistence. Because one of the factories in Edgware had been commandeered for the making of shells, doors and rocket-loading lifts, instead of brass instruments, he was

Letter from Leslie Boosey requesting the release of Alfred Kalmus, Erwin Stein and Ernst Roth from a wartime internment camp on the Isle of Man (1940)

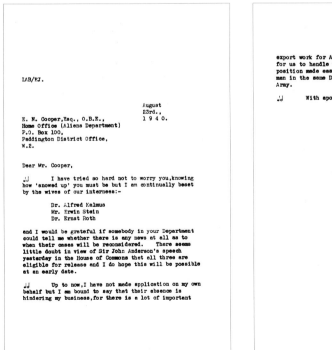

LAB/EJ.

August
23rd.,
1 9 4 0.

E. N. Cooper,Esq., O.B.E.,
Home Office (Aliens Department)
P.O. Box 100,
Paddington District Office,
W.2.

Dear Mr. Cooper,

    I have tried so hard not to worry you,knowing how 'snowed up' you must be but I am continually beset by the wives of our internees:-

        Dr. Alfred Kalmus
        Mr. Erwin Stein
        Dr. Ernst Roth

and I would be grateful if somebody in your Department could tell me whether there is any news at all as to when their cases will be reconsidered.   There seems little doubt in view of Sir John Anderson's speech yesterday in the House of Commons that all three are eligible for release and I do hope this will be possible at an early date.

    Up to now,I have not made application on my own behalf but I am bound to say that their absence is hindering my business,for there is a lot of important

export work for America which it is quite impossible for us to handle without their assistance; nor is the position made easier by the fact that the other leading man in the same Department has been called up for the Army.

    With apologies for bothering you.

        I beg to remain,

            Yours sincerely,

quizzed endlessly by the Aliens War Service Dept about the activities of
Roth, Stein and Kalmus. Patiently, he explained that their side of the
business was unconnected with the factories, and strategically emphasised
the role each man played in export: 'Our engagement of these men has
resulted in a very substantial expansion of our export business, not only
connected with Universal Edition but with our own English catalogue, and
their internment has compelled a cessation of these activities. Only in the
last fortnight I have had to abandon an important development in our
American catalogue ...' (This may have been an exaggeration, but it was
true that the publication of Britten, Bartók and Kodály scores was delayed
by the absence of Roth and Stein.)

LAB appealed to E N Cooper at the Home Office on every front: he was
'being bombarded by distracted wives'; their families were only surviving
thanks to 'the generosity of my company'; he knew they had already
'suffered great hardships at the hands of the National Socialists and they
were stripped of all they possessed before they were allowed to come over
here'. Eventually, in September 1940, Roth and Kalmus were released, but
Stein was kept in, writing to LAB with characteristically selfless concern,
'Some people think we ought to be glad to stay in a safe place. However
you will understand, to feel myself safe while my wife, my child, you and so
many other people are facing danger, is a most disgraceful position.' At the
end of August LAB himself was 'terribly distressed' to learn that Stein was
still to remain imprisoned: 'Poor little Mr Stein, he is no more a Nazi that
you or I.' Marion Thorpe remembers the time vividly: 'We had to move out
of our flat to cheaper accommodation. Father's salary was halved from six
pounds a week to three, and we had to live on that. It was a very anxious
time.'

Before the end of the year, Stein had returned to work, narrowly escaping
a delayed action bomb that fell in Portland Place in front of the Langham
Hotel and Broadcasting House. As LAB wrote to composer Julius Harrison,
'... we came off with nothing worse than one or two blown out windows
on the top floor and the doors of the basement blown off.' The Denman
Street premises were also bombed and the staff were often gathered in the
basements during raids and warnings. In spite of this, business, from
being 'dead' in the first months of the war, was beginning to gather pace
again, as LAB explained to Arthur Benjamin: 'Fancy, we are in the third
week of the intensified night bombing of London and yet we sold more
music last week than in the corresponding week of not only 1939 but 1938!
You see there's life in the old dog yet.'

In terms of new music, it was also an important year. In London there was the highly successful premiere of Britten's *Les Illuminations*, sung by Sophie Wyss with the Boyd Neel Orchestra, and in New York a well-received performance of the Violin Concerto with Antonio Brosa and John Barbirolli, about which even the curmudgeonly critic Olin Downes was guardedly enthusiastic. Conductor Eugene Goossens, who was also a fellow B&H composer, was effusive about the *Diversions for Left Hand* which Britten had written for Paul Wittgenstein: 'This is a truly amazing work and confirms again one's knowledge that Britten is the outstanding young man in the world of creative music today!'

Britten himself was still not financially secure, and was considering two offers of work, one from Ralph Hawkes to 'get you made a bandmaster or put you in a band' and the other from Winkler, to be signed up with a

BENJAMIN BRITTEN

LES ILLUMINATIONS
Poems by ARTHUR RIMBAUD

For High Voice and String Orchestra

Score (including reduction for piano and voice) $5.00

PRESS COMMENTS:

The Observer —

The music is certainly *the best that Britten has done so far*. One remembers many details as vividly as one remembers them in Schubert or Debussy, and this seems to come not only from clearness of conception but also from a mastery that is itself creative.

The Times —

A second hearing confirms the impression of the first, that they are *wonderfully clever* in the way they seize upon the essence of the words and in a few strokes delineate a whole scene; as illustrations they are both apt and vivid, as music they are fascinating; *well are they called "illuminations"*.

Musical Times

The work, which has been hailed as Brit-

ten's "best so far", is a song-cycle of settings of poems by Arthur Rimbaud, that wayward genius who flashed meteor-like into the realms of poetry between the ages of sixteen and nineteen, then wrote no more and ended his days as a merchant at Harrar, in Abyssinia, on the verge of a prosaic prosperity. The composer has well caught the spirit of Rimbaud's text. Often with little more than a hint or two he paints in a kind of tone-scenic background to each poem. Its outstanding virtue is the sureness of the composer's touch.

New Statesman and Nation —

This is *a truly remarkable composition and justified the expectation of great things from Mr. Britten*. I know of no modern composition by a British composer that has impressed me so favorably as this. What strikes one at once is his truly musical invention and its copiousness. *Each piece is a gem* perfectly finished and original in character.

financial retainer and to write 'simple marketable works' for schools and the like. Britten favoured Max's offer, and was working with W H Auden on the operetta *Paul Bunyan* under those terms, but by the end of the year he realised he was getting enough performances and commissions not to rely on either.

Ralph Hawkes's presence in the New York office for most of 1940 made it a hive of activity. 'It's wonderful to be here', he enthused in a letter home, cataloguing his breathless progress across the States, networking with the continent's musical movers and shakers. He hired Sylvia Goldstein during this trip, a formidable and lovable character, 'the backbone of B&H Inc' for forty years. She began as a secretary, put herself through law school and eventually became the Vice President and Head of Rights, revered by composers from Copland to Reich to Rorem.

In the early spring Hawkes and Heinsheimer launched the Boosey & Hawkes Artists' Bureau. The Bureau was originally intended by Hawkes to promote performances for his own composers, such as Bartók (who arrived in New York that October), Kodály and Britten, and to help them make a living in the new country. He could see that it would be hard for relatively unknown composers like Bartók to make a name for themselves without extensive touring, and as he had at his disposal the composer's former agent Andrew (André) Schulhof, who had left Hungary as war broke out, it seemed obvious to go into business.

The initial list included Beecham, Bartók, Kodály, William Schuman, Paul Wittgenstein, Benjamin Britten, Colin McPhee, Aaron Copland and Antonio Brosa. It was not long before the Artists' Bureau was taking on many other artists unconnected with the publishing firm, as Heinsheimer's enthusiasm soared. More artists sometimes meant awkward meetings in their particularly grim little offices: 'It was a very embarrassing experience to have Beecham in the main office and Bartók waiting outside in the caves assigned to us.'

But, as he recollected in his book *Fanfare for Two Pigeons*, it turned out to be more of an uphill struggle than they predicted. '[Andrew] couldn't figure it out. He had a fine list of brilliant artists. He certainly knew about the business – but somewhere, something was wrong … The *Tuesday Morning Musicale* in Oklahoma City was interested in our harpsichordist and the Provo summer school gave some thought to our chamber orchestra … but there was an enormous number of events where he had been unable to break in.' The two giant agents, Columbia Artists Management and the National Concert and Artist Corporation were already beginning to squeeze them out.

The inimitable Sir Thomas had come into B&H Inc in order to discuss his new editions of Delius and Mozart, which Hawkes was keen to have, and to ensure they undercut those of Breitkopf and Härtel on size and price. The flamboyant conductor was soon part of the Artists' Bureau but causing chaos: 'Sir T is annoyed we have booked him no New York date. Andrew [Schulhof] had one of the few bright moments in his life in suddenly suggesting he brought a Canadian orchestra to this country. Sir T was struck by this ... now this office is bristling with activity ... and we find ourselves involved in a scheme of utmost importance.' Hawkes, back in London, sounded a warning note: 'The greatest caution must be observed with Sir T, for although he is a magnificent attraction artistically, he is a positive menace financially.' He was already calling for large advances and name-dropping millionaire friends as (imagined) guarantors.

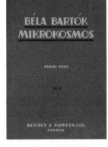

First edition of Bartók's
Mikrokosmos
(Permission British Library)

Financial wrangles were still delaying the signing of a contract with Kodály, who insisted on protection against the devaluation of the dollar. Hawkes felt his attitude was 'peculiar' but buckled on a request for a higher percentage of fees, with some minor provisos and against the advice of Winkler, 'who told me to stand my ground'. He was sufficiently concerned that another big publisher would take Kodály up. The composer was still perfecting the final manuscript of his 'Peacock' Variations, and Hawkes urged Heinsheimer to 'keep pounding Kodály with cables like the British pound Hamburg – I've got to have that score published by January, and you know what that means.' News came from a Hungarian newspaper that Kodály had been granted leave of absence to tour in the States in 1941 and he had readily signed up with the Artists' Bureau, much to Heinsheimer's delight.

The other composer Hawkes was in close touch with at this time was Arthur Benjamin, famous now for his *Jamaican Rumba* and a lively presence then on the light music and orchestral scene. Originally Australian, Benjamin had come to England as a young man and become Professor of Piano at the Royal College of Music, where he eventually became Britten's piano teacher (the young composer dedicated his *Holiday Diary* to Benjamin). When war broke out, Benjamin and his mother went to live in Vancouver. Hawkes's relationship with this composer was fond but workmanlike, and practical considerations came before Benjamin's muse: when he confides that he is working on a symphony, Hawkes is not impressed: 'Well, don't let me deter you but "times are 'ard"… I'm glad you like the idea of a Concerto for piano and strings. If you can, get this on the easy side without losing any brilliance in the solo part. I am sure that with your imaginative mind you can make it brilliant and exciting as a piece.' These were Hawkes's two favourite words when describing music, and when Benjamin suggested an overture based on a Negro spiritual he hastened to stop him, assuring Benjamin that the 'miserable' nature of such songs was not at all what the market required.

Hawkes would never have dreamed of influencing Britten in this way. When commissioned by the Japanese Government to write a piece celebrating the 2,600th anniversary of the Empire, Britten chose to pen his *Sinfonia da Requiem*, expressing his own 'anti-war conviction'; it seemed a 'disconcerting piece of irony', as Lennox Berkeley observed, that the Japanese Government should be commissioning such a piece, and when an official realised the import of the title, a letter of complaint arrived accusing the work of being 'unsuitable', 'too melancholy' and 'purely religious music of a Christian nature', which did not express 'felicitations'. Britten wrote a robust reply, and sought Hawkes's advice as to whether he should act as a private individual or as a 'representative'. In the end no music from composers of Allied countries was represented, and Britten and his publisher were spared the diplomatic disaster of attending an event where the Nazi salute was given during the Japanese National Anthem.

Arthur Benjamin (1940s)

'Like manna in the wilderness'

'Poor old London has been very knocked about,' wrote LAB to Arthur Benjamin. 'Everybody keeps wonderfully cheerful in spite of all the difficulties … though one must admit tempers are easily frayed these days.' He was feeling the pinch most acutely at home, not in the office. His house in Hertfordshire had become a haven for Booseys of every sort: 'I have had Ralph Boosey and his wife and two children, nurse and maid with me for the last nine months. Now my mother and father-in-law have had to come and join the throng, plus a maid. The cook, who has really been a Trojan throughout, has chucked her hand in. She says she cannot cook for so many and I do not altogether blame her. Another thing is the nurses do not get on as well as they might …' Two of his four children were away at school and the eldest, Anthony, in the navy. 'When they come home there will not be room for everybody with the best will in the world.'

Despite bombing and privations, business began to boom at Boosey & Hawkes Ltd. At the end of 1941 LAB announced that sheet music sales 'have increased throughout the trade to the extent of some 20% or 30% during the last twelve months. The irony is that we haven't had the paper to meet the demand.' The end result was 50% up on 1940, with no price increases. It was hard to believe it would last. Writing to George Cooper,

Leslie Boosey's home,
Bourne Orchard
in Brickendon,
Hertfordshire (1930s)
(Photo: courtesy Graham Irwin)

director of the Sydney office, who wanted to open a major street shop front, Hawkes, however, warns him 'not to get too carried away with the 1940 figures', believing the times to be too uncertain. LAB mused on a similar economic phenomenon during the First World War, when so many people were coming back from leave seeking entertainment. In comparison, the blackout had forced most entertainment underground, but he pinpoints people's buying power as the driving force: 'I suppose it is true to say that wages have increased substantially and … people's purchasing is limited by coupons and restrictions of all kinds in many directions, but not, of course, in music.'

He also notes that PRS revenues were only 6% down in 1940, despite the fall in the number of concerts. But as early as February concert life was showing signs of revival, with Myra Hess's weekly chamber music concerts in the National Gallery and orchestras coming out of the woodwork, as Ralph Hawkes noted: 'The LPO are really to be congratulated on what they have done …' The dance band leader Jack Hylton had saved them from bankruptcy by taking them on a tour of local dance halls and cinemas. 'Apparently,' continues Hawkes with satisfaction, 'they got tired of grinding out the standard classics and have now decided to introduce new works – they gave the first concert performance of

Wigmore Hall in London, venue for the Boosey & Hawkes Concerts between 1941 and 1947
(Photo: courtesy Wigmore Hall)

Programme for the first
Boosey & Hawkes concert
at the Wigmore Hall,
4 October 1941
(Courtesy Wigmore Hall)

WIGMORE HALL
BOOSEY & HAWKES CONCERTS

1st CONCERT, SATURDAY, 4th OCTOBER, 1941, at 2.30

*The Blech String Quartet: Harry Blech (1st violin), Max Salpeter (2nd violin),
Keith Cummings (viola), William Pleeth ('cello) · Eiluned Davies (piano) ·
Geoffrey Gilbert (flute) · Marie Korchinska (harp) · Sophie Wyss (Soprano).*
Notes by EDWIN EVANS.
(Author's Copyright)

Second String Quartet   HONEGGER
(1892)

Allegro · Adagio · Allegro marcato
Arthur Honegger's First String Quartet, in C minor, is a comparatively early work,
completed in October 1917, which helped to establish his reputation. Its successor was
begun in 1934 and completed in June 1936. Despite the interval of nearly twenty years
which separates them, the two works show a marked consistency of style, particularly in
the adaptation of the modern musical language to a classicism amounting almost to severity.

'' Psyche '' for Soprano, Flute, Harp, Violin, Viola and 'Cello   FALLA
(1876)

This setting of a poem by G. Jean-Aubry was composed at Granada in 1924. It is the only
one of Falla's later works that reminds one of his early French associations. As
J. B. Trend says: '' Falla's sense of language, his consciousness that, in their accentuation,
French and Spanish are at opposite poles, is reflected in the structure and feeling of the
music. Everything is vague and indirect; nothing is definitely stated; there is hardly a
single common chord from beginning to end.'' The composer has devised a delicate
instrumental background for a cantilena which the flute begins and then codes to the voice.

Household Music (1941) *(First Performance)*   R. VAUGHAN WILLIAMS
(1872)

Three Preludes on Welsh Hymn Tunes for String Quartet
1. *Crug - y - bar (Fantasia)*   2. *St. Denio (Scherzo)*   3. *Aberystwyth (Variations)*
These preludes are designed principally for string quartet, but the composer has envisaged
their being played by almost any combination of instruments which may be gathered
together at one time in a household.
Thus the string parts almost as they stand can be played by flutes, recorders, oboes,
bassoon, euphonium, according as their compass is suitable. R.V.W.

Theme and Variations for Piano (1941) *(First Performance)*   BERNARD STEVENS
(1916)

Bernard Stevens was born in London, 1916, and studied composition at Cambridge with
Dent, Rootham and R. O. Morris. He was awarded the Leverhulme scholarship and the
Parry prize at the Royal College of Music. He is now serving in the Forces. His works
include a String Quartet, two Sonatas for violin and piano, a Mass for unaccompanied
double choir and a Symphony. This Theme and Variations was composed in 1941. It
comprises a Theme, 17 Variations and a Finale in the form of a Passacaglia on a new theme,
at the end of which the two themes are heard in combination. Some of the Variations
maintain the harmonic basis of the theme. Others are free developments of characteristic
features of the theme.

Children's Songs from Op. 49   SZYMANOWSKI
(1883-1937)

*La Princesse se marie · La Pie et le Rouge-gorge · La Berceuse du Chrval brun
Le Geai insolent*
The death of Karol Szymanowski, March 29th, 1937, was a severe loss to Poland. Not only
was he the most eminent of her contemporary composers, but after a period of eclecticism
his work had acquired a nationalist colouring which linked them intimately with Polish
culture. His Children's Songs—or, rather, Rhymes—consist of twenty settings of nursery
rhymes by J. K. Illakowicz, composed in 1924-1926 and published two years later. They
are simple, mostly diatonic melodies, supported by piquant and sometimes illustrative
harmonies. These four songs are Nos. 6, 11, 19 and 20.

Three French Nursery Songs   ALAN RAWSTHORNE
(1905)

Je suis un petit poupon · Il pleut, il pleut, bergère · Fais do-do, Pierrot
Rawsthorne was born at Haslingden, Lancashire. He did not decide upon a musical career
until he was 20. In 1926 he entered the Royal College of Music at Manchester, where he
studied four years. He first came before the public in 1934 with a String Quartet. His
Variations for Two Violins and Symphonic Studies for Orchestra have been performed
respectively at the London (1938) and Warsaw (1939) Festivals of the International Society
for Contemporary Music. These Nursery Songs, which were first heard at a concert of its
British Section, the Contemporary Music Centre, are not arrangements of folk
tunes, but original settings of French Nursery Rhymes.

Sonate à Trois for Flute, Viola and Harp   DEBUSSY
(1862-1918)

Pastoral, Interlude and Finale
This Trio was composed in the autumn of 1915 and first performed at a concert of the
Société Musicale Indépendante, April 21st, 1917. The opening Pastoral foreshadows a mood
of spell of melodic invention based upon the modes and the songs of the Troubadours, but fated
to be cut short by the composer's death. The Interlude (tempo di Minuetto) almost
inevitably evokes the Trianon manner. The Finale, based on a flexible melodic line, is
perhaps the most original of the three movements. The whole, which was almost Debussy's
last composition, aroused differences of opinion recalling the controversies of earlier days.
Some found it tasteful but mannered, others a distinct revival of the composer's spontaneous
inventiveness which, had he lived, promised to be fruitful.

NEXT CONCERTS : Saturday Afternoons, Oct. 18th, Nov. 8th, Nov. 29th.
Write for programme leaflet.

TICKETS: 5/-, 3/6, 2/6, 1/6 each, from BOOSEY & HAWKES, LTD., 295 Regent St., W.1,
and WIGMORE HALL (WELbeck 2141).

Copland's *An Outdoor Overture* at Burnley, Lancs the other day, and now they plan to give Britten's Violin Concerto at the Queen's Hall just before Easter.'

Tragically, just after Easter 1941 the Queen's Hall was bombed and burnt, with all the instruments inside it. But by the autumn, Boosey & Hawkes was ready to roll out its very own series of concerts at the Wigmore Hall, which, in retrospect, became landmark events and, as LAB rightly said, 'like manna in the wilderness to the people who are really interested in modern music as there is nothing else of the kind available to them.'

Programmed and organised with the expert help of Erwin Stein, the concerts started off with a gentle programme of Rawsthorne, Villa-Lobos, Ireland, Debussy's Trio for flute, viola and harp, Vaughan Williams's *Household Music* for string quartet, and Bernard Stevens' *Theme and Variations*. The idea was to introduce unfamiliar works by established composers and new, younger voices, predominantly but not exclusively from the Boosey & Hawkes fold. Later programmes included Bartók's Sixth Quartet (just after its New York premiere), Finzi's *Dies Natalis*, and Britten's *Serenade for tenor, horn and strings*. The evenings provided a window on much of the musical activity taking place in America, while giving a platform to English composers whose works were being written in a vacuum, such as Rubbra, Lennox Berkeley, Elisabeth Lutyens (who had adopted the twelve-tone system) and Michael Tippett. LAB gave a blow-by-blow account of the concerts in his letters to Arthur Benjamin, commenting on a programme in 1942, he writes: 'The Bartók [*Contrasts*] was interesting: in fact, what might be described as the more advanced musical element there were very enthusiastic about it. I must frankly confess that the first two numbers were quite out of my depth, but the last one is amusing and exciting. The high spot of the evening was Britten's *Seven Sonnets of Michelangelo* [1940]; these had the most tremendous reception and I was not surprised.

When I heard them originally in the organ room at Regent Street,
I expressed the opinion that they were the most outstanding songs that had
been written in the last 25 years … the critics went further than that. One
described them as the finest songs that had been written in this country
since the 17th century.'

The Boosey & Hawkes series grew in ambition and scope, and in 1942
there was a performance of Schoenberg's *Pierrot lunaire* with Hedli
Anderson, conducted by Stein, and a 'galaxy of talent' performed Walton's
Façade, with the composer conducting and Constant Lambert narrating.
By 1943 they were presenting the Schoenberg arrangement of Mahler's
Das Lied von der Erde in a specially commissioned new translation done
by Stein. LAB's attitude reflected a generally-held
suspicion of both Bruckner and Mahler at the time:
'Mahler has had such a following on the Continent
that it is difficult to believe that he has not some
appeal here if properly presented to the British
public, but I 'hae my doots'. There is something in
both Bruckner and Mahler which either the British
public does not understand or does not appeal to
them.'

Much is due to Erwin Stein for inspiring British
interest in the composer he knew and loved. Had
he not been stuck one night in the basement with
Ralph Hawkes, it might have taken longer, as the
latter described in a letter to Heinsheimer: 'Last
Saturday night I was on duty here at the Office in
charge of Fire Spotting Patrol but as "Jerry" left us
in peace, we decided to do a little "Music Spotting"
instead. Our attentions were directed to Mahler's
Second Symphony and as Stein and [Ernest]
Chapman were on duty with me, we had our own
concert [both played the piano]. Gunfire it is true
was heard but this was from Mahler rather than

Hans Heinsheimer
(late 1930s)
(Photo: courtesy Frances
Heinsheimer Wainwright)

anti-aircraft guns.' Hawkes confesses himself 'quite sold on the idea' of
asking Stein to make an arrangement for small orchestra of the second
movement. Britten was already looking at the Third Symphony, and Alma
Mahler, then in California, was in principle happy with the idea of a
performing edition of movements for smaller orchestral forces, in order to
'introduce' Mahler to a new audience. In 1942 *Tempo* published Britten's

seminal essay in defence of the composer, 'On Behalf of Gustav Mahler'. The Mahler revival was under way.

Breathless in Boston

While Hawkes sat in that basement in London, Heinsheimer was frantically busy in New York with his composers and artists. Bartók had brought over the score of Kodály's *Concerto for Orchestra* which was finally premiered in March by its commissioner, the Chicago Philharmonic Society. Hawkes sent a petulant cable to Kodály to sign the final agreement and, after three years of negotiation, it was done. Heinsheimer had secured some engagements for the Bartóks, but it was an uphill struggle: 'Not many organisations were prepared to forego the commercial appeal of other two-piano teams for the unbending austerity of the Bartóks. Their appearance on stage in the company of two page-turners seemed old-fashioned and was easily misinterpreted as a lack of preparation or courtesy by audiences accustomed to flashier displays of virtuosity ... His bows were a concert manager's nightmare: stern, professorial, unsmiling to the extent of chilliness.'

Bartók had begun work at Columbia University in March on a collection of Yugoslav epic songs, but for the next two or three years completed no new compositions, apart from an orchestral version of his *Sonata for Two Pianos and Percussion*, a practical commission from Hawkes to assist him financially and perhaps get the work performed by orchestras. His Sixth Quartet was premiered by the dedicatees, the Kolisch Quartet, and was critically well received, but Hawkes later recalled that among concert promoters there was an 'apathy and even aversion to this kind of music to be found everywhere'.

Despite the lack of new compositions, some publications were being prepared by the fledgling American office. Heinsheimer was in almost daily contact with Bartók over scores of *Contrasts* and the 'Concerto' for two pianos, percussion and orchestra. Bartók was an exacting editor, and fourth, fifth and sixth proofs were sent agonisingly slowly between London and New York: 'The war was not permitted to interfere with the proper appearance of a semi-quaver. It was very, very trying once in a while, to work with a man with such sidereal principles.'

Although publications from the American office were improving, Hawkes was still anxious that they were not up to London standards. In an attempt

Letter from Bartók to
Ralph Hawkes (1942)

'2, Cambridge Ave, Bronx, N.Y. <u>Copy of a letter sent on</u> (Aug 5.) by air mail   Aug. 3. 1942.
Ralph Hawkes, Regent Street 295, London.

171.

My dear Hawkes,

end of May I began to write a letter to you; and then I got a high fever attack and I postponed the sending of the letter to a time when I will perhaps better news for you. This is unfortunately, not the case even now, but I don't want to postpone the letter any more. I would concentrate my letter to 3 or 4 main subjects

1. The events of Dec. caused the postponement of a settling of my non-quota immigration business. In Jan. I got news from the Montreal consul that no visa can be granted to me as a Hungarian citizen for the time being. I sent an application to Washington for reexamination and got an answer in Febr. saying that they will reexamine my case. Since that time no news! — In the meantime, however, conditions and circumstances got changed in such a way that I really wonder if I ever will be able to get that immigrant visa! It would be too bad if this circumstance would influence the sending over of my performance fees and of other due money from England, for I really badly need any money — — —. A few months ago I got a statement from the Performing Right Society about some amount (perhaps $ 60), this in fact did not yet arrive here.

2. I thank you so much for your kind help in my son's case. He arrived on Apr. 19, after a phantastic journey of almost 4 months, quite unexpectedly; found his way to the 231st street where we met by chance!

3. You probably know from Mr. Heinsheimer that I am ill since the beginning of April: I have every day temperature elevation, rising sometimes to 100°. And the doctors can not find the cause, in spite of very thorough examinations. Fortunately, I can continue my official work at Columbia Univ.; I only wonder how long this can go on, in this way. And whether it is perhaps a general break down? Heaven knows.

4. Just before my illness I began some composition work, and just the kind you suggested in your letter. But then, of course, I had to discontinue it because of lack of energy, tranquillity and mood — I don't know if I ever will be in the position to do some new works.

5. You remember you signed as a co-trustee (with Dr. G. Herzog) a kind of agreement (or what it is called) concerning my manuscripts. Now, that I see how conditions here are, I realise that the purpose I wanted to attain with these manuscripts, can never be ~~realised~~ attained. Therefore, I ask you to agree with the cessation of this "agreement" and to send me a statement with your declaration of consent.

6. The Performing Right Society asked me for a statement concerning the {transfer {forwarding of my share of performing fees to you, i.e. to Boosey & Hawkes, London. I don't know why a new declaration is necessary as I told them a few years ago to forward all these fees to. Nevertheless, I will repeat my request concerning this in a letter to P.R.S. in a few days.

I hope you are well, and your family too.
Yours, very sincerely
Béla Bartók
[BÉLA BARTÓK]

to recruit qualified editors, Heinsheimer had even suggested that Britten start working for them, but Hawkes decided he should not be distracted and might not be the most objective of editors. Heinsheimer assured Hawkes they would take 'all possible care to avoid mistakes and misunderstandings in connection with our future editions'. (It wasn't until *Contrasts* was finally printed in 1942 that Hawkes approved a publication and congratulated Heinsheimer on an edition 'worthy of London'.)

The Winkler culture of churning out editions and concentrating on sheet sales was perceived to be holding the music publishing department back, and both LAB and Hawkes began discussing the possibility that Boosey & Hawkes should drop the 'Belwin' (a name created by Winkler to honour his wife, Bella Winkler) from BHB, and bring the office under their sole control, something that only happened as the War ended.

Heinsheimer was certainly creating an entirely new reputation for the office. He describes to Hawkes a whirlwind trip to Boston: 'It is really a wonderful feeling to realise what Boosey & Hawkes already means to the American music world. Wherever I went I was received immediately.' At 10.30am the Boston Chamber Orchestra agreed to perform Bartók's *Divertimento*; by 11am the Dean of the New England Conservatory had arranged to hire *El Salón México*; by midday, Beecham was booked to conduct the Boston Symphony Orchestra the following January, and half an hour later he had persuaded the orchestral librarian to invest in Delius's *The Walk to the Paradise Garden*. More significantly, he spent the afternoon with Serge Koussevitzky, who not only agreed to perform Copland's *Quiet City*, but explained the complicated situation regarding Rachmaninoff rights and his own catalogues in Paris. He spoke 'with very high esteem about you and asked me to send you his kindest and sincerest regards.'

Hawkes's ultimate aim was to acquire the ageing Koussevitzky's important Russian catalogues, Édition Russe de Musique and Gutheil (which included works by Stravinsky, Rachmaninoff, Prokofieff), but he played a long game. As he explained to Heinsheimer, first it was important to win the conductor's trust – not to lose any opportunity of seeing him 'to cement the relationship' and to be seen to be 'helping him sort out complicated legal matters'. George Cooper, the director of the Sydney office, was not wrong when he urged LAB to keep Hawkes in New York as a director: 'There is no doubt that the progress up to date can be attributed to Mr Ralph Hawkes's special experience, his hard work and capacity to take advantage of the situation ... The lack of his controlling hand at this juncture might result in disintegration.'

One artist who seemed to charm everyone in 1941 was Sir Thomas Beecham, and Hawkes's previous scepticism was replaced by unalloyed enthusiasm. He described having 'a wonderfully exciting time' with him during a short visit to New York, and for having the 'utmost admiration for him'. No doubt the warm feelings were fired by the staggering $26,000 that Beecham had earned in an eight-week period, a fat percentage of which went to the Bureau. But the joyride was not to last. Despite significant work on his Delius edition and further conducting engagements, 1942 saw Beecham descending into personal chaos, with poor Heinsheimer standing helplessly on the sidelines. He had been having an affair with the pianist Betty Humby, and was spending money like water. He begged Heinsheimer for more advances, and then threatened him. Hans cabled Hawkes for moral support. 'No more cash!' came the reply, to Hans's relief: 'If I have to walk through minefields I would much rather do it in Africa than in Madison Avenue, New York City,' he writes with feeling, explaining that 'nervousness and strain' were damaging Beecham's reputation. The following year he would be dragged in as witness to the conductor's secret marriage to Humby.

Bartók was also having a difficult year. It started well with the arrival of his son Peter in April, who had been stuck for over three months in Lisbon on his way to join his parents, and who had only been allowed out of the country after Hawkes intervened strenuously on his behalf, using his Foreign Office contacts. Bartók, writing to thank him, describes how 'after a phantastic journey of four months' his son 'found his way to 231st Street where we met by chance!' There followed a successful ISCM evening in Bartók's honour at the MacDowell Club, at which his Four Pieces for two pianos were premiered. 'To the shocking disappointment of the large gathering of "atonalists",' wrote Heinsheimer gleefully, 'the pieces are very melodious, lyrical and brilliant. If played by a more fascinating team than the Bartóks they should be very successful.' But soon afterwards the composer lapsed into a high fever he could not shake off, the first sign of the leukaemia that was eventually to kill him. Unaware of the gravity of his illness, Hawkes wrote cheerfully in May asking for new works from him, giving him the choice of a series of small concertos – along the lines of the Brandenburgs – or 'a work for orchestra lasting ten to fifteen minutes'. Hawkes blithely suggests that 'if this is based on Folk music and does not present too many difficulties in performance, I feel certain that it

An advert in Tempo for the new Hawkes Pocket Score series
(American Edition, September 1942)

should do well.' (One can understand why Marion Thorpe said Hawkes could be 'brash', but composers tended to forgive his frank proposals, presumably because they felt his respect was genuine.) Bartók took nearly three months to reply, explaining how ill he had been: 'I began some composition work, and just the kind you suggested … but then I had to discontinue it because of lack of energy, tranquillity and mood – I don't know if I ever will be in the position to do some new works.' He still had not been diagnosed and was trying to continue his work at Columbia University, but he did not know how long he could keep it up and wondered if: 'I am having a general breakdown? Heaven knows.'

This year also marked a crisis in orchestral life in America. Boston was on its knees, Detroit collapsed in October and the New York Philharmonic was only saved at the eleventh hour by the sponsorship of the American Rubber Company. Heinsheimer was determined the Bureau should do its bit to initiate more performances, and joined forces with the Town Hall's Kenneth Klein to present four concerts devoted to new music by William Schuman, Ernest Bloch and Copland. Yet still the Artists' Bureau lurched into loss, and soon Heinsheimer, who always erred on the side of optimism, was having to take some hard advice from Hawkes: 'Cut your coat according to your cloth … and from what I can see your coat should now be practically a vest.' He urged Hans to concentrate on artists who were 'directly interested with us in publication be they composers, arrangers or conductors.' Later that year he went further and suggested drastically reducing the Bureau: 'In view of your report I suggest closing bureau down to one really efficient, loyal American girl, salary 40–50 dollars weekly.' He recommended getting rid of Andrew Schulhof, who had been the subject of repeated complaints. A month or two later, Schulhof resigned anyway, and Heinsheimer took the decision to merge with another agency, LaBerge, who had Louis Krasner and Alexander Tansman. He could no longer sustain the Bureau on his own with all the publishing work that was in progress.

For this was a year of notable successes: Copland's *Lincoln Portrait* went down well at its premiere in May by Kostelanetz and the Cincinnati Symphony Orchestra, who then repeated it in Toronto and several other venues. Heinsheimer notes early in 1943 that 'Copland not only earned his advance for 1942 but got an additional $334 in royalties plus a bonus of $150. The *Piano Sonata* has been performed in New York by five different pianists in the course of one year.' Hawkes was delighted to see that 'Copland is a seller' and arranged with Robert Helpman and Constant Lambert to produce *El Salón México* at Sadler's Wells, also commissioning a 'curtain raiser' of 'hot afternoon music' to fill the programme. This year also saw the first performance of *Fanfare for the Common Man*, which went straight to the hearts of Americans whose country had just entered the war.

Another figure to gain rapid prominence in America this year was Bohuslav Martinů, who had escaped France with the help of Paul Sacher

Bohuslav Martinů playing music from Symphony No. 1 to Serge Koussevitzky
(Photo: courtesy Martinů Foundation)

and Ernest Ansermet, and arrived in New York as a 'blacklisted intellectual'. He was soon absorbed into the lively émigré network of New York, and Copland invited him to take up a teaching post at the Berkshire Music Center. Koussevitzky had been sufficiently impressed with his *Concerto Grosso* to commission a first symphony, and Heinsheimer proudly notes it had already been played in Boston twice, and in Cambridge, New York and New Haven, and was due to be repeated in Boston, Providence, and Hartford, making a total of $415 in hire fees. He was to write a symphony a year for the next four years, and all six would end up in the B&H catalogue. Hawkes was enthusiastic, urging Heinsheimer to get a contract together: 'There is no doubt that Martinů is one of the best of the youngsters and you should tie him up as we arranged.'

'Britten has gone straight to the top'

Signed photograph of Britten (1940s)

Britten had made the decision to return to Britain by the end of 1941, but spent the early months of 1942 awaiting clearance for his passage. One of the reasons for returning to London was the lack of income he had received in 1941 (he was often relying only on his small allowance from Boosey & Hawkes) but since the decision, commissions flooded in: there was the suggestion of a clarinet concerto commission from Benny Goodman which he started but did not complete, and a harp concerto from a certain Mrs Phillips who offered him $1,000; Frederick Ashton expressed interest in a ballet on Spenser's *The Faerie Queen*, and Hawkes arranged for him to write an orchestral overture for Artur Rodzinski to conduct with the Cleveland Orchestra in New York, which he wrote in a great hurry but which was never performed. When it came to light in the sixties, as the 'Occasional Overture', Britten said he had no memory of having written it as he was depressed and having a creative block at the time.

It was Koussevitzky's commission for an opera in memory of his recently deceased wife, Natalie, that was to prove decisive: before leaving in April 1942 Britten had discovered Crabbe's *The Borough* and was already dreaming up *Peter Grimes*. On the crossing he completed his last important Auden setting, the *Hymn to St Cecilia*, and the first draft of *A Ceremony of Carols*, equipped as he was with the two harp manuals he had acquired for the harp concerto commission, and a book of medieval poetry bought in Halifax, Nova Scotia.

Hawkes was glad to have him back, but was concerned that his conscientious objector status in Britain would hamper his writing: 'it is uncertain what his future position will be,' he explained to Heinsheimer, 'If his appeal is allowed, he will be able to write but if it is disallowed I do not know how much will come from him.'

Cover of Cavendish Music Company recording (1930s)

In the event, Britten's appeal was successful and although he was asked to do non-combatant work, he was highly productive in the first twelve months back in Britain, writing, among other works, *Rejoice in the Lamb*. Hawkes invited Britten and Pears to play through the latest American works in the organ room in Regent Street, before a specially invited audience. Julian Herbage from the BBC was greatly struck and recommended the works to Boult, resulting in an immediate BBC commission for some propaganda features. As Hawkes wrote in 1943, 'He has gone right to the top ... whenever there is a new work of his we get a packed house.'

In the world of light music, LAB was feeling the pinch, as he wrote to Arthur Benjamin: 'There is no longer the BBC Salon Orchestra for Leslie Bridgewater and his gang of "the best musicians in England" has now been broken up, some of them being called up and others dispersed into the various symphonies. However, your *Prelude to a holiday* is being played at this year's Proms.' Nevertheless, after a period of inactivity, the Cavendish Music Company recordings were relaunched, and Benjamin, along with William Alwyn, Haydn Wood, Armstrong Gibbs, Eric Coates and Clive Richardson, received numerous commissions to supply the newsreels and documentary films with the music of the moment, including the military band arrangements that were currently popular.

Hawkes was itching to return to New York, although he had much to settle in his personal life. Despite LAB's best efforts to assist Ralph's German first wife Erika and her daughter to join him in New York in 1940, there had been a damaging period of estrangement and the marriage did not survive. In 1942 Hawkes married the glamorous Clare Watson, who danced professionally as one of the Cochran girls under the name of Clare Presgrave. As the marriage produced no children, he adopted her sister's family, at first in an avuncular way, but later as his heirs. It was this succession that was to influence the politics of the company for decades.

Barwick Green, now familiar as *The Archers'* theme tune, on a 1940s recording

1941 recording by Harry Fryer, a doyen of light music who made over 140 *Music While you Work* broadcasts for the BBC

Telegram from Ralph Hawkes to the New York office about the Fürstner acquisition (1943)

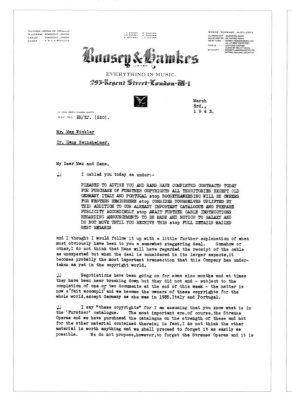

The creation of a musical monopoly

On the morning of 3 March 1943 Max Winkler and Hans Heinsheimer
found an extraordinary cable awaiting them: 'PLEASED TO ADVISE YOU
HAVE COMPLETED THE CONTRACTS TODAY FOR PURCHASE OF
FURSTNER COPYRIGHTS ALL TERRITORIES EXCEPT OLD GERMANY
ITALY AND PORTUGAL stop BOOSEYHAWKESINC WILL BE OWNERS
OF WESTERN HEMISPHERES stop CONSIDER YOURSELVES
UPLIFTED'. The cable went on to advise them to prepare publicity but
not to move until he had explained exactly how they were to proceed.
What Hawkes did not need to say was of what the Fürstner copyrights
comprised: the operas of Richard Strauss. Boosey & Hawkes had
acquired the rights to, among others, *Ariadne auf Naxos*, *Die Frau ohne
Schatten*, *Der Rosenkavalier* and *Salome*. It was, as Hawkes rightly
declared, 'a somewhat staggering deal ... probably the most important
transaction that this Company has undertaken.'

The negotiations had begun in secret nine months
previously when Berta Geissman, Furtwängler's
former secretary, also a refugee in London, came to
see Ernst Roth, and indicated to him that the
Fürstners, who had been living in London as
refugees since the mid-thirties, were in need of
money and might be willing to sell the catalogue.
Roth, Hawkes wrote, had been a 'tower of strength'
throughout the negotiations, which had at times
been near breaking down, and he noted that this
sort of business was 'right up his street'.

In fact Roth had known Strauss well in his former
life in Vienna, and in the forties was to become the
composer's close friend and most trusted business
adviser. It is likely that without his intervention, the
deal might never have come off. He was to play a
pivotal role after the war in restoring Strauss's
reputation and assisting him financially by
acquiring more works.

Galaxy, the company who administered the rights to
the Strauss operas in America, was to be served a
two-month notice: Hawkes could hardly contain

himself as he concluded his letter to Heinsheimer: 'You may have the "rose in your button hole" sooner than you think. In any event, I think you can tell Mr Edward Johnson at the Metropolitan – with my compliments – that nothing would give us greater pleasure than to deal with him over these matters in future. I am not yet prepared to buy either of you a tall hat and cane, a new tail coat or your wives a diamond tiara, in order that you may disport yourselves at the various opera houses in the US; let us hope that will come later. In the meantime "hold your horses" and await further instructions!'

The Fürstner deal put Boosey & Hawkes on to a completely different footing in the international music world. 'This is ... of great importance to us as it gives our catalogue an international standing which I should think is unique among British publishing houses.' From being a publisher of popular ballads and military music, to taking on a handful of important contemporary talents, the firm now represented a significant body of famous copyright operas, the grand rights of which were immeasurably more valuable than all their current orchestral works put together. Of course, Strauss's stock was low at the time, and in the years immediately after the war would sink lower still. But Hawkes had faith that these operas were works of genius, 'bright jewels', and would achieve immortality. He also recognised the advantage it gave them in the opera world internationally and was already plotting to maximise the opportunity. He mentions in the same letter to Heinsheimer, 'Operas such as these are bound to have a very wide performance on stage, radio, television etc. We shall stand in the forefront for the further acquisition of major copyrights. One cannot overlook ... the question of Artists and all this goes hand in hand with our general policy.'

Richard Strauss in the late 1940s
(Photo: Robin Adler)

The aim of the policy to which he refers was to become more involved in artist management, on an international scale. Despite the difficulties Heinsheimer had encountered in America, Hawkes was determined to have a finger in the performing pie, and thus to influence directly the choice of repertoire. Around the time of the Fürstner deal, another important bargain was being struck and in May he announced to

Heinsheimer that he had 'acquired an interest in Harold Holt Ltd. Leslie Boosey and I become directors of what is virtually the only impresario business in this country and one which has – if I may say so – a world-wide reputation and connection … one might almost say that 'nobody who is anybody' in the music world can get established in the concert business without going through his [Harold's] hands.' He explained that, given their Australian, American, Canadian and proposed South African offices, they could offer artists work 'for virtually two years'. While in Britain, Harold Holt would continue to promote concerts, Hawkes envisaged that in a territory like Australia, they could contract the artists 'wholesale' and therefore 'reap the benefit of the promotional angle in the concert field'. He accepted that they would have to tread more carefully in America where NBC and Columbia Artists presented overwhelming competition, but assured Heinsheimer that the relationship placed the New York office in a 'powerful position to negotiate business' and that it could 'act as a buying office to handle deals through other agencies'.

Hawkes tried to reassure Heinsheimer that this was not the end of his Artists' Bureau, and that Holt would be launching European careers in the States rather than stealing Heinsheimer's clients, but the latter must have seen the writing on the wall. How could so small an operation succeed when the managing directors in London had their sights set on globalisation? The Fürstner and Holt deals had set Hawkes's ambitions soaring: 'You see gradually how the chain is being forged. With our interests in composers and publications, operatic activity and artists, the whole thing becomes an international tie-up. Machiavellian it may be, but we have embarked on this course and we shall continue.'

Had Hawkes lived longer and employed more staff of Heinsheimer's calibre, it is likely he would have achieved his vision of a musical monopoly. Given LAB's long experience with artists and Hawkes's instinctive good taste, it would likely have been a benign monolith which served the cause of music well. As it turned out, the project flourished until the late fifties, when direction weakened and artists and repertoire matching became a trickier proposition.

In 1943, however, Hawkes could see a clear way through, and advised Heinsheimer to ensure all the singers on his books had Britten's songs and his *Les Illuminations* in their repertoire. The correspondence between Hawkes and Heinsheimer at this time is intense, and Heinsheimer pleads with him to come over to New York again as it is 'nearly two years' since they have worked together. During this time, LAB and Hawkes had been heavily engaged in setting up the new group of factories at Edgware dedicated to the wartime manufacture demanded by the government. Hawkes had characteristically relished the new challenge: 'the work was entirely foreign to me and whilst I developed a tremendous enthusiasm in the organising of them ... this has waned somewhat ... Production has reached the figures anticipated and I find it boring to sit in an Office and conduct what I call "strictly routine" business day by day and at the same time have to listen to petty arguments as to whether Miss Jones or Mr Smith are to have a halfpenny or penny an hour more and why. The profiteers of this War are the working classes; they have to be bribed to do pretty well everything' (a common sentiment among business managers of the time).

Hawkes longed 'to get back into the creative side of musical life' and Heinsheimer's letters transported him into the middle of it. He had just heard Martinů's Second Symphony – 'most unusual. It was again a tremendous success and the press are simply raving.' He also heard, and acquired, Milhaud's 'most charming' suite for harmonica and orchestra specially written for Larry Adler. Bartók was still not well, but underwent a transformation when Koussevitzky visited him in hospital, at the request of Tibor Serly and Fritz Reiner, who, like many of his friends, were concerned for his health and financial state. He commissioned Bartók to write a major orchestral work, again for the Foundation he had set up in memory of his wife. Bartók typically refused the advance, saying he could not promise to finish a work in his present condition. Koussevitzky would hear none of it, and said the terms of the commission were fixed: he must accept $1,000. They talked for an hour, Bartók becoming flushed with a 'new and very touching confidence in life' and 'an incredible recovery set in', Heinsheimer recalled, which enabled him to complete the Concerto for Orchestra in just two months.

Programme for premiere of Britten's *Serenade* at the Wigmore Hall, 15 October 1943 (Courtesy Wigmore Hall)

Back in London musical life was buzzing, as LAB described, 'The streets are crowded with people in uniform, night after night the theatres and concert halls are packed out; there are more orchestras than players so it's hard to get good work out of men who are jaded from playing night after night ... people have money, more money than ever before and nothing to spend it on, business is booming.' From out of this hive of activity, as Roth put it, 'Britten's genius rose like a meteor'. Hawkes found his *Serenade for tenor, horn and strings*, premiered in 1943, 'a remarkable composition ... The horn soloist was Dennis Brain and I can safely say I have never heard the horn played so well before.' LAB was typically suspicious of immediate success: 'I still think I prefer *Les Illuminations* and in any case I am distrustful of a work of this character which causes too much enthusiasm at the start.' The Proms were packed out and when Britten and Clifford Curzon performed his *Scottish Ballad* for two pianos and orchestra the audience demanded an encore – 'an unheard of event at the present day Proms.'

Behind the triumphant deal-making was LAB's guiding hand, and it was in this year that he achieved an unsung, but highly significant, victory for British composers through the PRS. In 1940 BBC Radio began broadcasting three-and-a-half hours of music a day entitled 'Music while you work' to 'lessen strain, relieve monotony and thereby increase efficiency' in the factories. By 1943 nearly 7,000 large factories were relaying these broadcasts, a figure that rose to 9,000 at the end of the war, reaching an audience of over five million. Gillette Industries claimed that the broadcasts were in effect private performances in privately-owned buildings, and therefore there should be no charge for the music. LAB led the case against, and proved that it constituted a public usage. Two appeals took place, which prompted a wave of damaging press comment, claiming the PRS was 'blackmailing' the factory owners and trying to profit unfairly from the war effort. Eventually the judgment went in favour of the PRS: a substantial new revenue stream had opened up.

Rescuing Covent Garden

'I was lunching with Harold Holt in the Café Royal.' LAB recalled the day, decades later: 'He said to me "I have a letter from Phillip Hill today in which he says if somebody cannot be found at once to take Covent Garden for Opera and Ballet, Mecca's Dance Hall lease will continue for another five years. Is it any good to you?" As a first reaction I said "No". Then I thought what a wonderful patriotic gesture it would be if Boosey & Hawkes took the lease of Covent Garden for five years and made the theatre available to run Opera and Ballet. I was convinced that the Government would then never dare let it lapse once its value as an opera house was realised.'

He immediately telephoned Hawkes, then back in
New York. Naturally, Ralph leapt at the chance
and the two pulled the Board with them. It was
clearly in the interests of their business to have a
thriving national opera. That said, it was
a huge investment, and in essence an altruistic
one: the firm did not stand to make any profit
from it, since the plan was that CEMA (The
Council for the Encouragement of Music and the
Arts) would take it over. LAB's next move was to
take Mary Glasgow, Lord Keynes's private
secretary, into his confidence on the matter: 'I said
it would have to depend on Lord Keynes' agreeing
to transfer the headquarters of CEMA to Covent
Garden. She conveyed this to him and he was as
enthusiastic about it as we were.' LAB agreed to
take up the lease for five years provided Keynes
would be responsible for opera and ballet. An
appointment was made to see Keynes in
Washington: 'I shall never forget the reception we

Covent Garden in the 1950s
(Photo: Gordon McLeish & Associates)

received,' recalled LAB. 'We were told by the receptionist, "He won't see
you, he doesn't see anybody." To which Ralph replied quietly, "Never mind
your views on the matter, perhaps you will be good enough to tell him that
Mr Leslie Boosey and Mr Ralph Hawkes have called to see him." The
receptionist went up looking very dubious but returned shortly afterwards
looking sheepish, "He says I am to take you up".'

The incident is a nice illustration of the two men's strengths: both were
ambitious, but where LAB had the more strategic and systematic mind,
Hawkes had the confidence and personal charisma to set his plans alight.
Later on, without Hawkes's support, LAB's leadership was critically
undermined.

An agreement was made that year that the Covent Garden Opera
Company was to have use of the stage and everything connected with the
production side for a nominal fee, while Boosey & Hawkes agreed to pay
the lease and all the expenses connected with the front of house. It cost
the firm £10,000 a year and they never received a penny from the
Government. The only influence they were to have was over the choice of
Manager. Anthony Gishford, a cousin of Ralph Hawkes who had been
involved in opera, suggested David Webster, and after having met a

number of candidates Hawkes announced to LAB he thought he had 'found the right man'. Indeed, he had, as David Webster was to lead the House triumphantly out of wartime darkness and into the international spotlight in the next decade.

Later that year, LAB was writing to Arthur Benjamin about the situation: 'The plans for the future are beginning to take shape, and we have received the most gratifying support from the highest quarters. Whether our endeavours will meet with any more success than those of the past is in the lap of the gods, but we mean to have a good try to put opera on the map over here.' Unfortunately, the story would have a bitter end, but for five years the directors of Boosey & Hawkes had the satisfaction of witnessing the rebirth of Britain's premiere opera and ballet house, knowing they had made it possible.

Tempo, Boosey & Hawkes' musical newsletter and later contemporary music journal, was published erratically during the war, but in 1944 a bumper edition was issued to keep readers up to date with the house composers. In this edition Britten was praised for his ability to write for occasions and commissions: 'although deeply immersed in plans for an opera commissioned by the ever-munificent Koussevitzky, he is not averse to sparing the time to write a short cantata for the anniversary of a

Covent Garden as a dance hall with Teddy Foster's Band (1945)
(Photo: courtesy Royal Opera House)

provincial English church.' This was the *Festival Te Deum*, written for a church in Swindon, and the opera, of course, was *Peter Grimes*. At the time, LAB had to apply to the Ipswich Police Constabulary for permission for Erwin Stein to make weekly trips to Aldeburgh to assist with the parts of *Peter Grimes*. As an enemy alien, Stein needed the permit to travel near the sensitive East coast. LAB explained his role and assured the Chief of Police that Stein was the 'only person with sufficient knowledge of the composer's work' who could carry out this task.

Tempo also listed Copland's recent ballet successes, *Billy the Kid* and *Rodeo*. This was also the year he completed his masterpiece *Appalachian Spring*. Kodály created the final version of his *Missa Brevis* while Hungary was suffering Nazi occupation, but resolutely refused to leave. Meanwhile, by October 1943, Bartók had completed his *Concerto for Orchestra*, which would become his most profitable work, and had accepted a commission from Yehudi Menuhin to write a solo violin sonata. He spent a peaceful four months in North Carolina, living on funds made available from the American Society of Composers, Authors and Publishers (ASCAP), and completed the sonata, which Menuhin initially thought 'unplayable' and later felt was 'the most important composition for violin alone since Bach'. Bartók also sketched the Third Piano Concerto for his wife Ditta, which he almost completed just before his death in 1945. (As Heinsheimer mused, 'In the last pages he ever wrote he set a small, lovely monument to the birds of North Carolina'.) He spent the summer of 1944 at Lake Saranac working on the texts of Wallachian folksongs as part of a commission for Columbia University, and would not begin work on another piece for almost a year. In December 1944 he attended the New York premiere of his *Concerto for Orchestra*, the last time he would appear in public. Heinsheimer was there too: 'He knew that this time he had touched the hearts of his audience, and he was present to hear it and to take many of his gentle, very touching, terribly serious bows.'

Peter Grimes and the death of Bartók

During the final weeks of the war, rehearsals for *Peter Grimes* were in full swing and it was agreed that Sadler's Wells Opera Company could return to its own theatre for the season. Determined to maximise publicity, which was already intense, Boosey & Hawkes engaged the principal singers to give excerpts from the opera at a concert in the Wigmore Hall, with Britten at the piano. After attending the evening Edward Sackville-West announced that London was about to hear 'the English equivalent of *Wozzeck*'.

The premiere production of
Peter Grimes at Sadler's
Wells with Peter Pears in
the title role
(Photo: Behr 1945)

The first night, on 7 June, caused a sensation: there were fourteen curtain
calls. Joan Cross remembered, 'The stage crew were stunned; they
thought it was a demonstration. Well, it was, but fortunately of the right
kind.' Ralph Hawkes threw a lavish party at the Savoy. As Britten, who
clearly knew the worth of his work, wrote, 'It looks as if the old spell on
British opera may be broken at last.' For Boosey & Hawkes, the success
had another significance: with newly forged links to Covent Garden and
Harold Holt, an international network of offices, and the operas of Strauss
in its armoury, the company was perfectly placed to promote the work of a
new opera composer. Ralph Hawkes lost no time, as Roth recalled: 'There
was still much scepticism. "This is not the first English opera which will
disappear after four performances," said an official to me when I applied
for thirty tickets for the foreign press. We had to buy them. "First blood!"
cried Ralph Hawkes the next morning when the Royal Opera House in
Stockholm and the Municipal Theatre in Basle asked for contracts.' The
opera's dissemination after the war was sensational by the standards of
any new work. Hire library records show that within 18 months of its
premiere it had been performed in Stockholm, Antwerp, Basle, Milan,
Brno, Vienna, Berlin, Copenhagen and Tanglewood.

That same summer, Bartók was on Lake Saranac continuing work on the
Third Piano Concerto and sketching the Viola Concerto for William
Primrose. Hawkes had seen him in New York at the end of 1944. He had
been planning a new Wigmore series for the 1945 autumn season during
which all six quartets would be played, and in February commissioned a

Hire Library records showing rapid early spread of *Peter Grimes* performances (1945–47) seventh string quartet, which Bartók had expressed a desire to write. Hawkes had tried to give Bartók an advance of £250 to purchase the copyright on the projected quartet, but every such payment had to go through the Bank of England, as B&H was an English company. Hawkes was quite wrongly accused after Bartók's death of not doing enough to finance the composer's time in America, but his long, pleading letter is evidence of the stranglehold the Bank had on such advances, and Bartók would never have accepted an informal hand-out. Other attempts had been made before, both by Hawkes, who tried to add on money to a cheque from ASCAP (Bartók insisted it be accounted for and when it could

not be, returned the money), and by Heinsheimer and the owner of a small record company who had issued an LP of Bartók playing his own piano works. Instead of sending him the royalties for the few hundred that had actually sold, it was agreed they would say 10,897 were sold. Initially Bartók was delighted, but when his much smaller royalty cheque from Columbia records arrived he smelt a rat: '"I want you to investigate," he said with stern determination. I felt my swivel chair turning to molasses,' recounts Heinsheimer.

Sylvia Goldstein remembered Bartók at this time as 'so beautiful and radiant, he had an aura – though I now realise it was his illness that made him glow like that.' In September, Bartók was taken to hospital for the last time. György Sándor arrived just as he was leaving the house and took the second proofs of the *Concerto for Orchestra*

Bartók's grave in New York

that the composer had been correcting. Earlier that year Hawkes had suggested they go ahead with publication without sending them back, but Bartók had clearly insisted he proof them himself. Sándor remembers that one of his comments in the margin criticised the inaccurate use of a capital letter in an Italian term: 'It is so typically *German* to set words in such a way!' A prejudice with which Stein could sympathise. Sándor completed the proofs before Bartók's death on 26 September, and a few months later would be the first to perform his friend's Third Piano Concerto.

When Bartók died, almost overnight he became a famous composer in the country that had been so reluctant to listen to his music. It was considered scandalous that ASCAP had to pay for his burial and coffin. A few years later, Hawkes pointed out that ASCAP itself had been at fault in that they had made no attempt during this period to organise a department for serious music or to collect his royalties. 'Whatever gifts they made to Bartók were no compensation for his just performing fees. To have given money at all after denying the principle of collecting seems but a hypocritical attitude to whitewash their faults.' Their system of radio royalties awarded the same sum to a popular song as a symphony. Hawkes was charged early in the war by PRS in London to alter the American attitude and, together with LAB, he achieved the aim seven long years later. In an American obituary of Hawkes, the achievement was given its due: 'the victory he was proudest of was getting ASCAP to give the works of serious composers adequate rating.'

But in the late forties, such was the backlash against Boosey & Hawkes that Friede Roth, then a publicist for the New York office, felt the need to address the issue of Hawkes's maligned reputation in her memoir of him: 'All those who looked away in embarrassment when Mr Hawkes begged engagements, performances or commissions for Bartók, stormed loudest. Ralph Hawkes was the natural whipping boy. It is time to put a stop to this sham. The truth is that Ralph Hawkes did more than anyone else; he stood behind Bartók when few even dreamed of his genius.'

The war was over. Bartók had lived to see himself elected to the new Hungarian parliament. He would have been satisfied to know that his great friend Kodály had been appointed head of the new arts council and president of the musicians' union. A letter from Hawkes to Kodály in 1945 congratulates him and enquires as to what he is writing and whether there are new works to be published. The relationship would continue until Kodály's death.

Hawkes was, as ever, impatient to return to New York now that travel easier. But before he could leave in October, a host of new initiatives needed attention. There was the founding of the Anglo-Soviet Press, a wholly-owned subsidiary of Boosey & Hawkes whose sole purpose was to publish Soviet

Letter from William Walton to Ralph Hawkes declining offer of publishing contract (1945)

> March 16ᵗʰ –
>
> Dear Ralph Hawkes,
> I am sorry that I have been so long in making up my mind as regards your proposal to publish my works with your firm.
> After much consideration & consultation I have reached the conclusion that it is almost impossible under the circumstances to leave the O.U.P.; for they have expressed the

works in Britain in conjunction with the Soviet government's own rights organisation, as a way of obtaining copyright protection in Europe. It would open the doors to a relationship with Shostakovich, the later works of Prokofieff, Kabalevsky and Khachaturian, and was made in the nick of time. As the political frost of the Cold War set in, such an optimistic business venture would have been almost impossible to set up. Alfred Kalmus was chosen to manage Anglo-Soviet, and duly installed in 23 Berners Street.

Dr Ernst Roth, fresh from his Straussian triumphs, was made Music Publications and Production Director, while Anthony Gishford, a cousin of Ralph Hawkes and, crucially, a close friend of Britten, was appointed Press Relations Officer for Covent Garden. The job tied him only peripherally to Boosey & Hawkes itself, but eventually led him into the firm, first as an editor of *Tempo,* and then as one of the directors of the company. His starting salary in Press Relations was to be £1,500 per annum, a reasonable sum in comparison with one of the staff at the factory music department, who earned £7 a week at the time.

determination to keep me with them at all costs. Seeing this, and the fact that they started publishing my works in the first place & have continued to do so for so long a time makes me feel that I am under a certain obligation to stay with them.

But I should like to say how grateful I am to you for your generous offer & how sorry I am that I cannot see my way to accept it.

If I am ever in the position to do anything in return I should be only too happy to do so.

Has Lord Berners communicated with you as yet? I told him you wanted to get in touch with him in regard to other things beside his music & he is anxious to meet you. If I had been in London I would have arranged a meeting personally.

I hope that we may meet sometime in the near future.

Yours very sincerely
William Walton

In the summer of 1945, Hawkes went to Paris to secure world distribution rights to Éditions Belaieff. Cesare Grechi, who had been managing Éditions Hawkes since before the war, was instructed to purchase the Belaieff stock for approximately 100,000 francs. Hawkes also continued negotiations with Mr Paitchadze, who was responsible for Édition Russe, with its works by Stravinsky, Rachmaninoff and Prokofieff, the first moves towards an acquisition that would transform Boosey & Hawkes. He made one final effort to persuade Walton to leave OUP and offered him a major opera commission; Walton turned him down again but said that he would offer him his *Clytemnestra* ballet.

Hawkes left for New York at the end of September and was soon joined by LAB who helped oversee the establishment of Boosey & Hawkes Inc. Hawkes had secured from the Bank of England 'a 51% participation in the formation of the new company'. Max Winkler was bought out, though his son Harold continued to work for the firm for some years, and Hawkes's Manhattan base was finally established in 57th Street.

The last days of Richard Strauss

Having acquired the rights to Strauss's operas without the composer being present at any of the negotiations, Boosey & Hawkes went on a charm offensive after the war to assist its new composer and secure further works from him. Late in 1946, LAB was in Paris and heard rumours that other publishers were attempting to acquire the composer's latest works. Roth was dispatched forthwith to Switzerland with an agreement for all future works. He recalls in his book, *The Business of Music*, how Strauss appeared after so many years: 'He met me in the corridor, a little bent but still very tall, his face a little more wrinkled than I remember but otherwise hardly changed.' When Roth explained how his publishing firm had acquired the operas, the composer asked seriously, 'But do you really think that I am still a business proposition?'

Ernst Roth in the 1950s
(Photo: Fayer)

By 21 January 1947, he had signed the new agreement and wrote to the Boosey & Hawkes directors: 'As present conditions do not allow me to take care of my rights and interests myself I herewith authorise you to take all the steps concerning publication and safeguarding of my artistic and financial interests of the works listed below' (these included *Metamorphosen*, his Oboe Concerto, the Horn Concerto No. 2 and other works written since the late thirties).

Like many in Europe, Strauss was penniless after the war and had no means of income; there were no conducting engagements and a large proportion of his royalties had been appropriated by Allied Property Control. He was living in a hotel in Baden and had given its owner some original manuscripts to put in the safe as surety.

Hawkes, enjoying relative wealth in America, sent out parcels of clothes, food, penicillin and cigarettes. (Strauss was not the only composer – Britten was the lucky recipient of hams, sugar and, surprisingly, furniture.) Hawkes even suggested to Strauss that the clothes he was sending might 'provide fuel'. One amusing exchange between Roth and Heinsheimer notes the composer's request for Loxol, 'No. 8 bright, ash blond', an

American brand of hair dye that his wife Pauline used: 'Let's get it – it is more important to keep Pauline in good spirits than Richard!' Their son, Franz, also benefited from Hawkes's charity, sending a touching letter in 1948 thanking him for the 'beautiful wool … so necessary as my eldest boy is beginning as stage manager now in Coburg with *Daphne*, and has really nothing dark and good to dress.'

Roth, meanwhile, was brokering the sale of manuscripts in London – each was priced at over 20,000 Swiss francs, but Strauss repeatedly asked in letters how he was going to find more money to live on. He was depressed and embittered by the hostility with which he was viewed in the music world, having been for a period President of the Reich Music Chamber before the war. Although he was eventually cleared by the De-Nazification tribunal, the fact that he had stayed in Germany placed him under suspicion, and his musical reputation was at a low ebb. His Oboe Concerto got a cool reception in London in 1946 as a work which 'exhales the atmosphere of a culture that has crashed in ruins since Strauss was writing this sophisticated, yet fanciful, elegant yet half-poignant music thirty years ago or more' (*The Times*). A review of some essays on Strauss in the same paper a year later is more critical of his 'apolitical' stance, claiming that 'his egotism, revealed in his indifference to men and affairs, is, unlike Beethoven's or even Wagner's, a sign of spiritual frigidity'.

Strauss arrives in London for a festival of his music in 1947
(Photo: Associated Press)

Throughout 1947 and 1948 his wartime record was being investigated by officals. In one letter he complains bitterly to Roth: 'I was never a party member, but always against the Nazis. Goebbels even considered me "impossible" … Some affidavits, from Lotte Lehmann and God knows which other people, I have dismissed as unworthy of me.' His requests to leave Germany during the war had been repeatedly refused by the Gestapo, but the Swiss regarded him with suspicion and in 1946 cancelled a planned performance of *Ariadne* in Zürich in protest at his presence in the country.

It was absolutely in the interests of Boosey & Hawkes that Strauss's reputation be rehabilitated, and Ralph Hawkes was an energetic advocate. He wrote to Strauss in 1946, 'You will be glad to hear that Dr Koussevitzky, who sends his best wishes, will give the first performance of *Metamorphosen* and the New York Philharmonic will give the Oboe Concerto in April. You may have already heard of the success of *Ariadne* here.'

But it was Roth's inspiration to organise a 1947 Strauss Festival in London, with Beecham as the principal conductor, and to bring the maestro before a British public, who might not have realised this musical giant was still alive. It was a brave undertaking, involving co-operation from the highest quarters. The British authorities were persuaded not only to give this enemy alien a visa but to lift the embargo on his royalty payments. Roth knew what a risk he was taking and, just before they set off together for the flight, wondered whether the octogenarian composer would survive the ordeal at all. 'Strauss, my wife and I sat in a DC3 aircraft at Geneva airport, waiting for the moment we should fly into the cloudless blue. It was only then that we realised our heavy responsibility. At 83 Strauss was making his first air journey. How would it all go? The unreliable London weather, the concerts, the people, the Press! But Strauss was happy as I had not seen him for a long time. The flight gave him a sensation which he enjoyed like a schoolboy.' Roth had judged the moment correctly: when Strauss entered his box for the first concert in Drury Lane, he was greeted like a king. Beecham conducted two of the concerts but Strauss himself conducted the Philharmonia in the crowning concert at the Royal Albert Hall where an audience of 6,500 people turned out to hear *Don Juan, Burlesque, Symphonia Domestica* and the waltz from the second act of *Der Rosenkavalier*. As he wrote to his grandson, 'The two-hour concert did not tire me in the least. The applause was incredible and there was no unfriendly remark in the press.' It was an historic occasion, and Roth's part in it was not forgotten: Strauss presented him with a manuscript memento of themes from *Der Rosenkavalier*, inscribing it: 'in gratitude to Dr Ernst Roth the true helper and courageous organiser of the London Strauss Festival.'

The occasion marked a turning point in the composer's reputation. *Arabella* became as successful as *Der Rosenkavalier, Friedenstag* ran for 40 performances in Brussels, and *Die schweigsame Frau* for over 50 in Berlin. The beauties of *Capriccio* and *Daphne* were discovered and the 'workshop' pieces of his war years, such as *Metamorphosen*, were played all over the world. When he returned to Switzerland, his health deteriorated, but there was more music to come. Boosey & Hawkes was paying for his hotel bills at the Palace Hotel in Montreux, and Roth was in constant touch. Throughout the summer of 1948, at the famously casual suggestion of his son Franz ('Papa, stop writing letters and brooding ... write a few nice songs instead'), he started orchestrating some songs. Ernst Roth commissioned and paid for five, but ultimately only received four, one of which, *Im Abendrot*, was dedicated to him. The title, *Four Last Songs*, was chosen by Roth, who published them after Strauss's death. To the ears of the millions who love them, there is an inevitability about the shape of this famous cycle, but it was Roth, not Strauss, who grouped and ordered them, surely one of his most significant contributions to music.

Strauss underwent an operation on his bladder early in 1949. 'It looks as if he will never get well again ... please don't mention it to anybody,' wrote Roth to Hawkes. Roth received an SOS from the family and arrived just in the nick of time to find the lawyer from Garmisch 'dividing up the kingdom' between the family members, but more alarmingly attempting 'to alter existing agreements in favour of heirs'. Roth was in his element in such a crisis, and there is a sense of keen satisfaction in his account in a letter to Hawkes: 'I refused any discussion and gave them a slight shock by showing them the documents by which Strauss agreed to the transfer from Fürstner [to B&H] and by which he gave us 20% for *Arabella* and *Die schweigsame Frau* ... The matter with Fürstner will come to a head in February and we have agreed that we shall administer all Strauss works in Germany on a 20% commission ... I reckon that could give the German

The showroom at
295 Regent Street (1946)

business a turnover of some 100,000 marks per year and could solve the problem of capital.'

The 'German business' he is referring to was Boosey & Hawkes GmbH which Roth had been charged with setting up in the British Zone in Bonn in 1949 (though ultimately the Fürstner rights in question were to be administered by Schott on behalf of the Strauss family in that territory). Roth was not one to allow sentiment to cloud his financial judgement, but Strauss left a huge gap in his life after this short period of intense friendship. Roth said later he would often read the composer's letters from this time of 'sorrow' – Strauss's last letter to him had described the 'torture chamber' that awaited him and was signed 'yours desperately' – and drew comfort from ever-increasing numbers of performances and devotees of Strauss in every corner of the globe.

Spreading the net wide

The directors of Boosey & Hawkes had spent the war cooking up ambitious plans for expansion and they lost no time in the forties in pursuing them, despite less than propitious economic conditions. Besides the German office, a South African branch was set up in Cape Town, after months of negotiations with a certain Mr Weiss, whom Hawkes accused of 'seeking to establish a very advantageous situation for yourself'. An in-house candidate, Mr Golbourn, was sent out to be managing director of the office for three years. Although the company had always had a colonial, military relationship with South Africa – great ox carts of brass instruments were loaded up by the reps at the Cape in the early years of the 20th century, and would make their stately progress to East Africa and on to India, visiting royalty along the way – it was a risky move. As one South African director put it some years later, 'This is drum and bugle country' and it was never going to be fertile ground for promoting expensive contemporary operas. But the market for instruments, Hammond Organs and sheet music, particularly light music, was sufficiently large to make it a viable business, as it remained for the next four decades. Another colonial outpost, Delhi, was doing less well: in 1946 the agency showed an annual loss of 46 rupees. The Sydney office, having boomed during the war, showed a poor result in 1946, and Hawkes travelled to Sydney in 1949 to update himself on its activities. LAB's second son Simon had gone to work in the Sydney office on leaving Malvern College, and Ralph invited him to come and work in New York. Simon was eager to join the Manhattan team and accepted with alacrity. It was a great misfortune that he did not work longer with Hawkes, since he would very likely have become the director's chief protégé and might have been in a position to heal the rifts that were to develop between the Boosey and the Hawkes sides of the business.

LAB also travelled abroad after the war, and visited several countries in South America in his capacity as President of CISAC (International Confederation of Authors' and Composers' Societies). The firm took on Roberto Barry of Buenos Aires to be the exclusive representative of Boosey & Hawkes publications and band instruments, a relationship that has lasted to the present day, despite a rocky start. LAB's mission in Argentina was to try to persuade officials that Argentina should join the Berne Copyright Convention, which so far only Brazil had signed up to. He was received by no less than President Perón, who listened to the deputation and promised support, as did the President of Uruguay. While there he visited Rio to chat with Villa-Lobos and witness Brazilians dancing to their 'own peculiar rhythm', the samba.

Back in Regent Street, staff conditions were examined and a canteen set up jointly with the Performing Right Society, which shared the adjacent building in Margaret Street. Female staff, many of whom worked on Saturdays, were granted one hour's shopping leave a week to ensure there was food on the table at home. Boosey & Hawkes's reputation was high but the attitude towards staff famously mean. Bassett Silver, the highly successful composer and arranger in charge of light music, requested a three-week holiday at this time and was turned down. Salaries were extremely low, partly because the Booseys themselves were thrifty and did not choose to draw large salaries for themselves. It is still shocking to read that the eminent music editor Erwin Stein was so hard up he had ask for a loan of £500 for living expenses, which Roth made him work off by doing freelance editing at night. (Roth and Stein were not friends, and there is a hint of humiliation about this episode.)

The triumphs of the war were rather overshadowed by two outbursts of litigation. Firstly, Universal Edition challenged the validity of its 1939 agreement with Boosey & Hawkes, claiming unfair advantage had been taken of their firm when it was 'under Nazi duress'. Dr Roth was put on the case immediately and proposed to withdraw the previous and, as B&H saw it, generous offer to hand back the Mahler and Weinberger copyrights to UE. (This was eventually settled in UE's favour). Secondly, after the glittering opening of the Royal Opera House in February 1946 and a dinner in LAB's honour when the contract ended in December 1949, the Ministry

of Works claimed a far larger amount for dilapidations than Boosey &
Hawkes had allowed for. It was something of a kick in the teeth for the
company that had set Covent Garden back on its feet. The wrangling over
amounts went on for more than two years, and its sad end lies in the next
chapter.

A Russian Spring

The great acquisition of this period was the fulfilment of Ralph Hawkes's
pre-war dreams: he finally bought the key catalogues associated with the
visionary and influential Russian conductor, Serge Koussevitzky.

In Moscow in 1909, Koussevitzky and his wealthy wife, Natalie, had
founded Russian Music Publishing, with Rachmaninoff as a key member of
its council. The company had rapidly contracted leading young composers
– including Scriabin, Medtner, Prokofieff and Stravinsky – and in 1914
Koussevitzky bought the long-established Russian publisher, Gutheil, thus
securing the rights to most of Rachmaninoff's major works. Companies
were established in France (Édition Russe de Musique) and Germany
(Russischer Musikverlag) to establish international copyright protection,
which music published in Russia did not then enjoy.

Plaque at Covent Garden to
commemorate Boosey &
Hawkes's purchase of the
lease, and the reopening of
the house for ballet and
opera in 1946. (The death
date of Hawkes should have
appeared as 1950.)
(Photo: Donald Southern)

Serge Koussevitzky and his
second wife Olga at their
home (late 1940s)

By 1945 Koussevitzky was over 70 and no longer wanted the responsibility
of supervising the publishing house. As has been seen, Hawkes, who had
secured the sole agency for Édition Russe in 1923, was closely in touch
with Koussevitzky from the late thirties onwards and encouraged
Heinsheimer to cement a relationship when he came to work in New York.
Eventually, Hawkes approached the conductor formally, and a deal was
struck, thus giving B&H an incredible treasure-trove containing many
works of Rachmaninoff, Prokofieff and Stravinsky: highly desirable rights at
the time which were to increase in value as the century progressed. Today,
the 'Koussevitzky works', which include *The Rite of Spring* and *Petrushka*,
Lieutenant Kijé and the *Classical Symphony*, Rachmaninoff's Second Piano
Concerto and Second Symphony, and Ravel's orchestration of *Pictures at an
Exhibition*, are among the top earners in the B&H catalogue.

Not surprisingly, it was an expensive acquisition: a figure of $300,000 is
mentioned in 1946, and the bank had to be approached to help raise it.
This was not a single payment: numerous other payments for rights and
territories were to be made in the following years.

So much for the works of Stravinsky's youth: Hawkes was, as ever, looking
to the future. On the day that Stravinsky became an American citizen,
28 December 1945, Ralph Hawkes went to Beverley Hills to meet him, as

he recalled in an article in *Tempo*, 'in the incongruous but unavoidable setting of an hotel dining room complete with dance band and cabaret.'

They discussed his current works, the *Symphony in Three Movements* and the *Ebony Concerto*, though B&H did not ultimately obtain these. Stravinsky's future plans included a concerto for string orchestra for Paul Sacher, his first European commission for twelve years, and it was this, the *Concerto in D*, that was the first work to bear the imprint of Boosey & Hawkes. A full agreement was drawn up and signed in 1947, by which time he was working on the ballet *Orpheus* and planning a full-length opera in English. In fact, it was Hawkes's contract that had made the composition of an opera possible: Stravinsky was to be guaranteed a minimum of $10k a year rising to $12k after two years. Hawkes never underestimated Stravinsky's worth, as Friede Roth noted in her memoir of Hawkes: the agreement was 'so lavish that at last one composer could feel that something was being put over on a publisher'. By 1948 *Orpheus* had had a 'smash hit' reception at the Ballet Society in New York and his *Mass* had been praised at its first performance at La Scala.

The Rape of Lucretia **and a monstrous misrepresentation**

With Stravinsky now a house composer too, Britten would have to share the limelight, and the attention of Hawkes, LAB and Roth. The two composers could not help but be aware of each other. An exchange between them during Britten's 1949 recital tour of America reveals the outwardly dismissive attitude of the older to the younger composer: the Earl of Harewood recalls that when Britten asked if he would write a

Ralph Hawkes and Olga Koussevitzky (left), Clare Hawkes and Serge Koussevitzky (centre) and Leslie Boosey (far right) at Tanglewood (late 1940s)
(Photo: courtesy Nigel Boosey)

full-length opera, Stravinsky replied he was working on one, 'But opera, not music drama, is my interest – and I shall write it in closed forms.' When Britten suggested his own *Rape of Lucretia* was just such an opera, Stravinsky, to Britten's shock and anger, said 'Not at all'. (There was clearly another side to this story that remains unknown). Later when Britten heard Stravinsky's *The Rake's Progress,* he declared himself 'miserably disappointed' that such a great composer should have 'such an irresponsible and perverse view of opera.'

Britten's *The Rape of Lucretia*, his 'lovely piece' in Hawkes's words, was dedicated to Erwin Stein. As a short, chamber opera it was clearly not going to have the sensational success of *Peter Grimes*, but it did not lack exposure. The 1946 inaugural tour of the Glyndebourne English Opera Company, underwritten by John Christie, might have been financially disastrous but it helped towards the 83 consecutive performances in Britain and Holland that the opera enjoyed that year. British critics compared it sometimes unfavourably to *Peter Grimes* – only when it was performed in New York did Ferruccio Bonavia detect 'a widening range, a deepening sympathy'.

Britten's next opera, the Maupassant-based comedy *Albert Herring*, was also introduced by an impressively large tour of Britain, Holland and Switzerland in 1947. This time it was being performed by the newly-formed English Opera Group. Ralph Hawkes and Erwin Stein joined Tyrone Guthrie and Kenneth Clark on its board. After some initial reviews

Britten at Glyndebourne for rehearsals of *The Rape of Lucretia* with Eric Crozier and John Piper (1947)

dismissed it as mere 'charade', 'hardly an opera' and 'a diverting piece on the second plane', Peter Diamand of the Holland Festival tried to pull out of his commitment, but Britten insisted, and audience reaction was as joyous and amused as it had been at the Glyndebourne premiere.

Hawkes felt highly responsible for the New York production of *Lucretia* after the 'farcical' production of *Peter Grimes* at the Met in 1947. He wrote to Britten at the time, 'I didn't send you a cable after the Met performances, it would have been senseless and upsetting. I must guard against repetition of such farcical casting and scenic work in the future and intend to do so with *Lucretia* when I see Cardelli next week.' At first he tried to persuade Britten that the chamber opera should run on Broadway, a suggestion the composer rejected. Eventually, Agnes De Mille's production opened at the beginning of January 1949 and marked 'a milestone in the development of the operatic world here,' according to Hawkes. The veteran critic Olin Downes completely reversed his opinion on a second hearing, much to Hawkes's amusement: 'he changed his mind in the most violent fashion ... one should never lose sight of the fact that he cannot stomach an English success.' In the same letter he mentions that he has a date for *The Beggar's Opera* in Denver and that there have been many requests for *Albert Herring* but he is awaiting the right director as 'So much can be lost in this piece unless the producer knows it as it was done in London.'

A performance of *The Rape of Lucretia* in Rome in 1949 was the occasion of a serious row between Ernst Roth and Britten, the first open display of a brewing hostility between the two. It had been suggested by the British Council that *Lucretia* be performed after Purcell's *Dido and Aeneas*, a coupling Britten was unhappy with, feeling the two operas did not complement each other in mood or style. Roth had conveyed this to the organisers, but was pressed repeatedly and in the end wrote a letter explaining why he thought Britten did not accept the programming. To his great misfortune, Roth's letter to Sr Ravizza was read out at a dinner and thus leaked into the press. It contained for Britten a most unfortunate heresy: Roth claimed that Britten did not want *Dido and Aeneas* to be performed before *The Rape of Lucretia* because 'everyone' finds Purcell 'terribly tiring, not to say boring'.

Britten was incandescent: 'I am so horrified and made so furious by these two documents that I have immediately written to Faulkner [Music Organiser for the British Council] describing the opinion as 2% mine, the rest "a misleading, inaccurate and distorted elaboration" ... You build up a monstrous edifice of inaccuracy and half truths.' A few days later Britten wrote to LAB to explain what had happened, regretting the strength of his outburst to Roth. LAB, tactful as ever, was sympathetic to both parties, and encouraged Britten to send a press statement clarifying his position. Britten did so, noting: 'Purcell is the king of English music. I love him enough to be making a large edition of his works ...'

In his reply, Roth suggested that Britten's 'abusive' letter was part of a darker plot. At the end of his acid riposte, he notes: 'It grieves me more than I can say that your attitude towards me is always obscured by some suspicion of sinister intentions on my part. And there seem to be people who are taking a sporting interest in preventing a better atmosphere from developing between us. I cannot force your confidence. But I believe to have a justified claim to your fairness. And this, I trust, I shall enjoy as a poor but indispensable substitute for better things.' Roth summarised the situation perfectly: his relationship with Britten remained 'forced' and the 'atmosphere' strained for many years to come.

When Roth refers to 'people' poisoning the relationship he probably meant just one person: Anthony Gishford. The conservative, well-connected, homosexual Gishford, Britten's affectionate friend and skilful negotiator, was never a favourite of Roth's. Neither was he highly rated by his cousin Ralph Hawkes, who did not welcome him into the firm but kept him at arm's length working as press officer for Covent Garden, and only let him in by the 'back door', as it were, as editor of *Tempo*, a peripheral activity to the actual business. But by 1949 Gishford had been made head of publicity and would soon become a director of the firm. By then it must have been obvious that he was valuable as an important ally of Britten's (and it was a friendship that survived). Letters show that they shared precisely the same sense of humour, and rather enjoyed sending up the various characters at Boosey & Hawkes. During the fifties Gishford, next to Stein, became Britten's key contact in the firm, the insider whose loyalty to the composer was perhaps greater than his loyalty to his employer. Tensions would eventually come to a head.

Hawkes under pressure

Britten had agreed reluctantly to travel to Tanglewood in 1946 to hear the first American performance of *Peter Grimes*, a rather shambolic student affair conducted by the 28-year-old Bernstein. Throughout 1947 and the beginning of 1948, Hawkes tried to encourage Britten and Pears to come to

Copland and Britten at
Tanglewood in 1946
(Photo: Ruth Orkin)

America on a major recital tour. He always felt particularly proprietorial
about Britten, and he not only wanted to promote the artist and his music
in the States from a business point of view, but politically it was in his
interests to have them around as much as possible in 'his' own territory.
A major tour was organised for 1948; unfortunately, in February, Britten fell
ill with stomach problems while performing in Amsterdam and decided he
could not face the US tour. He cabled Hawkes: 'Urgently wish cancel
American tour. Start new large scale works needing several months
uninterrupted concentration. Very much regret causing trouble.'

Hawkes was devastated, and did not immediately accept the cancellation. It
put him in an extremely embarrassing position with venues and promoters
all over the States. At first he tried to reduce the tour but in the end
accepted a postponement to the end of 1949. As Britten commented, he had
been 'leading a rather mad existence these last years': since 1946 he had
written *The Rape of Lucretia*, the *Young Person's Guide to the Orchestra*,
Albert Herring, *The Beggar's Opera*, *Canticle I*, *St Nicolas*, *The Little Sweep*
and he was currently completing Koussevitzky's commission, the *Spring
Symphony*. He had also created an opera company and led two major opera
tours and founded the Aldeburgh Festival. The 'large scale works' he
mentioned in the cable were *Billy Budd* and his projected requiem for
Gandhi, a requiem that was never written, but which might have contained
the seed of his idea for the *War Requiem* a decade later.

There were more disappointments that spring: Britten rejected
Koussevitzky's invitation, via Hawkes, to come to teach at Tanglewood that
summer. Koussevitzky had hoped the visit would provide an opportunity for
the premiere of the *Spring Symphony*, but he and Hawkes then had to
swallow the fact that Britten had agreed to an Amsterdam first
performance in July of that year with van Beinum and the Royal
Concertgebouw. It was the second time Koussevitzky had been prevented
from hosting the premiere of his own Britten commission. Although Britten
did go to New York in September 1949 he wrote to Stein that it had become
'a terrible nightmare city'. Hawkes's dream of having Britten and Pears in
his musical sphere was not to be.

Britten's 'nightmare' city was Hawkes's El Dorado, and he was king of the
heap. Despite the pressures, he was building a fabulous business there.
Immediately after the war, he bought himself a brand new red Buick and a
plot of land in Bermuda on which he planned to build a residence for his
retirement. Arnold Broido, who came to work for B&H Inc in 1945 as a
stock manager and went on to become an editor and production manager,
remembers Hawkes's commanding presence: 'He was a monarch. When he
appeared at a musical function, people were drawn to him immediately.

The recording studio at
295 Regent Street (1940s)

He wasn't especially tall, but he carried himself beautifully, people naturally deferred to him and he had the charisma to make them feel good in his presence.'

He also remembers what a ruthless, and sometimes unpleasant, boss he could be. 'I remember one time Harold [Winkler], Ralph and I had spent the morning out on Long Island, on a business trip somewhere, having a fine old time. When he was in a good mood, Ralph could be the most charming man in the world. We all came back in good cheer and I passed a candy store on Fifth Avenue, and bought a box of candy. When I came back into the office I took the box in one hand, with its hinged lid up, and offered Mr H some candy. He snapped the top of the box hard down on my thumb and said between his teeth, 'Get back to work.' He was ruthless. It wasn't a personal attack: but business always came first.'

Despite the booming sales of sheet music in the States, and prestigious status of B&H Inc, Hawkes had personal reasons to be concerned by the end of 1948: while travelling in Australia in the early summer he had suffered his first heart attack. Britten was not the only friend to be alarmed by Hawkes's news: 'You must take care Ralph, and follow the doctor's orders to the letter! It will mean great boredom for you, but you are far too precious to many, many people, and your ideas are too valuable to go playing around with your health.'

Hawkes had put himself under extreme physical strain earlier that year during a yacht race from Cowes to Santander. Both he and LAB's eldest son, Anthony Boosey, who shared his passion for sailing and often crewed for Ralph, had entered the race. Hours after the start the boats were hit by a terrible storm and many bailed out before the major crossing. Typically, both Ralph and Anthony, in separate yachts, persevered through the turbulent Bay of Biscay, and just managed to reach the Spanish coast days later. But those who knew him have said that the experience shook Ralph and put his heart under strain.

Others maintain that a more direct cause of Ralph's heart attack was a particularly violent row with his brother Geoffrey. Geoffrey was similar to Ralph only in his entrepreneurial leanings, and their disagreements were legendary. He lacked his brother's keen intelligence and dedication, and would fly off with new enthusiasms at the drop of a hat. He 'wasn't terribly practical' as one colleague remembers, 'and was good at losing money on his business ventures'.

The first post-war Boosey & Hawkes International Conference (1949).
Standing (l to r): ?, John Little, Ralph Hawkes, Tony Gishford, Ralph Boosey, Cesare Grechi, Geoffrey Hawkes, ?
Seated (l to r): Ernst Roth, Edgar Bielefeld, Leslie Boosey, Betty Bean, Will Golbourn, Will Croombs.

Up to that point, Geoffrey had been more involved with the instrument side of the business. But when Ralph moved to New York, Geoffrey naturally, but unfortunately, became his brother's representative in London. Lacking Ralph's grasp on strategy, and at times wildly undiplomatic, Geoffrey was bound to come into conflict with the gentlemanly LAB and with his absent brother.

Hawkes had been riding a wave of success since the day he and LAB joined forces, but by 1950 his position was being undermined by the lack of profit from B&H Inc. Although Copland's stock was riding high – his Third Symphony and Clarinet Concerto both had great success during this period – B&H did not have a large source of royalties in America, especially since so many works of the Russian composers were not protected in the States (there were no performing right fees, for instance, for Rachmaninoff). Already in a 1947 directors' minute it was noted that although the 'volume of sales is increasing' in the States, the 'expenses were also rising and Mr Hawkes did not hold out hopes of substantial profits'.

He was also feeling isolated. In 1948, in a rash moment of irritation, he had dismissed Hans Heinsheimer for publishing his amusing music business memoir, *Menagerie in F sharp*. Arnold Broido takes up the story: 'Ralph had come into Manhattan on the Queen Mary, and as soon as the ship was docked, Harold Winkler, who hated Heinsheimer and saw he had a chance to get one over on Hans, rushed to the ship clutching a copy of the book. He told him that Heinsheimer had written the book in company time and that now it was all over bookshops in New York and Chicago. Ralph came to the offices and summoned him. (You always had to wait for Ralph to speak, and the longer you waited the angrier you knew he was. This time he was in a rage.) He said to Heinsheimer, 'You will, of course, withdraw this book. If you want to continue working for me, that is.' Heinsheimer apparently turned and walked out. Within days he was snapped up by Gus Schirmer, President of G Schirmer, the biggest publishing competitor in New York, where he helped build a serious rival catalogue, including the works of Carter, Bernstein and his 'discovery' Gian Carlo Menotti. Hawkes's ideal replacement for Heinsheimer would have been Ernst Roth, but his trusted ally resisted all invitations to come out and spend time in the New York office, usually pleading ill health and his responsibilities to his wife and elderly mother as an excuse.

By the time of the Boosey & Hawkes international conference in 1950, Ralph was on the back foot: 'Mr Ralph Hawkes reported that the adverse balance of B&H Inc was gradually being reduced and that the position would continue to improve.' LAB and Ralph's brother Geoffrey were not willing to bail him out, explaining that while there was 'no desire on the part of the parent company to hamper development' of the overseas offices, 'finances of the London company were already stretched'. In LAB's last letter to Hawkes, the lines are drawn: 'I am very glad you are hoping to be in a position to remit money soon because the fact of our having to pay your royalties, together with many other calls which are not strictly day-to-day payment of bills, has made our position a somewhat difficult one for the moment in spite of the Bank's generosity.'

The sudden sense of division is surprising. Hawkes's wife's sister remembers him saying at the time that he wished Clare and her sisters had had some money so he could have 'bought out the Booseys', but this was apparently never discussed with other colleagues. The 20-year partnership had reached some kind of watershed. Hawkes wanted control of the publishing business in America, and was not interested in the instrument business, which he hoped the Booseys would continue to manage in London.

LAB's letter, that was to turn out to be valedictory, also touches on another source of tension between them: Britten. The cause of the young composer Arthur Oldham had been espoused by Britten for some time, and Hawkes had thought it politic to give the composer a contract, which he had rashly promised Britten he would renew for a period of three years. How LAB rated Oldham, we do not know, but he gets straight to the point: 'his Divertimento for string orchestra was rejected by Stein (which means a lot!) ... the only other work that could go into production is the *Chinese Lyrics* which is not bad but there is no sparkle of genius either. Commercially they are a dead loss.'

He ends the letter with an account of the first British performance of Bartók's Viola Concerto at the Proms with William Primrose as soloist. 'It is difficult and modern and there are places where the hand of Tibor Serly is quite obvious, but I think it ... is a work which will be in the repertoire of every leading viola player.' LAB's letter is dated 7 September 1950. Hawkes never read it. He had recently bought William Primrose's house in Westport, Connecticut, and it was there on the morning of 8 September that he collapsed and died of a heart attack while walking in the garden.

A Scotsman in New York

When Ralph Hawkes died, he was mourned by literally hundreds of people. Not only was he fêted in Britain, but in a short time he had made himself an indispensable part of the music world in New York. That very week would see the culmination of his idea to bring a Sadler's Wells Ballet season over to the Metropolitan Opera. As critic Irving Kolodin put it: 'In the post War musical life of New York, Hawkes was a new and stimulating personality. The idea of a publisher with a creative interest in contemporary music was something strange in this circle; almost as strange as a publisher who went perpetually to concerts and opera of all sorts whether they involved the works of men he published or not. In his modest person was contained a great power of decision over the creative spirits of his time … Surely his best memorial would be the preservation, through some kindred spirit, of the broad, adventurous enterprise he imparted to the firm of which he was so integral a part.'

Without that 'kindred spirit', B&H Inc was in trouble. Since Heinsheimer had been fired, there was no obvious successor. LAB flew out immediately and arranged to spend 'four to six months' overseeing the operation. Ralph's plans for offices in Los Angeles and Chicago were unpicked, and the search for a new director began. The current set up included two sparky and able women, Betty Randolph Bean, who was already a director and involved with press and promotion, and Sylvia Goldstein who would eventually become Head of Rights; several competent and some experienced men on the sales and production side, including Arnold Broido, then production manager, and the young Simon Boosey. In hindsight, it seems to have been a mistake to overlook the women, but at the time it would not have occurred even to Sylvia or Betty themselves that they should be put in charge of such an operation. Bean was a formidable character and very well-connected in Manhattan's music world, having come into the firm via Koussevitzky. 'I remember she had her own private secretary and a private, locked cupboard in the office,' recalls Broido. A photograph of an international sales meeting in the late forties shows her to be a lone female figure in a sea of besuited men, holding her own with a doughty hat and coat. Geoffrey Hawkes did not take to her, and shortly afterwards she was pushed out. But in 1950 she took on the organisation of a Ralph Hawkes memorial issue of *Tempo* as a personal quest, urging Gishford to help commission contributions: 'I do feel such a Memorial should be done promptly and well, for few people in the world are aware of the real qualities of greatness that were in Ralph.'

The firm's Chairman, LAB, was all-too aware of his colleague's exceptional talents and, as he himself approached retirement age, was extremely anxious about the American company. He wrote to Britten: 'We have decided not to make any definite appointments as yet but we have brought David Adams, our Canadian man, down to spend three weeks out of every four there until further notice, superintending the production and despatch departments. Betty is going to concentrate on the promotion side. Neither of them, however, has the experience which is necessary to run a concern of the intricacies of B&H Inc.'

David Adams was an amiable Scot, who had left school at 14 and earned a living as an itinerant organist for local churches. He had also worked as an assistant in the well-known Edinburgh music retailer, Rae Macintosh. He was considered very much a 'company man', who had done his time in various departments – 'a very good Hammond demonstrator,' remembers a colleague in the Edgware newsletter of 1964. He continues: 'Most of all we remember the wonderful job he did as a 'progress man' for aircraft parts ... like the 35 foot bomb doors which we made ... he was really good at it.'

When Hawkes died, Adams was the competent manager of the Canadian operation. The generally-held view of recruitment at the time was that it was best to appoint from within, which meant sending loyal staff out to the 'colonial' offices – such as Will Golbourn in South Africa and David Adams in Canada – to test their mettle, and then to reward them with positions in the more prestigious offices of New York and London. Everyone was fond of David Adams, as another colleague recalls: 'David was charming, and became seriously popular in New York: Copland and Stravinsky regarded him as a friend. [On one occasion Stravinsky actually signed himself 'Strawhiskey' in acknowledgement of a welcome gift of a bottle of single malt.] But he was timid and indecisive. He lacked judgement when it came to composers and he was shaky as a manager.' He may have been good at making aircraft doors, but a successor to Hawkes he was not.

David Adams, President of B&H Inc following the death of Ralph Hawkes, and later Director of Music Publishing in London (1970s)

Just how shaky his grasp of the American business was became apparent in the next few years. During the early fifties LAB spent several months over in New York, attempting to rescue B&H Inc, which was now running headlong into debt. There were members of the London board who were pressing for the American office to be closed, an extraordinarily short-sighted attitude given the size and wealth of the territory. 'This I opposed tooth and nail,' wrote LAB in a memoir of the time. 'I spent three or four of the most unpleasant months of my life, off-loading some of my best friends in the musical world who we were quite unable to carry on our staff. I hated doing it, but at least I had the satisfaction of keeping my promise not to lose any more money.'

He explained in a letter to Britten that the office had been in need of reorganisation anyway, hinting that Ralph had been over-investing. In fact the Bank of England was accusing Hawkes of having invested £100,000 in America without any permission from the Exchange Control Authorities, and was demanding that figure back immediately. 'How are we to do it?' LAB asked Adams in desperation. Hawkes had always been the spender, LAB the saver, and even posthumously, the Hawkes dynamo needed LAB's brakes. Roth, who, it must be remembered, had no interest in the American set-up, had a solution which involved only keeping a small office and appointing agents. LAB felt this was the last resort, and even suggested handing over the business to 'a first-class American publisher' (no doubt he had G Schirmer in mind) in exchange for its catalogue in Britain.

Sylvia Goldstein at her desk in the New York office (1950s)

In the end the business was put back on a better footing, one of the major savings being the selling off of part of the instrument business to C Bruno & Son Inc, a well-established instrument maker and importer. A new company was created called Musical Imports Inc, two thirds of which was owned by the company's firm in Texas and C Bruno in New York, a move which raised capital and reduced overheads. By the end of 1952, LAB reports in his Annual Review that 'our order books are full' and more importantly 'we have been paid up to date.'

During this period, LAB became very close to the staff in New York. Arnold Broido remembers that his management style was in stark contrast to Hawkes's: 'Leslie was the sweetest man. He was very tall, somehow disjointed and slightly awkward. He would come and sit beside me when I was going through submitted manuscripts and say "Do you mind?" and he'd go through them like lightning, he could tell immediately if they were any good by their handwriting. Once he came in after a long voyage, flung himself down at a desk in the office, put his

head on his arms and went to sleep. I'll never forget the time he came
to my home, and my one-year-old son climbed up on him and poured
a glass of orange juice over his head: there he was, the Chairman of
Boosey & Hawkes, sitting there smiling with juice pouring down
his face.'

LAB had a tendency to see the best in people,
and was prepared to trust Adams despite the
staff's view that his appointment was a 'a
triumph of mediocrity over reason' (Broido's
words). What was not perhaps appreciated by
others in the London office was that Simon
Boosey and Broido were running the publishing
and warehouse facility at Oceanside, Long
Island, with Betty Bean and Sylvia Goldstein in
charge of the New York office, leaving David
Adams to be the public figurehead and little
more. This became clear when a disastrous fire
destroyed the Oceanside premises in 1954, and
business ground to a halt for six weeks. 'He was
paralysed, he just didn't know what to do so he
did nothing,' remembers Simon Boosey. Taking
matters into their own hands, Arnold Broido and Simon brought in the
loss adjusters, sorted out the insurance at some cost and instigated the
rebuilding of new premises – all without assistance from Adams.

Stravinsky and George
Balanchine rehearsing *Agon*
with New York City Ballet
and pianist Nicholas
Kopeikine (1957)
(Photo: Martha Swope)

In terms of music, there was little composer activity in the USA during the
early fifties: Copland's output was restricted to an orchestration of his
Piano Variations while, aside from the *The Rake's Progress* premiered in
Europe, Stravinsky's main American premiere was *Agon* for the New York
City Ballet. The only new American composer taken on at that time was
the Russian-American, Benjamin Lees, who had studied with George
Antheil and Nadia Boulanger. Even he was initially published out of
London, as he was living in Europe at the time and became acquainted
with Roth while both were holidaying in Switzerland. Roth, says Broido,
regarded America as 'a colony, and a rather inconvenient one at that', and
even Copland was managed from London until near the end of his life.
Broido once asked the composer why he did not insist on London
relinquishing him to the New York office, and he said 'Oh, I couldn't do
that. They are still my publishers.' 'I think,' says Broido today, 'He really
was in awe of them.'

'An unutterable folly'

Once back in London, LAB was aghast to discover that rather than negotiate a settlement with the Ministry of Works over the Covent Garden dilapidations bill, Geoffrey Hawkes had decided to deny all liability and B&H was in the process of being taken to court. 'I told the Board that they had committed an unutterable folly, which would cost them another £50,000 and this turned out to be the case.' In fact Board reports suggest that this figure was whittled away again through negotiation, but it was still a heavy toll. The story says much about the differing styles of LAB and Geoffrey Hawkes. The latter was mercurial and combative, while LAB's instinct was to use personal contacts diplomatically: 'I thought I should go and see Sir Eric Normand, who was Head of the Ministry of Works, and known to me personally, and ask how much we really ought to pay.' He estimated another £15k would probably be acceptable. 'But without Ralph to back me up, no one would support me, so there was nothing I could do.'

Geoffrey Hawkes
(late 1950s)

This is the first hint that LAB was losing his power over the Board, and the sad result of the whole incident was that when the government awarded him a CBE for his services to music, an award he richly deserved, he felt he had to refuse it: 'I couldn't accept it without appearing to be looking after my own interests rather than those of the company.' Those close to him believe he also refused it out of loyalty to Hawkes, who he felt equally deserving of an honour and who had not been offered it before his death. It was the second time LAB had missed an honour: in the First World War he failed to receive his DSO because he was made a prisoner of war just as it would have been confirmed.

Geoffrey Hawkes's British factories were in a bad state too: just after the war he had acquired a harmonica factory and some other instrument factories in South Wales, assuming that the labour would be cheaper there, despite keeping on the Edgware plant. But by 1952 'serious and persistent labour and management difficulties' were proving too costly and the Welsh instrument factories were closed in 1953 at great expense, and the harmonica factory, in which B&H owned a minority share, was forced to close since the market had been re-opened to German manufacturers. It was for a time put into service as an aircraft factory: in fact, there was nothing that Geoffrey would not dabble in, be it ovens or radiators. In 1952 the sales of sheet music unexpectedly slumped, something which LAB put down to 'the very rapid expansion in the sale of television sets. I still have a vivid recollection of a similar drop in music

sales when everybody was buying radio sets in 1925 and '26.' This proved
to be a temporary drop and as the decade went on sales recovered,
although it was noted that fees from mechanical, broadcast, hire and
performance rights were going up at a much faster rate.

In fact, under LAB's firm leadership the company went from strength to
strength as the fifties progressed, and in 1956 B&H was listed on the
London Stock Exchange. In June of that year, at an Extraordinary General
Meeting, the 'reorganisation of capital' was approved, whereby 400,000
Ordinary Shares at 10 shillings were replaced by 1,600,000 Ordinary
Shares at 5 shillings, and the Issued Share Capital rose from £568,329 to
£712,228. While the firm had reached a size and importance that
warranted going public, the actual motivation for doing so was less than
glorious. LAB had been more or less bounced into it by Geoffrey Hawkes,
who had been selling shares for some time to fund his philandering. In the
end, Geoffrey needed to raise some serious money to support his
numerous mistresses, and persuaded LAB it would be a good idea. While
this action made B&H a company of great interest to the public and the
press, it was eventually to have serious and damaging repercussions, and
there was a collective sigh of relief when B&H finally went private again
in 2003.

Apprentices, aged between
15 and 21, in the brass
workshop at Edgware
(1950s)

The Rake's Progress, from London to Venice

Meanwhile, Roth was keeping an eagle eye on his side of the business; the creation of contracts and the collection of fees were his domain, and nothing would escape his notice. He took pride in his aggressively legalistic approach and did not trust other staff to agree contracts without his input. The only staff member Roth did trust was his devoted, authoritarian personal assistant, Rufina Ampenoff. She came from a well-connected Russian family who had fled the Revolution, and had been educated at the Lycée Français in London. Her mother had known Tchaikovsky and she herself had studied the piano with a pupil of Taneyev. With her musical connections (she and her two sisters were great favourites of the critic Ernest Newman, introduced to them by their other family friend, Koussevitzky) and with her six languages – Russian, French, English, German, Italian, Spanish – she was the ideal candidate for the job of personal assistant to Ernst Roth.

Having worked in the film industry before the war, she came to work for B&H in 1945, and immediately became involved in planning the 1947 Strauss Festival, which involved both exalted and menial tasks: 'I remember she was given Strauss's underwear to wash', recalls her sister, Nona, 'and it became the responsibility of our old nanny! Rufina tended to establish relations with composers very quickly, and they would become friends and come round to our house in Brondesbury Park. We entertained Strauss, Stravinsky, Petrassi, Xenakis, Boulez and Panufnik, to name but a few.'

Rufina Ampenoff, assistant to Roth, later Head of Rights and Performers (1964)

Having made her mark with the exacting Roth, Ampenoff stayed at Boosey & Hawkes for the next twenty-seven years. She never forgot she was a White Russian aristocrat, and acted accordingly. While her grasp of languages was a great asset when negotiating with foreign Intendants, conductors and composers, it also meant she could insist on having at least three secretaries to keep up with the different correspondences. Martin Hall recalls how she liked to arrange for different people to ring her in the afternoon when a composer or VIP happened to be in the office so they could witness her linguistic firework display. She made a vivid impression on Sally Cavender, who worked in the promotion department during the seventies: 'Oh, she was imperious, probably impossible, she dominated everyone, but she and I hit it off. She was terribly glamorous, and she'd sit there doing her nails, wearing the best scent and very smart clothes. She was a close friend of Elisabeth Schwarzkopf and when she

Opening scene of
Stravinsky's *The Rake's
Progress* at La Fenice in
Venice in 1951
(Photo: Erio Piccagliani,
courtesy Paul Sacher Stiftung)

went to La Scala, they would roll out the red carpet for her.' And she knew
her business. As her sister Nona describes it, 'Oh, she was a fighter, she
stood her ground! She would never let any infringement of copyright go
unchallenged.' She rose from assistant to Head of Rights and Performers.
Says Cavender, 'Once she noticed that the Israel Philharmonic were
coming to the Festival Hall to play Bartók's *Divertimento*, and they were
recording it the next day. She checked to see whether they had requested
the parts from the hire library and when she discovered they had
photocopied them, she hauled the manager into her office and gave him a
stiff talking to. The manager, unruffled, had the gall to say, "I know,
Rufina, but they are going to play it from memory!"'

She took up all Roth's crusades and shared his view that Britten was an
exceptionally talented composer, but not a genius like Stravinsky. She
served her 'Igor Feodorovich' with religious ardour, praying for him weekly
and fussing over the composer whenever he came into her orbit. Several
files remain of notes in long-hand Russian, written by Ampenoff and
returned to her by Stravinsky, his replies scribbled in the corners. Most
refer to practical matters and the all-important question of his health.

The two key European musical events of the early fifties were Britten's
Billy Budd, which Roth grumbled could not be a 'proper' opera without

any female roles, and Stravinsky's *The Rake's Progress*. While Roth makes no mention of the highly successful first performance of *Billy Budd* in his memoir *The Business of Music* – Anthony Gishford and Erwin Stein were the staff most closely involved with Britten at the time – he tells in great detail the story of the premiere of *The Rake's Progress*. The Royal Opera House had agreed 'with strictly controlled enthusiasm' to give the premiere at the Edinburgh Festival in August 1951; then La Scala would have the European premiere in Italian in December. Everything was going according to plan until one day in February Roth received a telegram from Stravinsky: 'Have promised first performance to Venice stop if you don't agree I cannot finish the work stop'. Roth soon discovered that Stravinsky had not been able to resist the offer of a very large sum of money for first performance rights from Italian Radio, who were sponsors of the Venice Biennale. Stravinsky had also agreed to conduct.

So Roth embarked on the long process of unpicking contracts. 'Covent Garden was easy enough. Without hesitation the gentlemen were offended and did not insist on their rights ... But the Scala did not give up ... they were determined to take the matter to court. Superintendant Dr Antonio Ghiringhelli threatened to appeal to the public, to have costumes, décor and music impounded in Venice, and to prevent the performance by every means. Before long I received a pile of Italian newspapers with long and uncomplimentary articles about Stravinsky and his publisher. In the Italian parliament a question was put to the Minister of Finance asking how it was that there were not enough dollars in the treasury to import badly needed flour but enough to pay for the first performance of an opera. A major scandal seemed imminent. I took the first plane to Milan.'

Roth took three such trips, always to be greeted with absolute refusals from every quarter. 'I had to admire these stubborn Italians. They fought tooth and nail for an artistic event that would bring them no material advantage.' Stravinsky, blissfully unaware of the rumpus he had caused, completed the third act and sent it to Regent Street.

Eventually, Roth persuaded all three parties to cooperate – for the production to be La Scala's, for the Venice Biennale to provide the theatre, the chorus and administrative services, and RAI to provide funding. It was a miracle. But it was not over yet: there was no rehearsal conductor, and no singers, and it was less than three months before the performance. Guido Cantelli nearly had a nervous breakdown at the thought of learning the score in three months; so Ferdinand Leitner from the Stuttgart Opera finally agreed, and Elisabeth Schwarzkopf and Jenny Tourel were engaged. The chosen producer Visconti, was in Australia, so Roth persuaded Carl Ebert to come from Glyndebourne, most reluctantly as he had at first been snubbed by La Scala. There was no Nick Shadow until Roth rang Otakar Kraus so many times he had to accept.

Then the time came for 'the longest dress rehearsal I can remember': 'Nothing worked. Stravinsky conducted with his head buried in the score as if he had never seen it before ... the interludes were too short for the old-fashioned equipment of the Fenice, and each time the scene changed and the curtain went up one could see stagehands running about between slanting props ...' On the day of the premiere Stravinsky was in despair and asked the singers to attend another piano rehearsal, which they refused to do. Roth tried to comfort him by saying a bad dress rehearsal was always a good omen.

Ernst Roth with Stravinsky in 1956
(Photo: courtesy Paul Sacher Stiftung)

That night, in the sweltering little Fenice, packed with film stars in furs, jewellery and fabulous dresses, Stravinsky's (for Roth) 'weird and gripping' *Rake's Progress* was born. The audience condescended to clap. The critics were agog. The next day the composer was welcomed by resplendently dressed dignitaries into the great hall of the Municipio. When the picturesque cortège led Stravinsky back to the entrance, he passed Roth and whispered, 'Have you got the cheque?'

'Between the poles of Schoenberg and Stravinsky'

Besides the extraordinary output of Stravinsky and Britten in the fifties, it would now be seen as the time when Messiaen, Boulez, Stockhausen, Ligeti, Henze, Berio, Nono and Dallapiccola began to emerge as important voices, with Ligeti making an impact after 1956. Of course, history-in-the-making is never so clear-cut, and the powers that be of the day had not necessarily recognised the talents of the future. A damning report in *Tempo* on the 1952 ICSM festival reveals a confused and unrepresentative picture. In Hans Keller's memorable words, the festival was an 'orgy of incompetence'. Each nation had been allowed to put forward works, resulting in dilettante music, amateurish efforts by 'untalented and defective' students. Britain was represented by just two short pieces by Humphrey Searle and Phyllis Tate; America by Don Banks, and Germany boasted 'Hindemith's well-worked trash, the *Symphonic Metamorphoses after themes of Weber*'.

Keller's acute ear picked out a piece by Boulez and another by Messiaen as works worthy of inclusion, and also praised Searle's Two Poems and a fantasy by Hanns Jelinek, but there is little indication of the revolution that was taking place in Darmstadt at the time. Keller suggested that most composers had chosen to 'settle down between the poles of Schoenberg and Stravinsky', and it is quite clear to which pole Roth was clinging.

André Jolivet

In fact, back in Regent Street, Darmstadt might not have existed. Roth, who was responsible for the signing of composers throughout this decade and well into the next, was extremely cautious. Hungary, now behind the Iron Curtain, had become a difficult territory in which to operate. But B&H still enjoyed a close relationship with Kodály, so it seems a deliberate oversight that no one from the firm capitalised on this connection to encounter the young talents who Kodály was generously supporting during one of Hungary's darkest political periods – Ligeti, Kurtág and Sándor Veress.

With giants like Strauss, Stravinsky, Rachmaninoff, Copland and Britten in copyright for decades to come, Roth had cause for complacency. Why risk money on an unknown, young composer? In his heart, he could not accept the Second Viennese School, even less the experiments of Stockhausen. He was happy to finish his musical education with Strauss, and if pushed, Stravinsky. His publishing philosophy was matter-of-fact: as he warned a younger member of staff, 'Always remember, you are not in business for the sake of music; you are in music for the sake of business.' He once said he would have been equally successful in textiles. So he did what any sensible businessman might do: he signed up a modest, but guaranteed earner. Henry Barraud, born in 1900 and by the early fifties a French establishment figure, occupied the powerful position of the Director of Music for Paris Radio. He would remain in post for more than twenty years, and naturally had a heavy influence on playlists, radio orchestra performances and the reputations of composers; in short, he was a rather useful contact. A little later, Roth also took on the gifted André Jolivet, who had studied with Varèse, and who founded the group La jeune France with Messiaen and others. Again, it was a canny appointment since Jolivet's

music had such a large pedagogical market – his *Cinq Incantations* for solo
flute still sell hundreds of copies a year, and by 1964 he was the most
frequently performed living composer in France.

Although these signings now strike us as opportunistic, Roth did make one
courageous deal, if under sufferance, which was political with a capital P.
Andrzej Panufnik had fled from Poland in 1954 in fraught circumstances.
A gifted conductor and an original, modernist composer, he occupied a
prominent place in Polish musical life. Since the war, he had gradually
been under more and more pressure from the government to act as a
cultural ambassador (he had even had to make a speech to Mao Tse-Tung
on one deputation). In 1954 when he was ordered
to start writing propaganda letters to his
colleagues in the West, his nerves cracked. He had
to get out. He and his first wife, Scarlett, who
fortunately had an Irish passport, arranged with
Zürich Radio for a special recording of his music
to be announced to the Polish cultural ministry
that would require his presence as conductor. He
was permitted to go, 'in the cause of Polish music',
and managed to slip out of the hands of his
minders.

While Roth may not have been instinctively in
tune with Panufnik's advanced style of music, he
recognised a true professional and was moved by
the man's bravery in the face of the Soviet
authorities, that he loathed. He decided to take on
all his existing works, which had been published by Polskie Wydawnictwo
Muzyczne (PWM), the Polish state publishers that Panufnik, ironically, had
helped to found. PWM had been ordered to destroy all copies of Panufnik's
music as he had officially become a non-person. But Roth knew that when
it came to copyright, you could not be too careful: he ordered Panufnik to
make small changes to each of his scores so that the Boosey & Hawkes
editions could be assigned anew. So it was with his revised *Sinfonia
Rustica* that Panufnik made his debut at the Proms in 1955. There had
been much publicity about his defection, and he was greeted with wild
enthusiasm and besieged afterwards with well-wishers and autograph
hunters. Later, the authorities did reply to Roth's letters and confirmed
that Panufnik's previous contract had been dissolved: he was free to
become a Boosey & Hawkes composer.

Andrzej Panufnik announcing
his escape to the West on
Radio Free Europe in July
1954
(Photo: courtesy Camilla Panufnik)

From a Polish refugee, to a composer sunk in the political minefields of Soviet Russia: Dmitri Shostakovich. After the formation of Anglo-Soviet Music Press in 1946, Boosey & Hawkes was entitled to publish Shostakovich's new works on the same day they appeared in Russia. This was not without its administrative difficulties, as can be seen by an intense correspondence between the Soviet music publishers, Mezhdunarodnaya Kniga, and Anthony Gishford. Violinist David Oistrakh was due to come to London in February 1956 to give the London premiere of the first violin concerto. According to the Berne Convention, in order for the work to be protected by copyright at all, it must be published first or simultaneously in a country that had signed up to the convention. As Russia was not a

Dmitri Shostakovich with his wife Irina at a Britten recital, Moscow Conservatoire, 1963 (Photo: Novosti)

signatory, Gishford duly requested a copy of the score so that they could start work on production in time. A certain Mr Belchenko had no objection, but the material was never sent. It was not until after the concert in which Oistrakh performed this moving work that Gishford went backstage and the great violinist pressed the score into his sweating hands.

Obtaining Anglo-Soviet scores became a regular nightmare. In March 1958, LAB wrote to Arthur Bliss, then Master of the Queen's Music, requesting that he join them for the London premiere of Shostakovich's Symphony No. 11: 'After *enormous* difficulties in getting a copy of the score over here and then getting the parts made, the first performance of Shostakovich's 11th symphony will take place at the Royal Festival Hall on Wednesday with the BBCSO under Sir Malcolm Sargent. I know that the Russians attach considerable importance to this as a landmark in British–Soviet relations, and I think it would be very much appreciated if you could possibly manage to be present.'

It is a sign of how little was really known about the life-threatening conditions under which Shostakovich was composing that Gishford could write to David Webster at the Royal Opera House in 1955, in response to his request for a score of *Lady Macbeth of Mtsensk*: 'there was some curious history attaching this work ... I was told by Mezhdunarodnaya Kniga that the material had been withdrawn, by the wish of the composer. You may remember that when it was first produced in Russia there was trouble about it on ideological grounds.' Moving swiftly on, he suggests instead Prokofieff's *Fiery Angel*, 'which does seem to me to have certain outstanding operatic qualities'.

Prokofieff by this time was also sequestered in Moscow, and B&H was not able to have personal contact with him, merely to communicate via the authorities. Having inherited some of his earlier works when Édition Russe was acquired, B&H brought out a handful of new and revised scores during the late forties and early fifties, including the Violin Sonata, the Cello Sonata, *The Stone Flower*, *Sinfonia Concertante*, Symphony No. 4 and the Piano Sonata No. 5. In the days of Édition Russe, Prokofieff had been a regular visitor at the company's shop at 22, rue d'Anjou, which then became Boosey & Hawkes's French office. In 1958 Mario Bois was appointed to run the office, following the retirement of the respected Swarzenski. Bois described the shop thus: 'My office was a little box on the ground floor, with shelves overloaded with orchestral materials and scores. When I came down to the cellar, it was in a tremendous disorder with mountains of paper and dossiers on the shelves and on the ground.' Eventually, Bois persuaded the 'adorable Mr Leslie' that he needed to move into more spacious premises on the rue Drouot, so the old offices were cleared. 'In the cellar I discovered an old dusty trunk, closed. In the presence of two colleagues, I forced the massive locks and we found ... things belonging to Prokofieff in there which he left when leaving for Russia in 1938.' The 'things' included a pair of yellow pyjamas, Christian

Serge Prokofieff with Mstislav Rostropovich who premiered the Cello Sonata in 1950 and Sinfonia Concertante in 1952

Science texts on which the composer had written, 'I am spiritual, consequently vigorous', his copy of the words of a French song 'Ma Normandie', a card from Leningrad: 'Je suis content de mon voyage en URSS. À Moscou, mes trois concerts ont été vendus le même jour.' And a picture from his son of the train which would bring his father home, with a touching note, 'Je pense chaque jour à toi. I am very lonsom [*sic*] without you. Je voudrais que tu viennes habiter avec nous.'

Poulenc attends a salon concert at the Boosey & Hawkes Paris office at rue d'Anjou (1961)

Bois also found the manuscript of an unfinished early opera called *Maddalena*, now published in an orchestration by Edward Downes. The contents of this trunk became the focus of a dispute many years later, when Prokofieff's first wife Lina came to live in England, and wanted to locate it, mistakenly believing that it contained some of her furs and jewellery. The long-serving Magdeleine Albert, who came to work with Bois in the rue Drouot, remembers that they used to sit on the trunk and use it as a desk. The new offices were rather elegant, and Bois formed a Club for musical soirées and events. There is a 1962 photograph of Francis Poulenc in the salon, attending a concert of works by himself and the Boosey & Hawkes composers Barraud, Jolivet and Tcherepnin. Stravinsky interested himself very much with this office, and tried to insist that they employ his friend Nicholas Nabokov as the manager at one point, when Mario Bois left to go to rival publisher Salabert. However, Didier Duclos had already been employed by the time Stravinsky's request came.

Most of the composers that had been signed or acquired during the 'golden' Hawkes era proved commercially and artistically successful. Of those still alive, Britten, Stravinsky and Kodály remained productive, Kodály during the period completing his Symphony in C, the famous *Missa Brevis* and continuing with his pedagogical choral programme which was having such an extraordinary effect in Hungarian schools. He was highly influential in his own country and all over Europe, but he still lacked many material comforts enjoyed by those in the West: in 1957 his young second wife, Sarolta, wrote to Roth to ask if her husband could be sent Quaker Oats for his digestion and Mint Alltoids for his throat. One composer who was faring less well was Bohuslav Martinů. He had spent the war in the United States, enjoying great success with a string of lyrical, neo-classical symphonies. Koussevitzky was a great supporter and premiered his first and third symphonies. But in 1946 Martinů suffered a serious accident which damaged his hearing and nervous system, and it took him more than a year to recover, in which time he composed only a string quartet. In 1953 he completed a sixth symphony before moving back to Europe and living as Paul Sacher's guest in Switzerland. But in 1952 he was feeling unloved: 'I have the impression to be put on the second line, I do not like this feeling and I think I do not deserve it. I have the impression also, that because of my mild and kind behaviour, somebody took me for granted ... I gave you five symphonies, several orchestral or soloist pieces, several chamber works, choirs which is lots. It really is not my fault if your Office do not distribute them more, because all these compositions have a big success.'

It is the eternal cry of the composer to his publisher: you are not doing enough for me! Martinů asked for a better and different contract by which he could offer works individually. Roth is a touch patronising in his reply: 'It was and still is difficult for us to keep pace with your output ... I have always said we should be given time not only to print but to promote your work.' Never one to mince his words, Roth points out the difficulty of promoting the current clutch of orchestral pieces: 'Therefore, you should not write so much of a similar nature. This cannot but be harmful in the end. You must not blame us for it.'

Erwin Stein, Britten's trusted editor and musical advisor (1950s)

Internally, there was some disquiet about the costs Martinů was incurring. When his contract came up for renewal in 1955, Roth wrote to David Adams in New York: 'We cannot keep pace with his output, which goes on with undiminished vigour and is becoming proportionately less interesting.' David Adams agreed, noting that 'he has not taken up his advances which amount to $4400, while his unearned royalty figure up to and including December 1954, is $5048.'

Contracts with composers were individually negotiated: while Martinů had a schedule of advances, Britten, for instance, felt uncomfortable receiving advances and simply wanted a modest fixed income and to receive royalties when they came in. In the event, a non-exclusive contract with

Martinů was agreed, which suited both parties, and on his arrival back in Europe he began to offer works to Universal Edition. These included the *Epic of Gilgamesh*, the luminous *Frescoes of Piero della Francesca* and his opera *The Greek Passion*, all three triumphs of his old age. It is unlikely that Roth thought of it this way, but it was a lesson in the rewards of loyalty, and the pitfalls of impatience.

'Your infinite tact'

The fifties were an even more fruitful period for Britten than the forties had been, with their interruptions of war, emigration and touring. *Billy Budd* was closely followed by *Gloriana, The Turn of the Screw, Noye's Fludde, Winter Words, The Prince of the Pagodas, Nocturne* and, as the decade reached its end, *A Midsummer Night's Dream* and work on the *War Requiem*. The expert Erwin Stein remained the careful midwife of his published scores, and Anthony Gishford's role as his 'man inside' was intensifying. Gishford had started to confide in Britten, who was now hearing about the inside workings of the firm and the politics of Roth, LAB and other members of staff. He had assisted with the libretto of *The Little Sweep* and Britten and Pears's jokey doggerel composed especially for him in thanks is full of in-jokes and betrays an intimate knowledge of the internal politics:

'Come, dear Tony, come less slowly;
Leave the low Roth, take the high.
Fear not Quilter, Gibbs or Rowley
Envious of your liberty.

Sonorous their echoes beckon –
Tyrant Hawk(e)s or g(l)awrie EOG!
Run poor boy! Not lightly reckon
(S)tiny stones or Boozy bog!

How we thank you that you aid us
In this crazier poetry!
Rhyme, sense, reason – all – evade us
Ever yours, PP – BB'

[Roth's name was pronounced as in the English 'rote'. *Sonorous* was the telegram code for B&H]

Curiously, there does seem to be an underlying message that Gishford should get out of the firm, no doubt provoked by the complaints he shared with them. Britten, too, had his grievances against the management as Gishford minuted in one 1952 meeting: 'You have some apprehension regarding our attitude towards young composers in general. You do not want to be enshrined as "the last of the young composers in our catalogue".'

Later in the year, Gishford drew Roth into a tripartite discussion in the hopes of getting a decision on the young composer Oldham, and the result was the renewal of his contract. Britten's other grievance was his impression that scores were being required 'to suit the comfort and convenience' of his publishers. By 1954 LAB, always sensitive to the needs of his major British composer, was openly asking Britten for 'practical suggestions in writing before we next meet' as to how he should like the company to progress, an invitation that would have horrified Roth, whose power base was always in danger of being undermined by Britten and his 'cronies'. But the composer did begin to feel that his voice was being heard and, at the end of that year, he wrote to Gishford: 'I confess I feel more confident about the New Year than I have done for ages, and one of the reasons is certainly the new improved relations at B&H. That is certainly due to your splendid, & tactful efforts in 1954. I do understand a little of your problems there, enough to admire and be very grateful for your solving of them.'

By 1955, Gishford felt more positively towards his employers, though the problems had not entirely gone away: 'Life at B&H continues to be something of a tightrope walk, but at the moment I'm feeling reasonably sure of my balance. Ernst, fortified by a new agreement, has suddenly become much more agreeable, and not being a very courageous character, has conceived the idea that there are many matters in which I might be his spokesman. This in a curious way is giving me a new feeling of strength in relation with the two chief proprietors. I would love to tell you more, but I'm no Dostoevsky.'

Three years later, Gishford would become too involved in a truly Dostoevskian intrigue and spectacularly lose his balance.

A trip to New York

In 1958 Roth was 62 and at the height of his powers. As a Vice President of the music section of the International Publishers Association he was responsible not only for numerous important decisions on contracts and copyrights, but had created an entire system of contracts between publishers and European broadcasting stations that is still in use today. Despite his vigorous mind, he had been unwell for long periods and was now planning for his retirement.

Geoffrey and LAB were understandably nervous, and in order to soften the blow of losing his incomparable knowledge, they had suggested he sign a contract for five years after his retirement so that he would be available in an advisory role to his successor. Roth never lost an opportunity to exercise his influence, and in this case he insisted that he would only agree to the proposal if his successor was *not* Anthony Gishford. This caused consternation on the Board, since Gishford was the obvious candidate, having had the greatest involvement with composers, performers and the production of scores.

Anthony Gishford (1949)

Roth and Gishford had always belonged to separate camps: Britten, the Steins and Gishford on one side, Roth and Ampenoff on the other, with poor LAB struggling to keep the peace in the middle. But Roth, who claimed Gishford was not sufficiently responsible, must also have been determined not to let Britten get a foothold in the management of the company by this backdoor route. Playing for time, he craftily suggested that Gishford go to New York and be Vice President of B&H Inc for two years, in order to 'prove' himself. Only then, he claimed, would he reconsider Gishford as a candidate. Gishford had no intention of leaving London, sensing that he was simply being sidelined. He did, however, agree to accompany LAB to New York in May 1958 in order to produce a full report on the business, after some rather dubious accounts in 1957.

In New York, Simon Boosey – who had now been in the company for ten years, including a stint in the Paris office – was champing at the bit for a promotion. Executive Vice President David Adams had established himself as a benign figure in the Manhattan music world and there were no openings in sight. Of the two Boosey sons in the business – Anthony was in sales at Edgware – Simon showed signs of having the vital entrepreneurial streak, and Sylvia Goldstein, a shrewd judge of character, felt he had promise. Looking back, he now realises, 'I was a handful ... I was aiming

Leslie Boosey (right) with his
son Simon (1950s)
(Photo: courtesy Nigel Boosey)

high and tugging at the reins, and I was liable to fall out with those standing between me and my goal. [My father] had to pick me up more than once.' Broido describes Simon as a man who could come up with 'one hundred ideas, one or two of which were absolutely brilliant. He needed a sounding board, someone to work with who could edit him, develop his ideas. David Adams was afraid of him and his potential power. He was plodding and methodical. It was the worst kind of partnership.' (Broido, who could have been that partner, had left the company in 1955 to be director of a publishing group, and would eventually become President of Theodore Presser Inc).

Simon knew, too, that both Roth and his father (who was by now over 70) must leave soon, and he badly needed the reshuffle to result in a new job. He resented Roth's power in the firm – 'he came between me and my father' – and never quite lost the feeling that Roth was an intruder, a stranger in their midst who had usurped the throne. On his visits to London, he hated to see Roth sitting 'in Ralph's old office' at 295 Regent Street. That is where Simon wanted, eventually, to be sitting himself. But there was no immediate prospect of that.

Restless and dissatisfied, early in 1958 Simon had taken a three-month sabbatical to join the team designing the new Palais des Arts in Montreal. But he was back to assist his father and Gishford in auditing the stock. LAB stayed around in New York to meet the staff and go through all the accounts, taking, in Gishford's words, a 'great deal of time and trouble' to teach his younger colleague as he went. When LAB went back to London, Gishford took matters into his own hands. He offered Simon three months on half pay in order to look for another job; Simon felt that was unacceptable so at this point Gishford 'decided to dispense with his services forthwith and offer him six months' full pay'. He then asked for a press release to be issued announcing that he had been 'elected' President of B&H Inc, in succession to Leslie Boosey.

The timing of the two actions conspired to effect maximum damage on the Boosey family. To the outside world it looked as if Gishford had either ousted both of them, or had been given an office which he had used to sack the Chairman's son. The truth was more complex. He had, in effect, been offered the post of President of B&H Inc when asked to go to America for two years, and Simon Boosey had been wanting to leave for a while unless the terms of his contract could be vastly improved. Simon had grown the sheet sales from $20k to $80k, and wanted more responsibility and recognition, but no one was prepared to force David Adams's hand on this matter.

It is not clear what lay behind this extraordinary action. Stein's daughter, Marion Thorpe, who knew Gishford well, finds it quite out of character for a man who was naturally retiring. Some have suggested that Roth put him up to it, in order to get rid of Simon, but then changed his mind when he saw how others reacted. It seems unlikely that Gishford was acting on Roth's orders given the lack of trust between them. Whatever the truth, Gishford seems to have acted as if he had been sanctioned, at least in theory, by someone in London. Broido puts it down to the culture of spying and intrigue that existed at the time: 'Oh! it was a scorpion's nest. There was so little trust, everyone was suspicious of each other. There were staff who considered themselves Hawkes's people, and others on the Boosey side, there were managers spying on other managers in the foreign offices. And there in the middle was poor old Leslie, who would do nothing to help his son Simon because he felt it would be improper.'

The London Board, when all this was discovered, was furious. It had created bad publicity for the company and almost suggested a mutiny. Back at Regent Street, Gishford was severely reprimanded by LAB, who offered his own resignation in protest at this apparent humiliation of both himself and his son. This might have been accepted had the company not recently gone public, and the Board feared the Chairman's resignation

would affect the share price. Geoffrey Hawkes insisted it was Gishford
who should resign, and brought up his poor handling of the agreement
with the Argentine agent, Roberto Barry, as evidence of his incompetence.
Roth weighed in with his reservations about Gishford's capacity to take
over as publishing director, and dismissed his entire report on the US
businesses as 'an unsatisfactory document that meant but little'. The
writing was on the wall. LAB noted in his personal diary that a breakdown
in trust had occurred which would have far-reaching implications.

The battle of Britten

What no one had anticipated was the reaction from Aldeburgh. LAB
recalled later how Britten had rung him in a
towering fury and 'put me on the spot'.
Britten suspected that Gishford had been set
up, and that this was all a plot to undermine
Britten's own position and to change the
policy of the company. LAB tried earnestly
to reassure him: 'This upheaval was not the
result of some deep-laid plot… it arose
because of an action of Tony's [Gishford] in
New York which had made my position
quite impossible.' He goes on to reassure
him that his affairs will be dealt with in the
meantime by Ernst Roth. Unaware of the ill
feeling between the two, LAB suggests that
Gishford was only a puppet to Roth anyway:
'However attached to Tony you had become,
the "deus ex machina" was Ernst Roth. In
all things that really matter his was the
guiding hand.'

This was the last thing Britten wanted to
hear. The loss of Gishford was a 'grievous
blow'. Not one to give up easily on a cause,
Britten went to see LAB with his accountant
Leslie Periton with the intention of
reversing Gishford's dismissal. For him to
leave Aldeburgh on such a matter when the
Festival was less than two weeks away – he
was moving into the Red House and

Letter from Britten to Leslie
Boosey following the
resignation of Anthony
Gishford (1958)

THE RED HOUSE, ALDEBURGH, SUFFOLK.

18th June, 1958.

Dear Leslie,

I had hoped to write again to you sooner, but the Festival
here has taken all my time these last days.

Thank you for the prompt way in which you reacted to my
letter written on the 4th, and for your efforts to seal the unhappy
breach – even though unsuccessful, I am sure that they were worth-
while, since nothing that has happened has impaired my personal
regard for Tony's abilities.

Had it not been that there seemed a chance of the
restoration of the old position, I would have made, earlier, one or
two comments on our talk together. As this restoration is now
impossible, I think I had better do so now.

So far as the pursuance of serious music publishing is
concerned, you suggested that one of the ways of implementing it
(and to which I agreed) was to strengthen the serious music
publishing side of the Board of Directors, either by adding a new
Director, or even splitting the Board into two

        (a) Instrumental, and
        (b) Music publishing.

If this is done, however, I do hope that the music
publishing business will be so placed financially as to make its
future reasonably secure. I assume that you will now immediately
start looking for a new assistant for Ernst, who will now be doubly
pressed in his work, with a special directive to look after my work
(although I should like to say, aside, that it is the _whole_
catalogue of serious music which interest me, and of course which
also indirectly affects the health of my own published works).
I gave you one or two names as possible candidates for this position,
and will continue to try and suggest others; but I must add that
if people such as we are discussing are approached it may well be
that they would not be interested unless there was a possibility
of a directorship in the near future – otherwise I cannot imagine
that they could be enticed away from their present important
positions. In the meantime you yourself and Erwin Stein will be
able to step in and handle such matters as Tony has been handling
for me, and would have in the future handled, which would be too
much for Ernst with all the important matters in which he is already
involved. I will enclose a list, as complete as I can, of the
current matters, but of course it will be difficult since so many

overseeing the first performance of *Noye's Fludde* – is a measure of its importance to him. The ever-attentive LAB succeeded in smoothing ruffled feathers, and Britten's next letter is more temperate, explaining that while he had thought that he personally might be able to 'heal the breach' he now realised that 'matters had gone too far'. He stressed again his complete confidence in Tony and his hope that 'there will not be a complete break. Differences have been brought to light, and perhaps could be settled for the benefit of all.' LAB replied that he, Roth and Geoffrey Hawkes had discussed the possibility of a 'via media' with Gishford and, of course, rejected it as unworkable. 'The tragedy lies in the fact that we had not recognised we were heading for trouble and taken action long ago.' Presumably, LAB means by this the jostling for position, the question of Roth's successor and the relationship that Gishford enjoyed with Britten, which was never approved of by Roth.

were discussed verbally, and some quite casually. The way that the interim regime should be worked would have to be discussed in great detail with Erst, of course, with whom closest contact will have to be kept, profiting by his enormous knowledge and experience.- before the unfortunate occurrence in the near future of his retirement.

Youdalso said you would reconsider the position of the Educational department, which was so splendidly handled by Ken Straker during his short sojourn. This is a branch of Boosey & Hawkes which you know I am, and have been, particuarly concerned with, from the days of Friday Afternoons (which I was surprised to learn, accidentally, had been allowed to go out of print) to Noye's Fludde. This branch besides will, I should imagine, become more and more important if music teaching continues to grow as steadily in all kinds of schools as it is now growing. We all agreed that Ken Straker's loss was most unfortunate – the circumstances make it doubly so.

I have had an additional idea since we met, which I hope will interest you. Using our London house for the next few months is Mr. John Mundy, who will not be unknown to you. He is an old and trusted, musical and personal friend of mine. He was also a close friend in New York, where he lives, of Ralph Hawkes. He and his wife, Clytie Mundy, a famous singing teacher, have an unrivalled knowledge of American musical life. He was for many years orchestral Manager of the Metropolitàn Opera House orchestra. He has now retired from the position, but although no longer young, he is full of vitality, and is a strong and wise character. Could he not be of some use to us, either in the New York business, or even here in an advisory capacity? You mentioned that you would consider new directors to strengthen the musical side, and it seems to me that he would be admirable if he would consider returning to England. I should add that he has no ambitions to start a new great career, but he is profoundly interested in music, in Boosey & Hawkes, and has a regard for my works. I would have deep confidence in him. Could you not meet him one day soon and discuss things, even casually, with him? I have myself discussed the general position with him, which was of course natural as he has been a close friend for many years.

I have already said how pleased I was to learn that your views coincided so much with mine and that you had sufficient confidence in me to discuss these matters so openly.

Yours sincerely,

'I need in my publisher', Britten wrote in a letter to Roth, who was now his contact in the company, 'someone interested not only in my music as a "commodity" but in me as a person'. 'I am the last person to treat music as mere business,' Roth replied, 'and I am quite confident you will find that I am fully aware of the necessary human element … believe me, you will find that I never fail you in this respect if only you will give me the opportunity.'

Roth protested too much: throughout the awkward correspondence that follows, his open, almost abject desire to be loved and accepted by Britten was bound to irritate the composer. Britten had always appreciated Roth's handling of business affairs ('Ernst has dealt splendidly with the ballet trouble,' he noted after a choreographer kicked up a fuss over one production of *The Prince of the Pagodas*; 'I'm so glad Ernst is going to Milan to unscramble it,' he mentioned on another occasion) but there was some natural antipathy, no doubt with sexual and cultural undertones, which neither could ignore.

Britten's reaction to the news that Roth was to be his 'personal contact' was dramatic: putting the question of Gishford aside, he grasped this opportunity to lay out exactly how he thought Boosey & Hawkes should be reorganised. He wanted the Board to be split in two – into Instruments and Music Publishing – and for a new director (chosen by himself) to be appointed to the publishing Board. A new assistant must be recruited for Ernst 'who will now be doubly pressed in his work' – 'with a special directive to look after my work (although I should like to say, aside, that it is the whole catalogue of serious music which interests me, and of course which indirectly affects the health of my own published work.)' He suggests that he put forward names of possible assistants, but warns that unless there is the possibility of a directorship 'in the near future' they may not attract a high-calibre candidate. He stresses that in the meantime he would like Erwin Stein (who was then semi-retired) and LAB to look after his affairs, *not* Roth. He then demands that a new manager be recruited for the Educational Department: 'This is a branch of Boosey and Hawkes which you know I am, and have been, particularly concerned with, from the days of *Friday Afternoons* to *Noye's Fludde*.' Ken Straker, who was for a short time in charge of the department was respected by Britten and 'his loss most unfortunate'. Lastly, he suggests that John Mundy, husband of Pears's one-time singing teacher Clytie Mundy, be

Premiere production of Britten's *Noye's Fludde* during the 1958 Aldeburgh Festival

recruited to the board of the American company in an advisory capacity. Mundy, manager of the Met orchestra, had been a friend of Hawkes.

LAB did not immediately address Britten's suggestions, but there was one request with which he simply could not comply. The lovable Erwin Stein was not up to full-time work and a month later died suddenly of a heart attack. It could not have come at a worse time for Britten: although Gishford had been an important ally, Stein was a far more significant figure in Britten's life, as friend, teacher, collaborator, critic and editor. He was practically family: Pears, Britten and the Steins had all shared a house in St John's Wood during the war. Britten had wanted Alban Berg to teach him, but it was Stein in the end who became his life-long teacher, imparting his wisdom on Mahler, Webern and Berg which he had so desperately craved in his musically-stifled early days. As Stein's son-in-law Lord Harewood wrote, 'Stein's death has deprived this country of the sort of musical influence we could least do without – someone with the whole of European culture behind him who yet lived and thought in the present and was able and prepared to impart this wisdom without preaching.' Stein was famously the only person whose criticism Schoenberg welcomed. He, in turn, revered the Viennese composer, but his acquaintance with Britten's music , with its utterly contrasting aesthetic, stimulated and excited him. For Britten, who wrote the preface to his book *Form and Performance*, Stein's 'rare gift for musical analysis, and at the same time warmth and understanding' was, in his experience, unique. There was no one on the staff who could match his profound musicianship.

But Stein was gone. The silent Spinner remained as a trusted editor, but the only person capable of dealing with publications and performances now was Roth. All the following correspondence is with Roth, who threw himself into the production of *Noye's Fludde* parts and translations for other territories with his customary vigour. He was assisted in this by John Andrewes in the promotion department, a musically able and energetic advocate of many composers, who had laboured tirelessly and selflessly on Britten's behalf. In all the discussions as to an 'assistant', he was left out, possibly because of his lack of assertiveness, and because, according to one staff member, he was 'kept down hard' by Roth and Ampenoff.

On 9 July 1958, the sun shone for the first and last time on the Britten-Roth relationship. Ernst and Käte spent a summer's day in the Red House garden, with Britten and Pears playing genial hosts, and put the world to rights. Roth's gratitude is almost cloying: 'Let me thank you once more for the afternoon in your beautiful home. I cannot tell you how relieved I am knowing that any possible misunderstanding concerning the new situation at B&H has been removed and that I shall enjoy your full confidence and friendship, and I want to reassure you once more that I shall do everything to justify it.' Roth even seemed comfortable to discuss Britten's suggestions for his eventual successor: Gerald Macdonald is mentioned, and the critic and musicologist Eric Walter White, who had worked for the Arts Council but who decided not to take up a job in the 'rough climate of what, after all, is a business.'

This *entente* was not to last. Roth had no intention of allowing Britten 'his own man' in a position of power in the company. Only a week before Roth had sent an angry letter to LAB violently rejecting all Britten's suggestions as to the reorganisation of the business and expressing outrage that LAB should even appear to be entertaining them. 'The splitting into two companies would be quite contrary to the existing reorganisational plan, and the appointment to the Board of an outsider nominated by Britten would recreate precisely the same situation which we now, for the first time in ten years, have an opportunity of remedying.' Roth, it must be remembered, was closely involved with Stravinsky at the time: he could not countenance priority being given to the demands of a local composer whom he considered the lesser talent.

Moreover, he took all Britten's comments personally: 'I am profoundly shocked at the recurring argument that the Board needs strengthening, apparently against me.'

He declared that this matter must come before the Board, knowing that he would be able to persuade Geoffrey Hawkes to defeat the proposals. He did, but the problem would not go away. Britten pushed yet again for the company to be split, and in 1960 a catastrophic result in the instrument business gave him the ammunition he needed.

A crisis in the instrument business

Although Anthony Gishford had officially 'sacked' Simon Boosey, his subsequent resignation quashed the action, and Simon remained on the staff, first coming to London and then returning to New York to take up what was, in effect, the Vice Presidency of the business in all but name. In 1959 he discovered important information about B&H's arch rival in the

United States, It seemed that Gus Schirmer's brother had inherited the company on Gus's death and would be willing to sell it. G Schirmer, with the copyrights to the works of Samuel Barber, Gian Carlo Menotti and Leonard Bernstein, was a hugely valuable business. A merger with Boosey & Hawkes would have created the biggest, most significant music publisher in America, if not the world. Simon knew that trade rules would make it hard for the London company to buy Schirmer while B&H Inc remained a separate company in the same market. But if Schirmer could be persuaded to buy B&H Inc, then the London company could buy the lot. His letters to his father are breathless with excitement: it would be a huge investment, but it would set the seal not only on the future of the business in America, which had had its share of troubles, but his own future.

LAB could see the importance of this opportunity, and even persuaded Ernst Roth and his wife to go to New York with him. It was the first of only two visits. Sylvia Goldstein remembers the occasion: 'The Roths were both very uncomfortable. Dr Roth took one look at the books in B&H Inc and said dismissively, "you should just concentrate on choral and band music".' (On the second visit to America in 1964, Käte Roth was invited to tea with Lady Bird Johnson and travelled to Washington by train, as Goldstein also recalled: 'She wasn't the least impressed by the White

Woodwind manufacture at Edgware (1950s)

Shop front at 295 Regent
Street (1950s)

House but, as a doctor of plant biology, she got talking about the genus of
a certain pot plant. She couldn't do small talk!')

LAB examined Simon's proposal and saw that it was possible but knew
how much opposition there would be from the Board, most particularly
from Roth. To join with Schirmer would make New York the power base of
the music publishing business, the fulfilment of Ralph Hawkes's vision.
Given his imminent retirement, it is hard to understand the strength of
Roth's opposition, but he was a passionate European and never fought off
his prejudice against the United States as a profoundly uncivilised country.
LAB left New York a sadder man. 'I remember him saying,' recalls Simon,
'there's no fire in the belly to achieve this'. But LAB could not reveal the
extent of the pressure building up against his family, nor the new pressure
from shareholders. The outside scrutiny to which they were now subject
made the Board more cautious, and no doubt influenced the decision not
to invest in G Schirmer. (The opportunity would come again in the 1980s,
and, for a second time, the Board would shy away.)

On the Board at the time were the chief accountant John Little, a Hawkes
employee from before the amalgamation, and his assistant, the long-

serving Alan Clapham. Both were more involved in the instrument side of the business than the details of music publishing. Time and again in its history, the publishing side of the business suffered from under-representation on the Board. LAB had stepped down as Chairman of the company in the late fifties in order to give Geoffrey Hawkes a turn. The latter's comically self-congratulatory 'letter to the staff' in the 1960 Edgware newsletter reveals a tactless leader: '1960 has been a strenuous year – so strenuous in fact that I am in need of a rest ... it is time someone appointed a Committee to consider how the time and energy of Chairmen and Managing Directors can be saved.' No mention of anyone else's hard work. Martin Hall, who joined the publications department in 1960 remembers Geoffrey as 'outrageous'. 'He would march through the office shouting out the wrong names to people and once pointed to a wall saying "move that back by six feet"!' Geoffrey had always been associated with the factories, and used to complain bitterly about his brother's interest in 'long-haired musicians' who lost the company money. In fact, it was Geoffrey who had the real talent for turning profit into loss.

By 1960 the company was on the brink of disaster. Profits of £188,290 in 1959, slumped to £52,176 in 1960, due to massive losses in the instrument manufacturing business. Correspondence with Ed Sonfield, owner of C Bruno & Son, the US instrument importer, who was working with clarinettist Reginald Kell to develop a new professional clarinet, reveals a problem with cracking clarinet wood which had not been properly dried. Competition from American manufacturers was intensifying, and Sonfield was dissatisfied with the quality of B&H instruments. He wanted them to concentrate on developing a student clarinet in a cheaper material called sonorite, and a professional model. His recommendations were finally agreed to a couple of years later, and the famous 10/10 clarinet was developed. A radical reassessment in 1964 saw the factory reducing its number of distinct instrument models from 82 to 28.

The 1960 loss was so great that the Chairman's annual report had to be cancelled and redone, and the AGM postponed. LAB's eldest son, Anthony Boosey, had commissioned a report on the factories from a certain Mr Aird from the Radiation Group: his recommendations were not palatable. He stated that unless Geoffrey Hawkes was fired, the factories would continue to fail. LAB and Anthony wanted to bring in Aird to run the factories on the retirement of Mr Draper, on the understanding that Radiation might eventually take them over. Geoffrey, of course, resisted. For several years the costs of turning a small, craft business into a mass-production business, and trying to make the factories and distribution efficient, had put the management under huge strain – and would continue to do so.

But news of the loss in the instrument business was already out in the press, and Britten was now openly threatening not to sign his contract. He had even heard rumours that the company was up for sale, and he had been approached by three other publishers offering him a contract. 'If [B&H] are not seriously interested in publishing, then to my profound regret I could not sign a new contract and I could not leave behind the works of 30 years.' He ends that 'mere verbal or written assurances' would not do: 'something more was required'. This time, even Roth could not stop LAB from reorganising the firm. Six days later, the deed was done. A new publishing Board was set up, with Geoffrey Hawkes's blessing, and Britten signed his new contract. LAB protested that the formation of a separate publishing company was a plan 'I have been advocating for several years'. He goes as far as to say that he had been prepared to resign on this matter.

The truth was Britten's power over the Board was by this time much greater than LAB's. There were the usual internal squabbles about who should sit on the new Board: Geoffrey Hawkes was barred and consequently would not let Ralph Boosey belong to it either, despite his long experience in the light music department. Britten insisted on the appointment of Royal Academy of Music director Sir Anthony Lewis to the new music publishing Board, an instruction duly carried out, and threw in a final insult by requesting that LAB should not be Chairman because he was not confident of his interest in his (Britten's) music. LAB's response, explaining his apparent 'aloofness', is heartbreaking: 'I was acutely conscious that I belonged to an older generation and had been brought up in a completely different musical world and I had the embarrassed feeling that my company must be boring to a young musical genius like yourself and so I contented myself with telling you … that if at any time you needed any help you had only to let me know to be sure that I would do everything in my power to help you … I wonder how many people are accused of being aloof when they are really only shy?'

Exit Hawkes, Exit Boosey

At this critical juncture, Geoffrey Hawkes died. He had been suffering from leukaemia for some months, though he was still trying to work as best he could. Unfortunately, his doctor had persuaded him to rest instead of signing his new will one evening, and he died that night. His old will left nearly everything to his estranged wife Mabel, who died shortly afterwards, intestate. His new will would have taken account of his many lady friends, and would have been far more detailed as regards his interests in the company. The whole episode was to have far-reaching consequences for the ownership of the business. Death duties payable on Geoffrey Hawkes's death (and the fact that Mabel's relatives were not interested in the company), had necessitated the placing of substantial blocks of shares on the market. These were now being purchased by other manufacturers – Stammers and Aird, who were part of the Radiation Group, and the American cymbal manufacturer Zildjian, and a private American publishing company called Carl Fischer, who purchased 5% after Geoffrey's death and were looking to purchase a considerable amount more. With Geoffrey Hawkes gone, the Hawkes family interest needed a new representative. Step forward Kenneth Pool.

Pool, a chartered accountant with little commercial experience, was Ralph Hawkes's brother-in-law (his wife was Clare Hawkes's sister). On his death, Ralph had left his interest in the company, which amounted to just under 20%, in trust, to Kenneth's elder son, Anthony. Hawkes had paid his nephew special attention, and ensured he had some musical education: 'he was like a fairy godfather' remembers Tony Pool. 'He would come over from New York with fabulous toys for his wife's nephews and nieces,

Printing music at Edgware (late 1960s)

I remember he gave me my first gramophone and a marvellous model train set which I still have. I visited their flat in Lowndes Square on one occasion only, when he was to take me to my first ballet. But I do remember the black marble bathrooms – the lot.' (This was the apartment in Lowndes Square which had been occupied by the distinguished mezzo Conchita Supervia.) Pool was only ten when Hawkes died, but by 1960 had graduated from Cambridge in Classics and was prepared to try his hand at the publishing business in which he had such a large stake. 'I arranged an escape route, however: I applied to do the LLB course at Cambridge that summer so that I could always go into law.' He was subsequently called to the Bar, and his legal training served him well in his future career. But he did decide to stay in the firm – 'I rather enjoyed it' – and at the beginning of 1962 was sent by Roth to the small publisher and retailer, Hug in Switzerland, as an apprentice to 'learn the trade'. He returned at the end of the year with fluent German and a knowledge of all the processes involved in publishing.

But this is to leap ahead. In 1961 on Geoffrey's death, Kenneth Pool, as the sole surviving trustee of the Ralph Hawkes Will Trust, was appointed to the Board. Pool had been involved in the company since the war, through his friendship with Ralph Hawkes. He had assisted in revaluing the shares just after Ralph Hawkes's death, and had persuaded the tax authorities to

Warehouse at Edgware printworks (late 1960s)

accept a very low value for them, thus saving everyone a huge amount in death duties. He now began to take a close interest in proceedings, but he was no expert in the publishing business, so he accepted advice from the other Board members, whom he conscientiously interviewed, and in particular from the member with the greatest experience and track record, Ernst Roth. It is not clear whether he realised at the time that Roth had embarked on a war against the Boosey family, but his loyalty must always have been to the memory of Ralph Hawkes.

Two events in the years 1961 and 1962 occurred to undermine the Booseys. The first involved a letter sent to Roth's assistant Martin Hall from Simon Boosey regarding the second printing of his new band series, which had already been a commercial success in the States. Roth proposed to double the price, which Simon described in the letter as 'madness'. The letter, which has not been kept, was clearly inflammatory and David Adams had pleaded with Simon not to send it. Hall, as a junior, thought there would be repercussions if he kept it to himself, so handed the letter on to Roth. All hell broke loose: Roth seized the opportunity to censure Simon. He called an extraordinary Board meeting and offered his resignation, no doubt hoping this time Simon would be forced out. In view of the controversy, LAB asked his mild-mannered cousin Ralph Boosey, in charge of Light Music, to chair the meeting. He was no match for the tempestuous Roth, who claimed that Simon had grossly insulted him: Simon now believes Roth had misunderstood the use of words and really thought Simon was branding him 'insane', but Roth's grasp of English was far too sophisticated for such an error. Simon was not dismissed, but he was hauled over the coals and led to believe a promotion to director level was now impossible.

A year later, in April 1962, LAB was in New York. He had a Victorian sense of family as management. He had always assumed that his sons would play a significant part in running the business on his retirement (he was already in his mid-seventies) and had left a proposal with the Board that Simon be promoted to Vice President of B&H Inc, a change of title, not role, with which David Adams, by then President of that branch, was entirely happy: 'a little encouragement and a recognition of the work he has done ... This proposal is completely innocuous: vice presidents are two a penny here.' Earlier, LAB had tried to get Anthony, his elder son, promoted to the Board but the members had resisted. This time, led by Roth and Kenneth Pool, the Board tried to resist once again in a tart communication from Pool. LAB was incredulous: he wrote to Roth, whom he had hitherto never suspected of foul play, 'I am told that I have been a naughty boy but they will do what I propose on this occasion. Frankly, this is not good enough.'

He goes on, bitterly, 'No member of the London board has done a hand's turn to help any member of my family since Ralph died. I hate having to ask for favours for them but I know perfectly well that they would be left as hewers of wood and drawers of water if I didn't do something about it ...' It is an extraordinary admission, given the circumstances, to suggest that his sons needed such intervention to succeed in the business.

He goes on to defend his record, something that was never in dispute: 'When I was asked to take over the chairmanship from Geoffrey, I had one thought and one thought only, and that was to give the last few years of my life to restoring to the company the dignity and standing and financial stability which I felt it should never have been allowed to lose.' He ends by saying he will not be a puppet of the Board and if there is nothing for his family in the company, they will all have to reconsider their position. There was still a chance that LAB could have restored some influence for at least one of his sons, Simon, but his stubbornness blinded him to reality.

Rufina Ampenoff with Kenneth Pool and his wife Patricia (1966)

His youngest son Nigel had been serving in the RAF in Canada and had expressed an interest in going into the firm. The Board's initial reaction was to insist that he take a degree first (a rather arbitrary condition given the staff's general lack of formal qualifications). So Nigel attended McGill University and duly graduated. But when LAB raised the matter of Nigel's employment once more, the Board went back on its original decision, and refused him. Hearing that LAB proposed to bring Nigel in at a higher level and on a larger salary than his own son, Anthony, Kenneth Pool strongly objected. Surprisingly, Pool and Roth were supported in their objection by Britten: while Nigel had been a student in Canada, Britten and Pears had come to Montreal to give a recital. Nigel's father had requested that he attend the concert and represent the family in an 'official' capacity. Preoccupied with his campus activities, Nigel had completely forgotten to turn up. Britten never forgave the snub. Forever after the Boosey family were tarred with 'having no interest in my music'. When LAB wrote the following in a letter to Britten some years later, it possibly contains a germ of truth: 'Roth told our Board that you had specially requested that he [Nigel] should not be brought on to the staff of B&H.' Nigel never entered the business; the Boosey sons were being systematically frozen out.

A year later, when Roth was due to retire, David Adams was asked to return to London and replace him as Director of Music Publishing. He was certainly not a first choice, and many others had been approached in consultation with Britten. Of course, there was no such thing as equal opportunities in the employment processes of the company at that time. Even LAB's headhunting yielded few results. The New York job was offered to Hans Heinsheimer, who said he would have taken the London job had they offered it to him, and to Rudolf Bing, who had just that week signed a contract with the Met. Simon Boosey, now no longer working for the company, put his hat in the ring and offered to take over the New York office if he could be a member of the parent Board, and if the disciplinary episode could be cleared from his record. No one ever replied. Some years later, when David Adams was nearing retirement, Simon asked him if there was any chance of his re-entering the firm in London. Adams did not encourage him: 'Never – there is too much hate,' Simon recalls him saying.

In the end Roth made the decision to appoint the director of the South African office, Stuart Pope, to the New York position, against LAB's express wishes (he was holding out for his son Simon). Pope was a former boy chorister at St Paul's Cathedral and was an organist. He had previously worked in the Edgware accounts department before and after the War, in which he also served, before going to South Africa. There were no further protests: Simon, having already resigned earlier in 1962, had gone to work for Scholastic Press in the UK; Anthony Boosey also left to set up an air-taxi firm.

Ever dignified, ever dutiful, LAB stayed on until early in 1964 to sort out various appointments, to close a major deal with Hammond Organs in Chicago ('my own brainchild') and to oversee a reorganisation of the factories. His sense of responsibility to Boosey & Hawkes outweighed any desire to seek revenge. Reflecting years later on his father's life, Simon felt that one half of his initiative had been shot out of him by his First World War experiences. 'He had learned to keep his head below the parapet and to run the regiment smoothly as a long-standing major.' The trauma of losing his brother and father had caused him 'to withdraw himself from spontaneous reaction'. He had only one – and for decades only needed one – management stance, and that was benignly paternalistic; he was incapable of scheming or hatching political strategies to his own advantage.

It was as if he could not drag himself away. As late as March 1964, LAB was still in attendance at a Board meeting in his new role as President of the company, antagonising the other members by suggesting that Stammers, who by now held many of the Boosey family shares, should be given representation on the Board. By this time Kenneth Pool was Chairman, with Clapham, Little, the factory manager Mr Draper, and Dr Roth, who would stay on the Board until his death in 1971. The Booseys had gone. The only hint of LAB's true opinion of Geoffrey Hawkes can be found in his farewell letter in the Christmas 1963 *Edgware Journal*, in which he rightly claimed credit for 'the tremendous recovery and expansion during the last two and a half years since I resumed the chairmanship'. It was a huge wrench for him to leave the company he had worked in for 55 years, for 29 of which he was Chairman, and his departure was overshadowed by bitterness: he was later heard to say 'there was a generation of vipers in my bosom'.

Old fashioned beauty versus 'contemporary noise'

During these years of internal turmoil, the publishing of music continued unabated. Britten's *A Midsummer Night's Dream* was a huge success in 1960, followed by the *War Requiem* in 1961. Roth had negotiated the contract for this with the Coventry Festival, managing to raise the derisory fee offered to a more appropriate £2,000. The first performance made a most unusual impact on many members of the B&H staff. For the first time, perhaps, Roth was profoundly moved by a piece of Britten's music and, to his credit, revised his opinion of the composer's abilities. He wrote to Britten, 'I had thought that Mozart and Verdi had said it all, I was wrong.' LAB heard it twice and wrote: 'it is my honest conviction that it is among the greatest, if not the greatest, Requiem that has ever been written'. His wife Ethel's heartfelt response echoes that of many: 'My feelings are too deep for words but in the midst of so much "contemporary noise" today it was like someone reaching out and saying "Take comfort – there is still timeless Beauty". I have never seen Leslie so moved.'

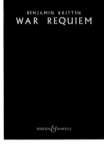

Vocal score of Britten's
War Requiem

By 1962, the 'contemporary noise' which Roth had tried for a decade to ignore, was growing louder. Therefore, he was grateful to attend the first performance of the venerable Kodály's Symphony in Switzerland. His neat assessment appears in a letter to LAB in the summer of that year: 'Kodály's symphony, his first and probably his last, is an old-fashioned piece, very Hungarian, very competent and in the traditional sense very beautiful. I expect the press to be mild but unfavourable, but the public was delighted and it will have many performances.'

The qualified nature of his comments says everything about the fraught aesthetic climate of the time. While Roth was coming to terms with the achievements of Britten (whose operas, surprisingly, he ultimately judged a failure: not works 'the public would regularly want to hear'), articles were appearing in *Tempo* on the radical approaches of Birtwistle, Alexander Goehr, Cornelius Cardew, Stockhausen and Iannis Xenakis. Mario Bois, the representative in the French office, had made a strong case for the latter, Greek composer, and John Andrewes, who shared his enthusiasm, had passed the scores to Roth. By this time, Roth had a slightly more relaxed attitude to new composer agreements since he was not going to be responsible for their commercial success in the future (he was to retire in two years). Commenting on *Pithoprakta*, he acknowledges 'it is hard to determine with any accuracy what this can sound like, because one just cannot read 46 strands simultaneously, but I have no

doubt that this is music as opposed to non-music'.
Metastaseis provoked his acid wit: 'I would
describe this as sound effects using musical
instruments. There is no economy of effort on the
part of the composer who takes 552 notes to make
a chord of octave G sharp.'

In fact, an agreement with Xenakis was signed in
1966, and he was, for a short while, a 'house'
composer. But examining the scores had given
Roth serious concerns about the future of music
publishing as he had known it. Increasingly,
composers were submitting works with electronic
elements to be assessed by the in-house arbiter,
Leopold Spinner. Roth notes in a 1966 Board
meeting: 'at the present time it is very difficult to
publish and promote the more advanced type of
music. The nature of the work makes it
impossible to print in the normal manner.' He
wrestled with what he saw as an aesthetic and
economic crisis in music, as can be seen in his

Iannis Xenakis in his studio
(late 1960s)
(Photo: Gilbert Rancy)

book *The Business of Music* – in effect, a valediction to his own profession:
'It must be said quite brutally that the new serial, electronic, improvised,
determinate or indeterminate music has no public – or at least no public
which could keep both music and its composers alive.' All creative effort
'is bent on "how" to the detriment of "what".' Stockhausen's famous claim,
'Whether organised sound is called music does not interest me', chilled
Roth's blood. Acoustic results had become irrelevant, composers were
struggling in the dark towards a new order that was 'nowhere in sight'. He
once confessed to Tony Pool that he could promote music he did not like,
but not music that he did not understand. No wonder the future looked
bleak to him.

Across the Atlantic, however, he signed a composer he *could* understand
and who was, moreover, eminently publishable in the 'normal manner'.
This was the Argentinian Alberto Ginastera, whose orchestral scores had
successfully married 20th-century orchestration with the rhythms and
colours of his native Argentina. The conductor-composer Igor Markevitch
had recommended Ginastera's *Variaciones concertantes* to Roth in 1953,
and this had been published as a one-off work. Ginastera at that time was
published by B&H's old ally Roberto Barry, who David Adams went to visit

Alberto Ginastera (1950s)

in Buenos Aires in 1962. By this time, Ginastera had developed more sophisticated, modernist techniques in his composing. They discussed the composer's wish to have more international exposure and his potential in the American market, which was clearly strong. After all, he was already working on an opera commission from the City of Buenos Aires, *Don Rodrigo*, which turned out to be a huge hit at its premiere in 1964. He subsequently came to live in New York at the Salisbury Hotel and was there to enjoy the success of the New York City Opera production of *Don Rodrigo* in 1966, featuring the young Plácido Domingo as the Don, one of the tenor's first major roles. Ginastera was inundated with commissions after this, including two further operas, and soon became a close friend of Adams and then Stuart Pope, who succeeded Adams in the New York office. In 1980, his back catalogue was acquired from Barry for $100,000 and today he is the 15th highest-earning composer for the firm.

Donald Mitchell and the final straw

Roth's suspicion and ultimate dismissal of the 'more advanced type of music' had prevented many composer signings during the fifties and early sixties. (Panufnik had been accepted under sufferance, but was an established and mature composer by the time he came to be taken on, as were Ginastera and Xenakis.)

Still, Britten would not give up his mission to revivify the catalogue with young talent and continued to put forward names to Roth and LAB of like-minded new music advocates who might join the publishing company staff. One of these was Professor Anthony Lewis of the Royal Academy of Music, who was duly elected to the Music Publishing Board. Another was Donald Mitchell, who, in 1962, had been editing *Tempo* for a short time. He had come to Britten's attention ten years earlier when he and Hans Keller published *Benjamin Britten: a commentary on his works*, the first serious study of the composer's music, which brought together contributions by the authors and by Stein, Harewood, Lennox Berkeley, George Malcolm and Arthur Oldham, among others. Britten was instinctively suspicious of musical analysis but was flattered by their initiative, and came to trust Mitchell's knowledge of the contemporary scene and his musical judgement (like Stein, Mitchell shared Britten's love of Mahler).

In September 1962, Roth agreed to meet Mitchell, to the composer's delight: 'I very much hope you had a satisfactory meeting with Donald Mitchell. I think the idea of him coming into the firm would be wonderful – he is a fine musician, a nice person and I should think extremely practical as well.' To Mitchell, Britten implied they would be working as a team within the business: 'I've been fighting a (lost) battle with B&H over young composers for years. I shall push and push for your coming in – if you can really face it! It would be wonderful to work together and get it really straight again and on the right lines.'

Roth – no doubt at the insistence of LAB and through gritted teeth – took him on. Mitchell says he was called a 'Music Adviser', and understood that he was to look after Britten's interests and to ensure that some new, younger composers were taken on. Other members of staff understood that Mitchell was 'Britten's man', but knew this should never be leaked to the other composers. If Britten was entitled to a personal representative, then what about Copland, Kodály, Stravinsky? (In fact, Copland *did* hear

Britten with Donald and Kathleen Mitchell (1974)
(Photo: Rita Thomson. Courtesy of the Britten-Pears Library, Aldeburgh)

about it, and did complain.) Roth had other ideas. As far as he was concerned, Mitchell was there to advise on new educational publications. That he could stomach. While he did not prevent Mitchell from looking into contemporary composers, he did not see this as the main task: Roth, after all, was in charge of the catalogue.

Peter Maxwell Davies
(1960s)

As far as Mitchell was concerned, his role was obvious: 'The idea was that I would be there and staff members like John Andrewes would keep me in touch with approaches made to Ben, and I would then discuss these proposals with Ben and with people who wanted to perform or commission a work – I was meant to be the interface.' He also took the remit to bring in new blood very much to heart. 'I was excited, probably naïve. I had no idea how bad relationships were in the firm at that time. Looking back I am amazed we achieved so much during that short period.'

Mitchell, with the assistance of Andrewes, who was also closely in touch with contemporary composers, recommended that Peter Maxwell Davies and Nicholas Maw be signed. They represented two very different strands in contemporary music: Maxwell Davies was of the 'Manchester' school, an *enfant terrible* of extraordinary vivacity with a highly original, almost violent relationship with his musical past; Maw was a naturally lyrical and dramatic composer who told radical stories in more conventional language. One can understand why Roth might have approved of Maw, who was wooed away from Chester by Mitchell with the promise of a better contract. But Maxwell Davies must have been accepted on the strength of the works he had written while teaching at Cirencester Grammar School. Britten himself admired what Maxwell Davies had done at Cirencester and did regard him by then as a successor in his pioneering work for the young. Of course, Maxwell Davies was already far more than that, and what Roth later made of *Worldes Blis* and *Eight Songs for a Mad King* we can only guess at.

Nevertheless, the suggestion to take him on must have had Roth's backing, since it proved a long negotiation. The young composer had been

Nicholas Maw, his then wife
Karen, and John Andrewes
(1970)
(Photo: Andrew Karney)

published by Schott for several years and was reluctant to leave: 'I shouldn't like to leave Ian Kemp [then in charge of Schott's UK office] now after all he did for me, disapproving of disloyalty …' he wrote to Mitchell. The latter arranged for him to be offered a generous contract which would inevitably lead him to question his current agreement with Schott. Maxwell Davies was excited: then on a fellowship to Princeton, he had already embarked on his opera *Taverner* and longed to be free to compose and not to have to find other work to 'earn a living' when he returned to the UK: 'Does this mean Boosey & Hawkes think my work will *pay*?! It wd be marvellous were it performed enough for that! …' Schott countered with a higher offer, and Roth wrote to Mitchell warning him not to try to outbid Schott once again, as he felt this would be 'unethical'. Max (as Maxwell Davies familiarly became known) was ready to sign, but Schott had not given up. They started issuing threats and accused Boosey & Hawkes of breaching unwritten codes of business honour. It was a very awkward situation: Mitchell was green in the ways of the music publishing business, and Roth, instead of lending him whole-hearted support, took the opportunity to wrong-foot him. The firm very nearly lost the composer, but Mitchell was passionate in his advocacy: 'I am convinced that PMD is a man of genius and the leading composer of his generation, and as such I should like to see him published by Boosey & Hawkes. More importantly, PMD now wants to be published by Boosey & Hawkes, which leaves us in the absurd predicament that though 1. PMD wants to come to B&H and 2. we want him to come, 3. we are deterred by

Schott's blustering.' It was also pointed out that Schott had been paying him a fraction of the amount now being offered by B&H. And so the deal was done.

One of the first works to be published by the firm was the *Second Fantasia on John Taverner's 'In Nomine'*, which, due to an administrative slip, turned out to be a very different piece from that requested. It was a commission from the London Philharmonic and the conductor John Pritchard had hoped to perform it with Webern's Symphony, so sent a note to Max via B&H, asking him to write for smallish ensemble. The note never got passed on, and Max wrote the piece heavily scored for full orchestra and an arsenal of percussion requiring four players.

The signing of these two composers represented a major triumph on the part of Mitchell and a change of direction in the publishing policy that had remained quiescent since Hawkes's death. Roth countered with the signing of a more conservative figure, the Austrian Gottfried von Einem, a pupil of Boris Blacher and teacher of the future B&H composer HK Gruber. His music was essentially tonal and he insisted his students mastered traditional counterpoint, doubtless an attraction for Roth.

Gottfried von Einem (1960)
(Photo: S Enkelmann)

Like Barraud, von Einem was an establishment figure in his own region, and highly influential. Since the 1947 Salzburg premiere of his breakthrough opera *Dantons Tod*, von Einem's new operas (he was to write six) had been widely taken up. He was a lecturer at the Wiener Konzerthaus-Gesellschaft for 18 years and was on the board of the Salzburg Festival administration for three years, until he was dismissed for helping Berthold Brecht to get an Austrian passport. This bizarre episode shows von Einem's independence of mind. He offered to help Brecht and in return commissioned him to write the *Salzburger Totentanz* for the festival. When opposition to Brecht's Communist views arose, von Einem was branded a Communist himself and declared 'a disgrace to Austria'. Brecht moved to East Germany, but not until decades later was von Einem pardoned.

To return to Mitchell, he was not only engaged in signing composers. He felt he needed to find out for himself, and for Britten, what was 'going on' in the business. He took the opportunity to talk to all the staff – 'to interview us', one said. Some resisted. Leopold Spinner, the ascetic editor on the fourth floor, famously refused Mitchell's invitation with 'I'm afraid I'm not very good at lunches'. The young writer was eager to look for composers abroad as well, and went to America 'on a mission … to talk to the existing American composers to see what could be done – I was hoping to start to get a feel for the whole market'. His intentions were positive. What he was not told was how circumscribed his remit actually was. He had no idea at first of Roth's attitude to his appointment and says his dismissal, in the autumn of 1963, came like a bolt from the blue.

In fact, there had clearly been tensions from the start. Roth, in a letter to Britten in December 1963 explaining his action against Mitchell, says that the advisory role required 'infinite tact and restraint', which was lacking. He goes on to describe Mitchell's chats with staff as 'submitting them to some sort of interrogation using your name freely and I had the unpleasant task of dispelling a widespread uneasiness that great changes were impending'. He accused Mitchell of speaking 'disparagingly' of the firm to the outside world, and even of suggesting that it needed reorganising – an idea that Britten may have planted some time before. He was 'particularly disappointed that DM did not produce anything in the educational field. He may say that the man at present in charge of the Educational Department is a man of little imagination, but the advice given should not have been simply of a general nature.' Here, Roth rises up on his hind legs to take a last swipe, 'Quite frankly, I do not need an adviser on principles. Bartók's *Mikrokosmos* would never have been written without me, and I advised Bartók in great detail on the principles.' He does give Mitchell credit for bringing in Maxwell Davies, 'but this alone cannot compensate for the considerable trouble which has arisen all round'. He ends his letter to Britten, 'Please do not say that your confidence in Boosey & Hawkes depends on any one single individual.'

Roth should have known better: of course it did. Britten was apoplectic. In a scribbled draft of a letter he writes, 'Heard news from Donald – horrified. History repeats itself. Another friend gone. Such relationships built up … this allied to what has happened recently has brought another colossal jolt in my confidence in the company. I don't feel I can say more until I have time to consider the implications … I hope no further action of any kind will be taken until I'm next in touch … perhaps misunderstandings can be cleared up before it's too late …'

It *was* too late. And in fact Britten took a very different approach this time. He ceased to write any further letters of complaint. He ceased to write any letters at all. He simply did not sign the new contract, and that was the end of his association with Boosey & Hawkes. There were no farewells, fond or furious. After all, the firm would still be dealing with nearly thirty years' worth of his scores, so relations were kept cordial. The only mention of the catastrophe is a short Directors' Meeting minute in November 1963 indicating that the composer's demand to reinstate Mitchell was unacceptable to the Board and therefore, to everyone's regret, Benjamin Britten would no longer have his new works published by Boosey & Hawkes.

When David Adams succeeded Roth as Managing Director of music publishing in London in 1964, no one drew his attention to the fact that relations with the greatest and most valuable living British composer in the catalogue seemed to have permanently broken down. Letters, unanswered, from Adams to Britten, throughout the summer of 1964 vainly ask for a meeting – 'we really must talk' – and suggest that he thought the relationship could be rescued. With Ralph Hawkes, Erwin Stein, Anthony Gishford and now Donald Mitchell gone, Britten felt no further connection with the company.

Did Roth know what a gamble he was taking? After all, by 1963 Britten's own annual royalty receipts from Boosey & Hawkes were in excess of £41k (over £400k in 2007 terms), a figure which rose dramatically in subsequent years. Says Mitchell now, 'I think it's pretty odd that Roth and his colleagues were prepared to go to that length to risk losing a composer who was 50 years old, who could have gone on composing for another 30 years. I don't think they really predicted he would leave.' Tony Pool, who was working there at the time, says that Roth firmly believed Britten was fully committed to the new contract, even if he had not formally signed it. He had already pooh-poohed the idea that Britten could leave the firm and go elsewhere, asking rhetorically, 'Where to?'

Britten had given the question much thought. In February 1964, when he was in Venice composing *Curlew River*, he wrote to Mitchell to commiserate with him on his dismissal from B&H and ended the letter, 'Don't worry ... I'm sure there'll be some future. I occasionally dream of Faber & Faber – music publishers!' Mitchell, who was by then the editor of the music book list at Faber, took the idea straight to the top. TS Eliot said, 'We must do it'. Director Peter du Sautoy supported him and immediately got in touch with Britten. Events moved quickly. By May it was public that a new music publishing company was to be set up, the first since Oxford University Press in 1925, managed by Donald Mitchell and with Britten as the first published composer. Britten deferred his fees for a long time to assist the 'lively new music publishing firm' he had, quite literally, dreamt up. His first work to appear under the imprint was the *Nocturnal* op. 70 for guitar, followed by the first church parable, *Curlew River*. What was the reaction of his former publishers to this humiliating defeat? 'They didn't take it seriously', remembers Pool. 'They were curious to know how a publishing outfit for Britten would fare, and thought that it wouldn't last.' One member of staff who Britten was eager to attract to the new firm was John Andrewes, who had served the composer with such devotion for many years. Interestingly, his loyalty remained to B&H, and no inducement could persuade him to leave.

Over forty years later, Faber Music continues to pursue the policies Britten set down at its inception and has built a leading catalogue of British composers, many taken on when very young. Its existence stands as testament to one composer's impatience with Boosey & Hawkes as it operated in the fifties and sixties.

Serving Stravinsky, and Roth's *Abschied*

Leopold Spinner, the senior editor in the production department, kept a diary of the manuscripts that passed through his hands for more than three decades. The diary is revealing in showing just how long a score could take to be produced and proofed – nine months at least on the bigger works – and also for showing the range of composers and works at any one time. In the early sixties, for example, the *War Requiem*, in all its various translations, looms large in the schedule along with *The Rake's Progress* in other language versions. There is Gottfried von Einem's opera *Der Zerrissene*, Nicholas Maw's *Scenes and Arias* and his *Sinfonia* (a commission paid for by Britten), Maxwell Davies's *Taverner*, several works by Jolivet and Barraud, Copland's *Organ Concerto* and *Letter from Home* and the odd score marked 'for Mr Boosey' (presumably Ralph, who still worked in the Professional Vocal Department) – mainly old songs that would have once qualified as ballads, including *In Flander's Fields*. Later, in the early seventies, von Einem's Dürrenmatt-based opera *Der Besuch der alten Dame* crops up for month after month until Spinner makes the first and last personal comment he was ever to allow himself: 'Bloody Alte Dame!'

Leopold Spinner, composer and Webern pupil, who was Stravinsky's editor in the 1960s

But the composer dominating the production department in that decade was Stravinsky, who was busy revising works throughout this period in order to earn new copyright fees. Stein had always been Stravinsky's trusted editor, but now Spinner was working on *The Flood* and *Abraham and Isaac*, the full score of *Pulcinella*, the *Requiem Canticles* and the revised *Symphonies of Wind Instruments*.

Rufina Ampenoff and Ernst Roth had been intensely involved in Stravinsky's conducting and composing schedule since the mid-fifties. As his state of health became more precarious in the sixties, they found themselves dealing with three people: the composer himself, his wife Vera and his assistant Robert Craft. The degree to which Roth and Stravinsky liked and trusted each other can be judged by the fact that Stravinsky entrusted the care of his granddaughter Kitty to Ernst and his wife Käte when she was studying in London.

In 1956, Stravinsky had come to Italy for the first performance of his *Canticum Sacrum* at the Venice Biennale. There had been endless wrangles before the performance because the Biennale's director felt his piece was too short. Stravinsky was having none of it: 'the contrapuntal nature of my music today ... makes it a must to keep the duration of a composition strictly within rigid limits. This is due to the requirements and possibilities of the human ear and because this kind of music is of the densest kind.' Of course, a solution was found: 'You, dear Dr Roth, are the only person I can rely on to settle the matter.' Roth was sanguine: 'it will all work out in the end', he comments archly, 'not by the efficiency of those in charge, but by a miracle apparently worked by St Mark the Patron Saint.'

In Europe that autumn, the composer suffered a mild stroke and had to cancel conducting engagements in Rome and London. Vera had been told by the doctors but wanted to keep the truth from her husband, and wrote urgently to the Roths: 'My husband must not know this ... I doubt he will attend Sargent's concert, because other conductors sometimes make his blood pressure go higher than his own conducting would!'

Stravinsky knew he was unwell, and his immediate thought was money. If he had to give up conducting, he needed a guarantee of income. In 1955 his annual royalties from his B&H works already amounted to $31,566, so it was not over-optimistic for Roth to arrange for him to be paid an advance of $25,000 a year in case royalties became his sole source of income.

In fact, this was not to be. Stravinsky, in his 75th year, rallied and by 1957 Roth was busy acting as his agent once again and somewhat alarmed to find that the composer had agreed to take on ten concerts that Bruno Walter had cancelled due to a heart attack. One engagement was a source of particular irritation to Roth. He writes to Craft: 'I am not happy with the arrangements with Boulez. Whatever his talents as a composer he is certainly very adroit in making publicity for himself, and I am not quite sure to what extent he helps himself to Stravinsky's fame … at any rate, I sincerely hope that Boulez is not the arranger of this concert in Paris, and that we, Boosey & Hawkes, shall have no dealings with him.' 'Dear' Roth as a friend was incomparable; as an enemy, he was pitiless.

In 1958, Stravinsky was devastated to learn of Stein's death. He had written to him three years earlier to express his pleasure that Stein, in semi-retirement, was to devote himself solely to the editing of Stravinsky's scores. 'The news of Stein's death made me very very sad. I sent a cable … asking to convey to his family my feelings of a deep sorrow', Stravinsky wrote to Roth. The cable was never passed on. Roth did not reciprocate with any fond memories. A civil *froideur* had existed between the two men since their early days in Vienna, which had never melted through all the trials and successes they shared. No one could have been less like Roth than Stein, once described by John Amis as 'an absent-minded professor … never with the right spectacles on his nose'. Stein's daughter Marion says of Roth: 'He was a tough man, a businessman. He was known to be ruthless.'

Stravinsky, too, could be ruthless. He – and, increasingly, Craft – juggled financial offers, waiting for a better one, and left Roth to disentangle the agreements. In 1961 he suddenly decided that the 'paltry fee' of $1,500 to conduct for Brussels Radio was not enough and cancelled the concert. There was an arrangement for him to come and perform the British premiere of *Abraham and Isaac* at the Proms. At first he complained the Proms were an 'inappropriate' occasion suggesting, to William Glock's indignant surprise, that they were merely a festive knees-up. When he was reassured by Ampenoff of the seriousness of the concerts, he wanted to cancel the Proms appearance anyway, favouring a date at the Royal Festival Hall with the Philharmonia who were paying 'full expenses and everything'. In the end Norman del Mar did bring the work to the Proms in 1965, to great acclaim: 'One of the most consistent manifestations of Stravinsky's genius has been his ability to invent not only new music but new vessels for it,' wrote the *Times* critic. Personal loyalty sometimes won over money, however. His ballet *Agon* had been written for George Balanchine and the New York City Ballet, but after Roth had signed agreements, with Stravinsky's blessing, with La Scala, Düsseldorf, Zürich and Berlin, the composer changed his mind and said that the New York City Ballet should have exclusive rights for a year. The planned performances never took place at La Scala or in Zürich, and B&H faced damages.

As Stravinsky aged, there were more opportunities for celebratory gestures. But when Roth suggested a promotional photographic calendar for 1962 he was having none of it: 'I could never welcome honours or similar things in connection with anniversaries when it concerned myself. So I ask you frankly, please drop your idea and forget about it. Thank you.' He did, however, graciously accept the gift of the original manuscript of *The Rite of Spring* as an 80th birthday present from B&H.

Aged 86, the composer came over to Europe in 1968, assisted by Ampenoff in every small detail, from the driver of the car to his welcome at the Savoy. (The strength of her ardour can be gauged by her note to him on losing a letter he had sent her: 'Igor Feodorovich: something terrible has happened.' He scribbled a reply that he had forgotten what his request was anyway.) In London he was now greeted as a deity and his new '*Aldous Huxley' Variations* were admired. In the summer of 1968, with the departure of Mario Bois for rival publisher Salabert, he pushed for Nicholas Nabokov's son, Ivan, to be given the job of manager of the French office, claiming that the Paris office had let him down

Stravinsky's *Movements*, published in the Hawkes Pocket Score series in 1960
© Copyright 1960 by Hawkes & Son (London) Ltd

badly and that his music 'was no longer heard in France'. Ampenoff played advocate, stressing that Ivan's wife was the daughter of the Minister Joxe and a 'wealthy woman'. It was one of the few times that Stravinsky indulged in any Britten-like intrusions into the running of the company, but since Didier Duclos had already been appointed, he could not be obliged.

Stravinsky was still very much aware of the composer with whom he shared a publisher and remarked in a letter to Ampenoff after a performance of his *Abraham and Isaac* in 1965: 'I really tried! Well, what can you do, it's not for everybody to have Benjamin Britten's success with the critics.' The following year came his *Requiem Canticles*, of which he said: 'The original title was *Sinfonia da Requiem*, but I seem to have shared too many titles & subjects with Mr Britten already.'

When Roth officially retired in 1964 Stravinsky signed a photograph of himself: 'Love and kisses (many) to my dear friend Dr E Roth who promised me not to leave me before I am going away, Igor Stravinsky.' It must surely have been Roth's greatest treasure. And, devoted to the last, he survived Stravinsky by four months, dying in July 1971.

Mario Bois with Stravinsky and Vera at Orly Airport, Paris (1960)

Roth was mourned by many. A memoir in *Tempo* by George Newman, who had worked for him as an editor, perhaps best captures the playful wit which bubbled beneath the formidable exterior, and which can be seen twinkling in photos: 'He was extraordinarily gifted as a translator. Everything he did he finished in record time: for instance, he translated the text of a Martinů opera into German in three days. He put into English, practically without hesitation, some of the most difficult German lyrics for the new edition of the Richard Strauss songs. It was during that time that he gave me the *Six Songs*, op. 68, which he was in the process of preparing. "We will both translate these six Brentano poems over the weekend and then compare the results" he said. On Monday he triumphantly produced his six translations. I had only managed to do the first poem by sitting up until the early hours. "That's because it's called *An die Nacht*", he said, and roared with laughter … When the printer asked

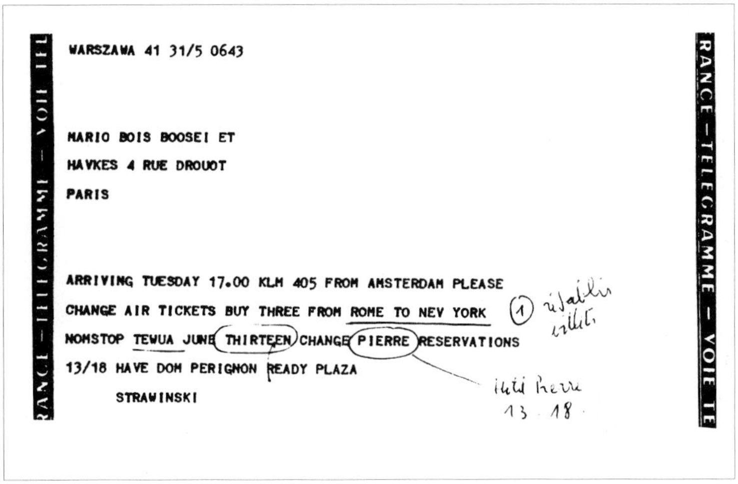

```
WARSZAWA 41 31/5 0643


MARIO BOIS BOOSEI ET

HAVKES 4 RUE DROUOT

PARIS



ARRIVING TUESDAY 17.00 KLM 405 FROM AMSTERDAM PLEASE

CHANGE AIR TICKETS BUY THREE FROM ROME TO NEV YORK

NOHSTOP TEVUA JUNE THIRTEEN CHANGE PIERRE RESERVATIONS

13/18 HAVE DOM PERIGNON READY PLAZA

        STRAWINSKI
```

Telegram from Stravinsky to Mario Bois (1960s)

why, on the title page of Strauss's *Four Last Songs*, "September" was the only title "in English", he replied, "September is September is September".'

His death was acknowledged by Britten, who had always recognised his qualities despite the lack of trust between them. He wrote a kind note to Käte regretting their estrangement. Her reply is impassioned. She could not forgive him: 'My only great sorrow is that Ernst has not lived to know your change of feelings. He himself has never had anything but admiration and true understanding for you.'

A Stravinsky postscript

Stravinsky's last years in California were overshadowed by illness and frustration. 'Can you imagine what it is like to wear a harness with 32 steel hooks from the spinal column to the shoulders in this heat?' asks Craft. Ampenoff said 'all my prayers for IS's recovery', and busied herself bidding for his manuscripts that came up at auction in London. As Craft explained, 'his lawyers say that the manuscript is not worth that for a resale but is worth many times more as a tax deduction.' She even accompanied the composer, his wife and Craft to Basle in 1968 to inspect his Swiss bank account, when he began to suspect his lawyer was working on behalf of his son-in-law.

Stravinsky with Ernst Roth
(late 1950s)
(Photo: Lotte Meitner-Graf)

Stravinsky's message to Roth
on his retirement (1964)

There was, however, one less than glorious legacy from the close relationship between Roth, Ampenoff and Stravinsky. It had been a dream of both Roth and Ampenoff that Boosey & Hawkes might publish all Stravinsky's letters and papers after his death. In the late sixties, Roth was no longer in the office, but Ampenoff worked tirelessly to get an agreement drawn up in which Stravinsky would assign the publishing rights to Boosey & Hawkes and his Paris-based friend Pierre Souvchinsky would edit them. Vera convinced Stravinsky that this was a way of helping Souvchinsky financially, and he signed a contract in 1968, giving Souvchinsky sole editorship for a stipend of £3,000 a year. Robert Craft was clearly not happy about this, and Ampenoff prepared further contracts, finally arriving in New York in 1969 with an agreement that appointed Souvchinsky and Robert Craft co-editors of the Stravinsky archive, a contract Stravinsky signed. However, work began to photograph all the letters and documents in his library. Craft complained that it was done in a haphazard and ill-informed way, with the musical scores and many of the photographs being ignored. On Stravinsky's death, factions in the family began a long litigation over the inheritance – chiefly Vera and Craft on one side, and the children of his former wife on the other. The Stravinsky archive became yet another bone of contention, but work had started. Other editors were brought in to assist and soon the costs were spiralling out of control. Craft complained in the *New York Times* that valuable archive material was now inaccessible because of the stalemate between the fiduciaries and Boosey & Hawkes. Tony Fell, who became Managing Director in 1974, remembers that when he arrived £80,000 had already been spent editing the still incomplete first volume. He took steps to sell the rights back to Vera Stravinsky in 1977 and the project was abandoned. The bulk of the archive remained in boxes in Stravinsky's apartment in Fifth Avenue until it was finally sold to the Paul Sacher Foundation in Basle in 1983.

Ampenoff had been a close ally of members of the Stravinsky family for so long, they were inevitably upset when she was required to retire in December 1975. She was in fact past retirement age, and it was clear to

Tempo

Igor Stravinsky 17 June 1882–6 April 1971

Stravinsky memorial issue of Tempo (1971)

Hugh Barker and Fell that little progress could be made in the firm while she continued her autocratic and increasingly idiosyncratic rule over the key area of business affairs.

Fishing for shares

Sometime in 1967, there were reports coming through that someone was bidding for the company, driving the B&H share price unusually high. It was soon clear that this was the American music giant, CBS (Columbia Broadcasting System, Inc). There was a connection: its then President, Goddard Lieberson, was a close friend of Stravinsky and responsible for producing the complete series of recordings with the composer conducting that was being released at the time.

Boosey & Hawkes had been a public limited company since the early sixties, and after the upheavals between 1961 and 1964 large numbers of shares had been falling into other hands. The CBS approach was rejected, but what subsequently happened had a more subtle, yet more insidious effect on the company.

On Geoffrey Hawkes's death, a large percentage of his stake in the company went to the Massachusetts cymbal manufacturer Zildjian, whose products Boosey & Hawkes distributed. On LAB's retirement, and the resignation of his sons Anthony and Simon, many of the Boosey family shares had been bought by Stammers (Aird and Stammers partly controlled the Radiation group, and LAB had wanted them to take over the Edgware factories). In January 1967, a Mr Frank Connor of the American music publisher Carl Fischer had enquired about the possibility of acquiring shares, and had obtained a five per cent stake in the company. A month later the stock brokers were again 'seeking shares at any price': for whom was not known, but it was probably Fischer. Knowing that Fischer wanted more shares, Bob Zildjian approached Frank Connor and suggested they bid for Stammers' shares together. The next day, Connor had some news for him: he had gone and purchased all the Stammers shares. Overnight, Frank Connor had acquired a significant stake in Boosey & Hawkes.

Bob Zildjian of Boston cymbal manufacturer Avedis Zildjian (1960)

Zildjian, who still owned 22% of the shares, had been agitating to have a representative on the Board. Some were in favour, as the firm had been very supportive in supplying replacement stock when there was a fire at the Edgware factory. But Kenneth Pool, by now Chairman, refused on the grounds that an American would not be able to come over for monthly meetings and, once such a shareholder was allowed a representative, Carl Fischer would insist on one too. Zildjian, piqued by the rejection, broke a gentleman's agreement with Kenneth Pool that neither would sell shares to a third party without informing the other. He sold up to Carl Fischer too.

The Board Meeting minutes give nothing away: 'After discussion it was agreed that no further action was called for hereon.' What could they do? They had sat by and watched the company fall into the hands of a stranger. Frank Connor was now, with a 49% stake, the major shareholder and could dictate terms. Pool recalls a dinner at the Connaught Hotel in Mayfair in 1969, at which Frank Connor stated his intention of remaining a 'sleeping partner'. It was on that, as it turned out, false basis that he was allowed to nominate a single UK Parent Board representative, and Christopher Saunders was duly appointed. Before long, he would be joined by three others. Did the full import hit the company at that moment, or was it only later, when key appointments were controlled by the Connor family, that they realised who was in charge?

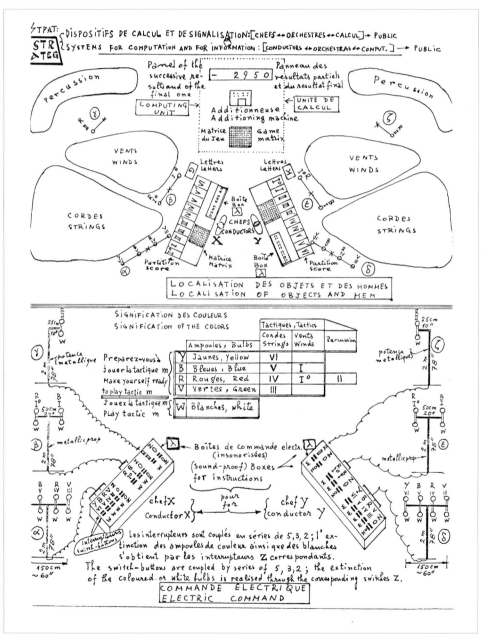

Strategies and *Eight Songs*

The late sixties and early seventies were a time of ferment in contemporary music, and the breezes of the new were beginning to steal under the heavy doors of 295 Regent Street. The stream of new works that had flowed from Stravinsky, Copland, Britten and Kodály (who died in 1967) had by now dried up, and while the copyrights were there to be milked, it was essential to focus on the next generation.

In 1966 Xenakis was signed, and *Pithoprakta* received its first UK performance, with *Eonta* going into production. *Pithoprakta*, with another contemporaneous orchestral score, *Metastaseis*, received a triumphant choreographic treatment by Balanchine and the New York City Ballet. As critic Clive Barnes wrote, 'In a sense this is organic music, better compared to sculpture than to drawing ... it is this three-dimensional element that appears to have attracted Balanchine, and enabled him to produce a work of tremendous power and interest. We are accustomed to music in which finite things happen, themes develop. This is not the way of Mr Xenakis, to whom sound is a cloud of sensation, an organic web of musical impulses.' Xenakis's extraordinary stochastic and conceptual scores offered a new set of challenges to the London production department, and there was much discussion as to how to publish *Stratégie*, Xenakis's 'game' piece in which a range of choices are open to the conductors and the 'umpire'. The piece generated a snow-storm of internal correspondence, with John Andrewes suggesting they published the score in the form of a box 'like a game', complete with coloured cards, rules, sets of matrices and an 'electric box'.

Unfortunately, by 1969 composer and publisher were embroiled in a legal wrangle as Xenakis first attempted to alter his contract and then sued B&H for breach of contract. It was a bitter end to what had seemed the start of a relationship with an entirely new kind of composer. Like some before him, Xenakis was fundamentally opposed to a standard general agreement: he did not like to be paid royalties as advances, as it made him feel obligated, and he did not want an exclusive contract: 'I want to have an equitable balance, that of a free man, not of an indebted one'. David Adams patiently explained the economics of music publishing – the need for a publisher to own rights since it was making all the investment in publishing and promotion, and received no subsidy of any kind. But the lawyers' letters continued to flow, quibbling over small amounts of money, for several years.

Premiere production of
Nicholas Maw's *The Rising of
the Moon* at Glyndebourne
(1970)
(Photo: Guy Gravett)

Nicholas Maw had already had success with his comic opera *One Man Show* in 1964, and in 1968 received an opera commission from Glyndebourne, which was to be *The Rising of the Moon*. But that year he was taken to hospital suffering from TB in both lungs. Rufina Ampenoff used all her powers of persuasion to secure him a loan so that he could buy a cottage to live in. It was a personally stressful period in Maw's life, but one that had the happy outcome two years later of a critically-acclaimed premiere of his opera and a repeat run the following year. Composer Anthony Payne, writing in *Tempo*, was one of its admirers: 'This is a traditional opera, but a tradition continues as long as there are works with vital breath of their own to sustain it.' He singles out the forging of a new language for opera – inspired by Strauss, Britten and Berg – as Maw's greatest achievement. Here was a born opera composer: 'the music, for all its fluctuating tempos and densities, does not need the story for explanation, it is itself the drama'.

The years 1969 and 1972 saw three important premieres from Peter Maxwell Davies. Having already caused a sensation in 1965 in New York with his Koussevitzky Music Foundation commission for voice and ensemble, *Revelation and Fall*, four years later he startled London audiences with *Eight Songs for a Mad King*. The work is now viewed as an enduring masterpiece, and some critics were excited by something 'so inventive and so new', but many condemned it as horrifying, offensive or just plain mad. It is still profoundly disturbing as a portrait of insanity, but its significance as a signature work was recognised by composer Jonathan Harvey in his *Tempo* review: 'In Maxwell Davies we have an unusually clear example of an artist working successfully both in and out of phase … he is true to himself in some works, such as the String Quartet and *Sinfonia*, and the *Second Taverner Fantasia*, and false to himself in the aggressively parodying and mocking series of works of which *Missa super l'homme armé* and the foxtrots are examples. In the former the spirit soars with intensity, in the latter we are astonished by the brilliance of the invention and by the daring of the wit.'

Eight Songs for a Mad King
by Peter Maxwell Davies,
performed by The Fires of
London (1972)
(Photo: Keith McMillan)

Eight Songs contained the kernel of Max's preoccupations: his intense, enriching relationship with the musical past, theatricality, expressionism and profound, political engagement with moral issues. The second major work – the tone poem *Worldes Blis* – caused more controversy. It was given at a Prom in August 1969 and provoked a strong reaction. Max, who stepped in to conduct it at the last minute, has said 'most of the audience walked out, and most of those who stayed booed'. The bleak 40-minute orchestral build-up of tension was heard as incomprehensible noise by many – Desmond Shaw-Taylor wondered if Max had not fallen into 'solipsistic megalomania' – though some listeners were beginning to penetrate its processes.

The third piece, the opera *Taverner*, based on the life of the great 16th-century religious composer, had been brewing for years – since Max's student acquaintance with Taverner's music in Manchester – and brought elements in the other works together on a grand scale. Although completed in the late sixties, it was not performed until 1972 for the simple reason that a producer or conductor could not be found to take it on. Ken Russell had initially agreed and then withdrew, while Georg Solti, then music director at Covent Garden, agreed to hear a play-through but rejected it. In 1971, he was replaced by Colin Davis, who was more supportive of Max and agreed that his enthusiastic assistant conductor Edward Downes should conduct the premiere. Although Max was far from happy with the production, the premiere was a success with audiences, and was performed first in the summer of 1972 and revived in 1983; further productions ensued in Stockholm the following year and in Boston in 1986.

It was viewed by B&H and the Royal Opera House as an important event, as can be seen by the extensive and glittering guest list for its premiere, and a whole issue of *Tempo* was devoted to its exegesis (provoking an internal memo from Rufina Ampenoff asking tartly if the first UK performance of von Einem's *Der Besuch der alten Dame* at Glyndebourne was going to be treated so lavishly: as a devout Orthodox Christian she had profound reservations about *Taverner*, and was devoted to the Catholic von Einem).

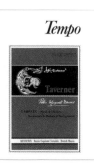

Tempo issue devoted to Maxwell Davies's *Taverner* (1972)

Tempo was edited during this period by the impressive Colin Mason, critic of the *Daily Telegraph* and Chairman of the Macnaghten Concerts Society. As composer Roger Smalley noted, 'he did not have his head in the clouds, but his ear firmly to the ground'. Certainly, Mason was always one step ahead of the other staff at Boosey & Hawkes at that time, with perhaps the exception of John Andrewes. He published an important survey of the younger Hungarian composers in 1964, drew attention to the Viennese MOBart & TonART Ensemble years before two of their number were signed, and counted among his enthusiasms Stockhausen, Malcolm Williamson, Bartók and Cornelius Cardew. In tribute Smalley writes, 'at a time when the majority of music critics seem unable to make up their minds about the value of contemporary music, and still less able to commit themselves to an unequivocal opinion of it in print, I found Colin's uninhibited approach splendidly refreshing.'

One of his great achievements was the commissioning of 'Canons and Epitaphs' in celebration of Stravinsky's 85th birthday in 1967. Composers included Edison Denisov, Boris Blacher, Berio, Birtwistle, Maxwell Davies, Hugh Wood, Schnittke, Maw and Tippett. He organised a complete performance of the works at the Cheltenham Festival that summer.

Mason died suddenly of a heart attack in 1971, and his absence was keenly felt. Had he been allowed a more active role in the firm at an earlier date, he would no doubt have influenced publishing policy. *Tempo* was a source of intelligence that was ignored at the peril of the publishing Board. It had been the source for recruiting Mitchell, and for signing Maw and Maxwell Davies. And it would be the source of the next great musical mind to come on board at Boosey & Hawkes.

The toffs and the workers: the real business of music

Board room battles between factions allied to the Boosey and the Hawkes families, or the new music and traditional music lobbies, did not represent the only divisions in the company. There were more obvious geographic and business splits.

'The toffs resided in Regent Street, the workers in Hendon.' Ian Julier, Production Manager at B&H London from 1976 to 2004, encapsulates one critical divide. Hendon in north London was the site for the production, engraving, printing and storing of sheet music, while Regent Street had traditionally been the location for the Head Office, promotion and the hire library.

There was also the fundamental divide between Musical Instruments and Music Publishing, a breach which had so concerned Britten. The instrument-making company, with its factory in Edgware in north London, was the more public, high-profile side of the business, and the area that was given disproportionate management focus for many years. In fact, the Musical Instruments division, after the radical shake-up of the mid-sixties, had had a period of high productivity and sales, and won the Queen's Award for Industry in 1971. The Music Publishing division had also been highly profitable, but what money was made was rarely invested in the

The new printworks at Hendon, a converted coachworks (1972)

publishing side of the business. Robert Cowan, now a well-known classical music presenter on radio, joined the advertising department in 1970 and remembers feeling the imbalance keenly: 'The instruments were given the big profile, the big image – and were perceived to have the biggest potential.'

The split in sites became more marked in 1972 when the whole production department, printing and warehouse was moved into a converted coachworks at The Hyde in Hendon, which was given its official opening by the Prime Minister Edward Heath. Up until that time there had been an editorial department in the basement of Regent Street, where Ian Julier's predecessor John Arthur worked for decades. A one-time engineer at Hoover and an active musician, Arthur had adopted and adapted the system of note-setting called Notaset, which worked by transferring notes on to grids rather like Letraset. In 1968 he hired a young copyist called Roger Brison on the strength of his ability to be the rehearsal accompanist for his Gilbert and Sullivan productions. Brison began his working life in that same basement. 'It was a very dusty place', he remembers. 'I once picked up a pile of transparencies of a von Einem opera. The dust rose up, I sneezed and dropped the lot! I remember Mr Arthur saying, "Do you think you're up to this?"'

Prime Minister Edward Heath opens the new printworks, with Kenneth Pool (1972)

Brison describes the laborious process of correcting scores: 'We would receive proofed, marked-up scores down from Leopold Spinner on the fourth floor. I would sit down with the razor blade, scratch out the mistake marked in soft pencil, and dip the mapping pen into ink and do the correction. I was doing Britten, Shostakovich and Copland scores at first, everything was done in a tremendous hurry for the first performances and then orchestras would gradually send corrected parts back with queries. I remember we did Prokofieff's *Fiery Angel* in three languages in two-and-a-half months, with four or five people working on it night and day. That would have taken nine months with the average staff. The costs were passed on to the piece of sheet music. If it was a rotten manuscript, the music could cost as much as £15 per page.'

Up until the eighties skilled artisan engravers were still employed to punch out the notes on metal plates for use on antique presses. The dry transfer method was retained up until the early nineties, when the first computer engraving programmes began to be introduced. Brison remembers that James MacMillan's *Veni, Veni, Emmanuel* and Max's tenth 'Strathclyde' Concerto were two of the last works to be produced in the traditional way.

The art of engraving used to astonish even senior editors like Brison: 'Those engravers needed seven years' training. When I started, there were two master engravers and four or five apprentices in the engraving shop. They used to have to put everything down in mirror image, like photographic negatives. I could never have done that; it was a real brain-teaser. But they knew how to space things in a way that has still not been transferred to other technology.' One of the most remarkable engravers, Jack Thompson, acquired the computer software Score in his late fifties and learnt how to use it. Says Brison, 'His work still has a better flow than that of most others.' Ian Julier mourns the passing of this unusual craft: 'It was a cumbersome, elaborate process. But I still think the quality of music engraving achieved – the interpretation of musical grammar on the page – represented a pinnacle of graphic achievement. But it hadn't attracted continuity. Youngsters didn't want to spend seven years in this Nibelheim with a hammer, banging away on a plate.'

Hand engraving music at Hendon (1970s)

Julier lived through the 'nightmare' hiatus during the late 1980s and early 1990s, when skill sets were not transferred across the technological divide: 'Composers and arrangers were not actively employed in the development of new computer software. So, tragically, you didn't have the musically literate people with note-setting experience transferring their knowledge to the new programs. The computer experts were able to work out facile programs but these couldn't cope with the demands of the type of music we were setting.' The computer had been seen as a quick solution to a cumbersome, problematic process, but it was never that simple. 'Gradually, a generation of programs emerged during the mid-nineties – Score, Finale and Sibelius – that were finally being configured with a degree of flexibility to suit serious music. A group of people who were both musically and computer literate at last emerged, at first consisting of a few of the prime users themselves, the composers. Eventually we were able to marshal a team of freelance originators who really knew what they were doing.'

Today many composers are able to submit scores on computer files, but the role of editors in making good those scores for publication is as vital as ever. Says Senior Editor Sally Cox, who came to work at B&H in 1977: 'Computer setting is still far from straightforward. There are composers who have mastered it well and their files do not need a huge amount of editing. But there are others whose digital files require so much work to

Shooting film for music printing at Hendon (1970s)

tidy them to publication standard – manipulating badly input data, respacing, moving slurs and other indications – that one would *prefer* to start from scratch. It can be soul-destroying work. In the past, engravers had served an apprenticeship and knew exactly how to lay out the music and, at proof stage, the job of editor was a musical check that all the notes were correct. Today, when I'm proofing, I often have to do some of the note-setter's job too. If not done with care, things like rehearsal numbers, dynamic markings and slurs may drift around, and a part automatically transposed by the computer may be littered with E sharps and F double sharps.' She remembers the first time a score was sent to be computer-set: 'It was Robin Holloway's *Scenes from Schumann*: it took more than four years, and we vowed never to do it again!' Of course, computer-setting has speeded up considerably in the last ten years, but the actual time spent preparing a score is not so much shorter today than it was thirty years ago.

Away from the engraving shop, the dusty, fusty atmosphere was something many commented upon on their arrival at Boosey & Hawkes in the seventies. Sometime in the early sixties the business seemed to have got stuck in a time-warp and stayed there. Robert Cowan remembers when he joined as a young man in 1970: 'You shuffled at Booseys, you didn't walk, you shuffled.' Ian Julier, six years later, was 'shocked to arrive in a company with such a huge reputation to see the astonishing level of laxity that was manifest in every department. It was riddled with old Spanish customs, stemming from people being there a long time. I half-expected to see someone in a corner covered in cobwebs.'

Lack of communication between the two sites had become endemic. Martin Hall, who had been there since the early sixties, and became Publishing Manager at Hendon, remembers the days when Roth would bark orders to him to give Mr Smeed and Mr Arthur in production. If Hall dared to take their side or pass on a complaint, Roth would say, 'Arthur's happiness is of supreme indifference to me.' Later in the eighties, when relations were significantly improved, Ian Julier and the hire library and promotion staff would have meetings once a fortnight, but the distance between the two sites was a still a problem: 'We couldn't just email things in those days. So much of what we were dealing with was hard copy – and a hard copy of an opera is a huge thing to lug about. You couldn't fax a whole set of parts: everyone had to wait.'

A staff review in the late fifties had allowed for men to smoke in all areas, but for women to smoke 'only in their tea break'. After much

Production office at Hendon, with Robert Cowan (seated second left) (1970s)

disagreement, it was decided a tea trolley would come around to each office so that no one had any excuse to leave their desks. By the early seventies not a great deal had changed: the London publishing staff were still treated rather like factory workers with clocking in and out at the start and end of the day and queuing up for the weekly pay cheque on a Friday. Smoking was still tolerated in most areas, and a slug of whisky before the morning meeting was a common occurrence in the offices of the top brass at 295 Regent Street.

Amidst the old customs and outdated management practices, a handful of whacky and unexpectedly 'with it' individuals came to work at B&H during the sixties, before their musical careers took flight. One was Trevor Watts, the jazz saxophonist and free-improvisation pioneer, who was then being groomed by Ampenoff to become a senior music editor before he left in 1968. Others included his jazz drummer colleague John Stevens, who worked in the hire library, Peter Knight, who sold violins in the Regent Street shop and joined an early line-up of the folk-rock group Steeleye Span, and Chris Squires up in the packing shop who had just founded what would become the legendary prog-rock band Yes. Other distinguished one-time employees in the hire library have included composer Malcolm Williamson and playwright Peter Schaffer, who was a cousin of Ralph Hawkes. Another surprising byway of this period was an unlikely, and ultimately unhappy, venture into pop and disco music in the late seventies with Robert Kingston Music. Apparently, young staff members would head off to Manchester and other places in the interests of 'market research', arriving back in the office on Monday 'looking wrecked'. The disco titles failed to hit the charts, but the deal brought into the catalogue a number of pop copyrights from the Tremeloes, as well as *Darlin'* and Jeff Christie's hit *Yellow River*.

New brooms

Tony Pool (1976)

The time was ripe for change, and David Adams was not the one to effect it. He was due to retire in 1975, and by 1974 the Board was discussing his successor. By this time Tony Pool, Ralph Hawkes's nephew and appointed heir, was one of the most experienced members of the team. He had gone to the New York company in 1968, met his wife Julie, and stayed there as Sales Manager for sheet music. He returned in October 1971 to prepare for the new operation at The Hyde in Hendon, North London, and in 1974 it was announced that he would be coming to work in Regent Street to understudy David Adams with a view to succeeding him at the end of the year. But the Board had not counted on the new power in their midst. The Connors of Carl Fischer, who by now owned nearly half of the shares, had other ideas about the succession. Despite the presence of Pool, Frank Connor had insisted that a head-hunter be appointed to track down a new Managing Director from outside the company; a year down the line, there was still no candidate.

In the mean time, Alan Clapham, the long-serving Board member from LAB days, had made it his business to meet potential managers while travelling to the foreign offices. The long tradition of appointing from within had resulted in three musically conservative but 'safe pairs of hands': David Adams, Stuart Pope and Ernst Roth. Clapham knew that the Connors were interested in bringing some fresh blood into the company, but he knew he would have to bring the Board with him.

While visiting the Boosey & Hawkes office in Johannesburg, he arranged to meet Antony Fell, the Managing Director of Hortors Printers and of Unimark International, the South African affiliate of an American corporate design firm. Fell, whose father had managed the Liverpool Philharmonic and Scottish National orchestras, had worked for the London music agency Ibbs & Tillett before penury had led him to join ICI and later accept a transfer to South Africa as publicity manager. He had experience of computer-aided typesetting and of newspaper and magazine publishing, and had founded and conducted the Johannesburg Bach Choir. A smart and enterprising manager, he had been looking to move back to London and the music world for some time (and had even been offered an interview for the job of Managing Director of Chester Music). Clapham admitted that head-hunters had failed to find a suitable candidate for Managing Director at B&H and that Fell appeared to have experience in four of the five key areas – music, management, printing and marketing (the fifth was law). He subsequently asked Fell to come to London for interviews, following which a competitive 'troika' of candidates was set up, consisting of Tony Pool, Terence Moss, Head of Light Music, and Fell, who would manage sales, production and print at Hendon. Feeling confident that he would prevail, Fell accepted the challenge. Just after he had sold his house and booked his air tickets back to London, he received an astonishing letter from David Adams saying that 'time would not permit the carrying out of our original plan' and that 'Anthony P Pool becomes Deputy Managing Director in July 1974 and succeeds to the Managing Directorship on the 1st January 1975', at the same time confirming Fell's appointment as General Manager of the Hendon operation and his seat on the Music Publishing Board.

Frank Connor of US music publisher Carl Fischer Inc

The Connors had other ideas. Hugh Barker, their representative on the Board, went to America to get approval for Pool's appointment, prior to making a public announcement. The Connors apparently refused, but Barker somehow misunderstood or misheard what they said, and the announcement was made public when he returned to London. Pool said to Barker: 'You know this will never go through, the Connors will never let it happen,' knowing that the American family, who now wielded such power, were antagonistic towards his father, Kenneth. Barker responded by promising to back Pool 'one hundred per cent'.

The Connors then decided that they needed three new representatives on the board: Frank Connor, his son Hayden, and his son-in-law Warren Mackenzie. By August 1974 they had persuaded the whole Board, still chaired by Kenneth Pool and including Hugh Barker, to overthrow Tony Pool's appointment: Tony Fell was made Managing Director.

The extent of the Connors' interest, now just under 48%, became public and caused a furore among the shareholders. 'Yanks go home!' was the hue and cry from shareholders and employees, who were now for the first time made aware of what had happened six years earlier. It was dramatised in *The Times* as the fall of *Land of Hope and Glory* into 'American clutches'. It was a painful moment for Kenneth Pool, who resigned his Chairmanship on his 70th birthday that year, and was succeeded by Hugh Barker. Despite their significant share ownership (18–20%) neither Kenneth nor Tony Pool was thereafter allowed a seat on the Board. The knives were out: it was no longer a case of Boosey *v* Hawkes. The Connors were determined to neutralise any former influence on the Board. They deemed that the Pools should appoint an outsider to represent the interests of the Ralph Hawkes Trust shareholding. A lawyer named Richard Crewdson took up this role, but the Pools were dismayed to find that, for whatever reason, he failed to keep them informed (specifically when an approach to take over the company was made to Kenneth Pool by CBS, to whom the Pools were willing to sell their shares). Crewdson even on occasion voted against the wishes of the Pools: when Sir Richard Young was suggested as a new chairman, Crewdson supported the appointment despite the Pools' objections. Crewdson turned out to be a relative of Young. When the Pools tried to appoint a new representative, they were blocked by the Connors. An untenable deadlock set in. To give him his due, Richard Young throughout his chairmanship did everything he could to break down the hostility between the Pools and the Connors, but it was all in vain.

The situation was particularly painful for Tony Pool, as he continued to put so much of himself into the company and had been publicly promised the promotion. As he still says, whatever the merits of the candidates, the bungled handling of the whole affair had a divisive effect on the team for a long time afterwards. He did not leave. 'All my loyalties were to this company – my own and my family's personal capital was tied up in it, and I just could not go and work for a rival. And I had a wife and new baby daughter – I could not throw it all in.'

Pool made a conscious decision to play an active role in the industry, and, following in the footsteps of the august LAB, he became increasingly influential in the Music Publishers Association, the PRS, and related international societies. He was on the Board of the ICMP (International Confederation of Music Publishers) and served as Chairman of the Standard Publishers Committee and President of the MPA, gaining respect for his incomparable knowledge, sound judgement and keen, legal intelligence. As President of the MPA he succeeded in consolidating the amalgamation of the MRS (Mechanical Rights Society) with the MCPS

(Mechanical Copyright Protection Society), and getting the new MCPS members agreement accepted. Says Arnold Broido, 'Tony is very smart. I remember the speech he made in the early eighties at an International Publishers' Association conference, when he triggered the idea of the extension of the term of copyright from 50 to 70 years after the death of the composer. We owe him a lot. It took a while, but he saw his idea bear fruit.'

'Running an atomic power station without any physicists'

Tony Fell, meanwhile, did a walkabout of the company and assessed what needed to be done. 'It was a bit of mess. There was no concept of marketing at The Hyde, let alone linking market knowledge to product development. There were accountants, but there was no structure for modern management. In the instrument factory, for example, there were no standard times for producing each instrument, so they didn't know how long it took to make a trumpet. How could they have a budget or a strategy without that information? David Adams had a secretary who also had a secretary. He would dictate letters to her and she would dictate them to her assistant. Rufina Ampenoff had about three secretaries – it was ludicrous!'

Fell introduced SWOT analyses (strengths, weaknesses, opportunities, threats) and set about devising a publishing policy. He brought in the design company Pentagram to give the publications a coherent identity. Some of the staff were bemused by the new regime. Cowan remembers a session in which Fell showed all the staff a film about an ice-cream-making business and how they had developed their marketing strategy. At the end he asked, 'So, what has Boosey & Hawkes got in common with that ice-cream company?' Cowan could not resist: 'Cornets!' he quipped. The room erupted.

One of Fell's most influential decisions was to bring in a new head of serious music. Although he was 'passionately interested' in music, he was

Tony Fell, Managing Director between 1974 and 1996 (1974)

no expert on contemporary composers and realised that an expert was required. He was not the only one to sense that a crisis of confidence had developed over the publishing of new music: the issue had been tackled at a Publication Committee meeting in August 1974, during a discussion about the possible signing of Hans Werner Henze. Henze, then published by Schott, had a commission on the table for a major new opera, *We come to the river* (1974–76). He was highly rated on the Continent, and had already had success with *Elegy for Young Lovers* and *The Bassarids* in the UK. Martin Hall noted that no major composer had been signed up by the company for the last ten years. 'It was absolutely vital', Hall argued, 'that we consider very seriously our publishing policy and if it was at all possible to derive a profit from the publishing of opera then we should put ourselves in a position to be able to publish the works of important composers, of which there were very few, in a proper manner.' In 20 years' time a number of their copyrights would expire, and there was a pressing need to look to the future. Ampenoff applied the brakes (it is unlikely she would have approved of the virulently left-wing Henze anyway): von Einem's *Kabale und Liebe* was already in production for a 1975 premiere, and resources would be overstretched. Geoffrey Cox, the Chief Accountant, countered with the question that would be asked over and over again in the next decade: 'The company should ask itself if there really was any future in music publishing. If we cannot get a realistic income from a man who would appear to have proved himself internationally, how could we be expected to be able to continue publishing new works of our living composers?' As Tony Pool has since pointed out, at that time the company could have chosen not to publish *any* new music and it would still have had a reasonable income for the next 40 years (because, as it turned out, there was a further copyright extension). This would have been a boring but legitimate option: if they were to decide to risk money on new composers and their works, the accountants needed to be convinced it was worth it in the long term.

At this point in the meeting the chief music editor, Leopold Spinner, was summoned to give a final judgement: 'He stated that Henze meant more in Germany than he did in this country and that the two operas which had been produced here had appeared because of their libretti by W H Auden and not because of Henze's music.' It was an odd and rather blinkered view. David Adams countered with the fact that *Elegy for Young Lovers* was in the repertoire of 32 opera houses. Spinner was resolute: 'it would be wiser to take each work separately but not commit ourselves to a general contract'. As an editor, the sheer labour involved in producing a new opera score weighed heavily in his decision-making.

Boosey & Hawkes never assigned the new opera, or any other works of Henze. When Martin Hall talked of 'proper' publishing, he was referring to the practice of giving major composers exclusive general contracts with a retainer attached. Having a few works by a composer was often unsatisfactory: the 'whole' composer could not be efficiently promoted, there was a lack of confidence on both sides and the long-term relationship could be compromised, with the best works ending up in another house.

Spinner was due to retire in two years, and his official responsibilities had always been those of an editor and not an adviser, despite the great respect in which his opinion was held. Submitted scores were invariably passed under his nose, and he was rarely impressed. John Andrewes, in Promotion, was also knowledgeable, but the structure was such that he had never held any management role. As Fell remarked at the time, 'This is like running an atomic power station without any physicists.' He urgently needed to find someone with their finger on the pulse of new music, who could be given a role of sufficient influence within the company to make things happen. Apart from Donald Mitchell, who had initiated a flurry of activity in the early sixties, no one had put into force a dynamic publishing policy since the days of Ralph Hawkes. Fell was looking for someone who could formulate a philosophy, and it turned out that the man was right under his nose.

David Drew and the new publishing policy

Fell went to talk to Nicholas Maw, who suggested he meet the current editor of *Tempo*, David Drew, and recommended him highly. Drew was a world authority on Kurt Weill, a scholar, writer and editor of *Music Today* as well as *Tempo*, who sat on a number of advisory panels. His fluent German and his friendships with many eminent composers and influential figures could open doors for B&H all over Europe and America. At the time he was asked to join the staff, he had many on-going commitments at home and abroad, including three book contracts and a major collaboration with the Berlin Festival on a Weill retrospective in September 1975. 20 years of professional involvements with some of the leading music publishers in Europe and America had left him with a passionate interest in the present and future of the industry; and despite the variety and stimulus of his freelance work, the offer from Boosey & Hawkes struck him as irresistible. The only other publisher that might have tempted him was Universal Edition: 'It was a unique example of enlightened patronage rooted in the grand tradition of Europe's Indian summer before World War I, coupled with the characteristically post-1950 acumen of the remarkable Alfred Schlee. But in the unlikely event of my being offered a job in that literally historic family firm, I would have reluctantly declined. I'd had a surfeit of advisory panels in ivory towers, and since I wasn't a composer or a practising musician, I wanted the challenge of working for composers in a publicly-quoted company. The knowledge that one is investing the shareholders' money would be salutary, or so I thought.'

David Drew (right) with
Copland at Tanglewood (1980)
(Photo: David Huntley)

The response of some of his friends was that he was selling out. The reputation of Boosey & Hawkes at the time was of a highly successful and wealthy, but apparently less than idealistic, publishing company: 'The relatively recent loss of Britten had left a widespread sense that "something is not right there", at a time when UE, Schott, Faber, OUP, and so forth were pursuing their clearly defined courses.'

It is striking how the subject of a music publishing strategy entered the agenda of Board meetings in the mid-seventies in a way it had never previously done. In the days of LAB, Ralph Hawkes and Ernst Roth, much of the strategy had been reserved for internal discussion and correspondence and had rarely been questioned in an open forum. The reasons were two-fold: the former directors were supremely confident in their own artistic judgement and ruled autocratically, never by committee; but, crucially, the classical music economy of the time had been sufficiently robust to support the composer choices made – eventually. By the seventies, a divide was opening up between the highly subsidised contemporary music world of European artistic institutions and radio stations, and the commercial sector where ticket sales drove programming. Fell made one tentative statement on the direction of the London publishing company in January 1975, before Drew arrived, when he reported: 'Further market research was essential before any firm commitment to the future development of this department. A judicious mix of serious composers (bringing long-term returns) and more popular (with certain early return) was required ... The Finance Director was to prepare a formula for returns on risk investment.'

Gradually the language of caution gave way to the names of real composers as Drew and Fell embarked on their journey back to a musical future. When Drew left, in 1992, Boosey & Hawkes was publishing John Adams, Steve Reich, Elliott Carter, Michael Torke, Kurt Schwertsik, HK Gruber, York Höller, Berthold Goldschmidt, Henryk Górecki, James MacMillan and Robin Holloway, and represented significant works by Leonard Bernstein, Roberto Gerhard and the entire catalogue of Igor Markevitch. They did not achieve this alone: it was the rich harvest of a true collaboration between Fell, Drew and key members of staff in the Regent Street, American and German offices. The sleeping giant had woken up and grasped the torch for the new once again.

MOBart & tonART

Fell remembers that Drew formulated a policy fairly rapidly after arriving. His précis of their strategy is characteristically pithy: 'In a nutshell, Drew said, "Yes, there is a problem in music publishing today. The post-War avant-garde is unlikely to do anything that will yield the kind of revenue that Stravinsky or Prokofieff or even Britten still yield. That doesn't make it

HK Gruber at rehearsals for *Frankenstein!!* (1980)

bad music, but it's a commercial fact. We've missed out on composers like Ligeti, Henze (ironically) and Berio – composers whose works have absolute quality and who still have a public – but that doesn't mean that there isn't another kind of music that in time will also have a public. Much of this modern music will fall away, so we need to find people who are turning the tide now, and we must go out into the world to find them. We must not be provincial!"'

Drew remembers a more gradual evolution of a policy, but he did appreciate Fell's prompt action in getting him a place on the Music Publishing Board: that was critical for decisions to become realities. Between the time Drew joined the company and the end of 1978, there were four important signings. Ironically, one of the most radical and unexpected composers came via a direct prompt from an established conservative on B&H's books. Gottfried von Einem sent Drew a postcard demanding in no uncertain terms that he see his former student, H(einz) K(arl) Gruber. 'I know what I say when I call him highly gifted.' He mentioned that he had a chamber opera at the 1976 Wiener Festwochen: 'I think it might be interesting to get hold of this man and his piece. Please have a sharp glance in and on it. It would be nice to have Mr Gruber as a grown up colleague.' Drew duly went to Vienna to hear *Gomorra* and Nali, as he is fondly known, worked his magic. Drew was enchanted by the exuberant chansonnier-composer. Gruber will never forget the day: '13 July 1976 at 1 am. David Drew telephoned me and said, "Nali, we have won the war, you are now a Boosey & Hawkes composer." I couldn't believe it – I was in a trance. I still say that it was the birth day of my new life. From that day I have had someone who trusts me, who supports me, who has given me a backbone so I can walk upright. In the War we were released by the Allies: that day I was released from Austria!'

Drew suggested as a first project a complete reworking of the music Gruber had originally written to underscore a recording of children's poems of HC Artmann. The composer had already extracted a so-called *Frankenstein Suite* for chansonnier and ensemble, but this was still in the nature of an improvisation, and as such, 'unpublishable and unpromotable'. The new version was to be a 'proper' composition scored for a 'normal–abnormal' symphony orchestra. Gruber worked on integrating new texts from Artmann's poetry and composing new music in intense discussion with Drew. 'Each week he would phone me and we would talk about it, and how the first performance was going to be prepared.' In this case, the publisher was entering the creative process in an unusually dynamic way. Simon Rattle agreed to conduct the Liverpool Philharmonic, with Gruber as soloist, and the 1978 premiere of the newly-created *Frankenstein!!*, complete with a bizarre range of plastic toy instruments, was a triumph. The piece was an instant, if subversive, hit and went on to become one of the most-performed scores of the next two decades. Gruber had previously been published intermittently by a small local firm, but after *Frankenstein!!* he was, to his great satisfaction, approached by Alfred Schlee from Universal Edition, whom he was able, politely, to turn down.

HK Gruber belonged to what had in the late sixties been known as the 'MOBart & tonART' group, which consisted of a handful of Viennese musicians who gave 'alternative' Salon Concerts. The ensemble they formed had three directors: Otto Zykan, pianist and poet, Kurt Schwertsik, composer and French hornist and the younger HK Gruber, double bassist and chansonnier. Their name hinted both at an 'urban gang'-like group and their interest in 'Tonart' – tonality. As Gruber remembers, at the time the word was almost taboo. 'I said to myself, tonality is possible. I can invent a musical world, and my chosen language will be this one.' Another person to make that brave choice, even earlier on, was Schwertsik: he had studied with Stockhausen but had become interested in the more free-wheeling experiments of Mauricio Kagel and John Cage. In 1963 he himself 'experimented', this time with tonality, writing the *Liebesträume*, a radical treatment of Liszt's *Nocturne*. Schwertsik criticised the forms of contemporary music which had become so complicated that 'it was only during the process of composition that the composer himself thought he understood them'. He himself was published by UE, and Drew was determined to poach him. He came willingly. Fell supported Drew, but there were others at B&H who were scandalised at a second Viennese being signed (Vienna then, as now, being considered somewhat provincial), and another composer who embraced tonality.

Kurt Schwertsik (1987)
(Photo: Sarah Ainslie)

Schwertsik's first work published by Boosey & Hawkes was the highly controversial 1977 ballet, *Walzerträume* or *Wiener Chronik 1848*, as it was later named. Commissioned by the dance company Tanzforum, whose composer-in-residence was Kagel, *Walzerträume* divided opinion with its unexpected diatonic lyricism, coupled with a kitschy, snowflake production. Drew remembers how 'the Tanzforum public was as shocked by Schwertsik's consistently tonal score as the traditional ballet audience was delighted with it'. The following year Drew attended the premiere of Schwertsik's Violin Concerto at the Styrian Autumn Festival in Graz – one of Europe's main *Neue Musik* events: 'The atmosphere during the performance was thundery, and the hisses and boos at the end were ear-splitting, but there was an old guy sitting next to me who seemed oblivious, applauded vigorously, and turned to me with a smile and said in broad Styrian "I think the composers are coming back to us". I was moved by that – but also by the hostility.'

The 'return of tonality' was heralded in a gloriously blunt article in *Tempo* in 1979 by the Polish composer Ladislav Kupkovič, entitled *The Role of Tonality*. 'If present-day music is evolving from the atonal to the tonal it is not headed towards "New Simplicity" but towards a degree of complexity which for most of today's recognised atonal composers would mean compositional suicide. Atonal composing, good or bad, can be mastered by anyone: as a rule one does not even have to be musical – if the music does in fact turn out to be musical, that's a terrible state of affairs. Tonal composing, on the other hand … is possible only for a few.'

Two more composers from very different backgrounds were given
exclusive publishing agreements in 1977. The first was Robin Holloway,
then in his early thirties and the possessor of an impressive œuvre,
including *Scenes from Schumann* and the First and Second Concertos for
Orchestra, which were acquired from Oxford University Press. He was in
some respects an heir to Britten, but in others a radical refractor of
musical styles – a technique which was later to be labelled 'post-modern'.
Holloway summed up his approach in a tribute to
Britten: 'If one spends months on end in one's
formative years listening to *The Turn of the Screw*
and *Peter Grimes*, mixed up with the Five
Orchestral Pieces and *Jeux*, *The Dream of
Gerontius* and the dances from *The Midsummer
Marriage,* the Four Last Songs, *Agon* and *Le
Marteau sans Maître,* curious transformations will
take place that won't allow one to lose any of the
elements, whatever the vicissitudes of later taste.
One gradually recognises that one *is* what one
assimilates.' By this time, it was acknowledged
that Holloway had moved, as Bayan Northcott put
it, 'beyond stylistic collage … into a quite personal
play of arabesque, gesture and colour'. The
majority of his new works were hailed by the
critical establishment, but there were times when
Holloway could disarm and disturb. After the premiere of *Evening with
Angels* he was accused by one critic of giving way to 'reactionary
temptations' and after *Domination of Black* another called him 'middle-
aged', revealing the knee-jerk reaction of the time to anything
approaching 'old-fashioned' music.

Robin Holloway (1985)
(Photo: Felicia Cohen)

That was not an accusation that could be levelled at the other composer
signed at this time, Tona Scherchen-Hsiao, the daughter of conductor
Hermann Scherchen and Chinese composer Hsiao Shu-sien. Drew was
always careful to balance opposing streams in modern music, and never
simply backed one 'type' of music, only individual composers he
considered interesting. Tona was educated to a high level in the musical
cultures of Europe and China. As Henze said to her: 'You have a Chinese
inheritance with which no one can compete. Don't let serialism shut you
away from it.' She had a somewhat tempestuous personality, and did not
always feel supported by her publishers as musical ideas and dreams
became more and more conceptual and she engaged in installation art.

Having joined B&H, she wrote twelve fine pieces between 1977 and 1979, but chose not to renew her contract in 1979. As she wrote to Fell in 1983: 'I would have been tied up artistically by your contract; therefore I preferred the apparent choice of total insecurity, real misery, but the freedom of mind.'

Scherchen-Hsiao was an example of a composer who evolved into another kind of artist, and she was not the only one. In the days of Strauss and Stravinsky, Roth had been dealing with composers who could be relied upon to pen publishable scores, but the sixties and seventies, as has been seen with Xenakis, were characterised by composers breaking beyond the limits of standard notation. One such was Wolfgang von Schweinitz, an extraordinarily original German musician, whose *Mozart Variations* Drew heard in 1977. The score was charming and witty, the composer personable and Drew was intrigued. There were positive political implications in signing a new German composer, and Fell recommended him to the board in 1979 as 'an eminently practical young composer'. His description was to prove ironic. Schweinitz had no intention of writing any more music like the *Mozart Variations*. A true eccentric, his next major task was an opera whose libretto, he insisted, must be the *entire* Book of Revelations. Drew, in vain, tried to persuade him otherwise, but *Patmos* grew into a monster. Ruth Berghaus's production was praised by critics at the Munich Biennale though the responses to the music were more equivocal. Schweinitz then headed into more extreme experimental territory, ceasing to write for equal-tempered instruments and insisting that orchestras re-tune to play his works. A minimum of ten weeks' rehearsal was essential. He did not need a publisher – he needed a patron. He is no longer a B&H composer, though relations remain cordial.

Reviving the past

Not all activity centred on living composers. Finzi's *Severn Rhapsody* was published and the decision made to complete the Finzi edition. Delius's lovely Violin Sonata in B (op. post. 1892) finally went into print in 1977, and acquired a vivacious advocate in the shape of Tasmin Little, who performed it often and made a fine recording in the 1990s. In the late seventies Drew arranged to buy from Keith Prowse/EMI some works by the Catalan composer Roberto Gerhard (further works were acquired in 1986). Drew had met Gerhard at Cambridge as a student and had become friends with him and his wife Poldi. Gerhard, who died in 1970, had studied with Schoenberg in Vienna, and became friends with Marc

Blitzstein while in the master's class. Forced into
exile by the Spanish fascists, he was offered a
research fellowship at King's College, Cambridge
and took up residence in Britain just before the
War. Although a disciple of Schoenberg, he
admitted to his teacher in a revealing letter of
1944 that he 'has not found it possible to work
consistently with the 12-tone series. I find the
desire to work with poorer series insurmountable.'
Gerhard owned a distinctive, Spanish voice and
was an original, lyrical heir to Falla and Granados,
as well as the rigorous Schoenberg. Once at King's,
his style expanded, and he wrote four ballets,
concertos for violin, piano and harpsichord, and
music for BBC radio plays, and made sophisticated
arrangements of Spanish operetta tunes. After his
death, however, his name fell into almost complete
obscurity. It was Drew's great achievement to
bring about the moving premiere of the exiled-
Gerhard's *Cantata* in his native Barcelona, and to
create a new performing version of his opera in
English after Sheridan, *The Duenna*, which received its premiere in
Madrid's Zarzuela Theatre in 1991. Nicholas Payne, then at Opera North,
was so impressed by the piece he mounted a new production of it in Leeds
for the opening of their 1992–93 season.

Vocal score of Roberto
Gerhard's *The Duenna*

Another such exhumation involved the works of the Ukrainian-born Swiss
composer Igor Markevitch. Markevitch had studied composition with
Boulanger in the twenties and conducting with Scherchen, been
commissioned by Diaghilev and achieved high recognition as the 'second
Igor', but had stopped composing during the Second World War, becoming
a full-time conductor. Drew acted as the catalyst for the premiere of
Markevitch's *La Taille de l'Homme* (set to a specially-written text by
Ramuz) by the Schoenberg Ensemble in Amsterdam and the US premiere
of *Le Nouvel Âge* in Tanglewood, both in 1982. Once again, the catalogue
of works was bought (from Schott) for a modest fee, and Drew went on to
set up a Markevitch Foundation and archive in Lausanne, laying the
groundwork for a series of recordings on the Marco Polo label. It was
tragic that, just as a revival of his music was under way, Markevitch died
in 1983, and the Sony recording of his oratorio after Milton, *Le Paradis
perdu*, was never made.

Igor Markevitch (1960s)
(Drawing: Elizabeth Valdez)

Leopold Spinner retired in 1976 and a concert of his works was held at the Serpentine Gallery, organised by Drew, who was a great admirer of Spinner's serial miniatures, with their Webern-inspired delicacy and precision. On hearing of the proposed concert Spinner said to Fell laconically, 'I suppose this was Drew's idea.' Spinner died in 1980, and indeed, Drew has proved himself an inspired advocate.

Max and Maw, more or less

In the late seventies, the two composers signed in the days of Donald Mitchell seemed to be experiencing opposite problems. Nicholas Maw, having completed his *Serenade* in 1977, was labouring over what was to become his massive 96-minute-long *Odyssey*. It turned out to be a transformative compositional journey, but the original commission, offered by the London Symphony Orchestra in 1972, had been for a 20-minute orchestral piece. As the date of the premiere drew nearer it was clear it would not be finished. In fact, it was not to receive its complete premiere until 1989, having been aired in an unfinished form at a Prom in 1987.

Maw had experienced a troubled few years, including his TB, a breakdown in his marriage and a period of financial instability with no fixed abode. He had written some of his most significant works, *Life Studies, Serenade, Personae I–III, La vita nuova* and part of *Odyssey* during the early seventies, but the turmoil in his personal life was taking its toll on the creative process. Things seemed to have ground to a halt at some point in 1978, and it was suggested that the general agreement was no longer working.

There was, however, great unease about losing a composer such as Maw, and in March 1979 the contract was renewed 'for a period of one further year on the same terms and conditions'. A year later it was not renewed, although B&H offered to continue to publish individual works on a work-by-work basis. Internally the reason was given that the 'gap between income and expenditure has not been satisfactory for the last 16 years'. Maw recalls that there was talk of the firm being under financial pressure, and that it could not support composers who did not earn enough.

Faber Music, where his old ally Donald Mitchell was Managing Director, readily signed Maw in 1981, and he has had a general agreement there ever since. Looking back, Drew can see that he had overlooked the symbolic effect and emotional implications of ending an exclusive contract. 'It was naïve of me to suppose that he would just walk away from the embers of a general agreement, and return in due course with individual works. As far as he was concerned, it was a breach of trust, and that was an end of the matter.' Fell and Drew also made the mistake of not communicating the decision to the promotion department first, which led to division and distrust from within.

An uproar ensued in the musical community about the apparent 'firing' of Maw, and conspiracy theorists put a sinister construct on what was in fact a combination of simple economics and inexperience of publishing psychology. Drew was unfairly singled out for condemnation, it being noted that Maw had recommended him for the job in the first place. Deeply distressed, he tendered his resignation, though it was not accepted.

Peter Maxwell Davies, on the other hand, now happily living on the remote island of Hoy in Orkney, was composing at a rate of knots, and manuscripts were piling up, unpublished, at 295 Regent Street. Max had originally dealt directly with Drew and Fell, who had given a loan to his ensemble the Fires of London at a critical time in 1975. But by 1977, when he was living in Orkney, his manager Judy Arnold was handling his business affairs. That year she made a list of all the works that needed

Maxwell Davies with The Fires of London (1985)
(Photo: Chris Davies)

publishing and asked for a timetable. Various such lists had been circulating since 1973, when *Worldes Blis* and *Taverner* were awaiting publication. Four years later the list included *Ave Maris Stella, Stone Litany, Revelation and Fall, Hymn to St Magnus, The Blind Fiddler, Ecce Manus Tradentis, From Stone to Thorn, Fiddlers at the Wedding, The Martyrdom of St Magnus* and *Westerlings*. In 1978 his new ballet *Salome*, which had been well received in Copenhagen, was added to the list with a proposed publishing date of 1980. Fell was already suggesting that the production department simply could not handle the sheer number of works and drew up a second list of 14 works that could not realistically be published within a two-year period. By 1979, the schedule contained no fewer than 20 works awaiting processing. It was an unprecedented situation.

In hindsight, there may have been a way in which all parties could have signed up to an agreed publishing plan, but, with B&H beginning to feel overwhelmed and with Max feeling insecure about his publisher's support, matters were bound to come to a head. In order to ease the backlog, Fell agreed to release certain works for publication by Chester Music, most importantly his atmospheric one-act opera *The Lighthouse*. In 1978 Chester published *Le Jongleur de Notre Dame*, followed by seven further works. Again, there was unease within the promotion department about this decision, especially when, in 1980, it was agreed that for a period of three years Max would offer all his new works to Chester in order to clear what had become 'a perpetual backlog'. An article about Max in *The Guardian* noted, 'He is writing so much music that Boosey & Hawkes, for over a decade his exclusive publishers, can't cope and has been obliged to share him with Chester.' In fact, the editorial team rose to the crisis remarkably. Three years later Judy Arnold wrote to Fell to congratulate his production team on 'an incredible achievement': in 36 months they had produced 23 scores, two of them major operas and one a 264-page symphony: 'this certainly is publishing history', she concluded.

Despite this, Max continued to have parallel agreements with both Chester and Boosey & Hawkes, an arrangement that has worked to this day with the further addition of Schott. Fell admits that by employing extra staff, they just might have been able to meet Max's demands that all scores be published within a year of the premiere. But the parent Board at that time did not contain any musically sophisticated or sympathetic members. When Fell had to justify costs in his division, there was no one on the Board who could understand the significance of one composer over another (David Adams had stepped down in 1975, though he continued to attend Publishing Committee meetings until 1976). 'There was a philistine culture on the Board', Fell admits. 'They were far more interested in the instrument side: light engineering, now, *that* they could understand. I had a real task arguing my case to that Board.' As far as Pool was concerned it was a practical matter of capacity: 'At that time Max was occupying nearly 50% of the total capacity. We still had our obligations to other composers as well.'

The end of a founding father

LAB was in his 90th year when he finally received in 1976 an honour worthy of his achievements: the CISAC Gold Medal (Confederation Internationale des Sociétés d'Auteurs et Compositeurs). It was only the second time the medal had ever been awarded, and LAB was the only President of CISAC not to have been a well-known writer or composer. He epitomised the prophet without honour in his own land: since his earliest days as an apprentice at Durand & fils, he had endeared himself to the French, and they recognised him as a negotiator second to none and had also made him a Chevalier de la Légion d'Honneur. The Royal Philharmonic Society was stung into throwing a dinner in his honour at the Garrick, and letters of congratulation were read out, including one from Britten.

Leslie Boosey
(Photo: courtesy Nigel Boosey)

Since his retirement in 1964 he had been unable to cut himself off from his life's work, though after a few years he divested himself of his shares. LAB's reply to Britten's note suggests that he still suffered from a sense of betrayal, and a suspicion that he and his family had been unfairly dealt with. It is pitiful that he still felt the need to prove his musical judgement: 'After many years in the music business, I know good music when I hear it. What is more I could go through a pile of manuscripts and pick out the ones that were really musical by the way the music was written. There wasn't a modicum of truth in the statement that I and my family weren't really interested in your music … I can only hope from your letter that you have realised how mistaken you were.' He goes on to say that he had decided to pull out of his own company when the Board refused his youngest son Nigel a job, claiming that it had been Britten's own request to ban Nigel. Did Britten *really* take such personal offence when Nigel failed to attend a concert of his? Nigel Boosey himself believes it was the beginning of a souring in relations. LAB concludes the letter, 'Nigel has been for years in the British Aeroplane Corporation. He plays the horn in the Bristol Orchestra and is a local JP but it was a bitter disappointment when he was told he couldn't join the staff of B&H.' He ends that Britten's kind words 'have done much to heal the wound'.

Certainly, the RPS occasion and the CISAC gold medal touched LAB deeply. He was a man who had achieved much behind the scenes, and for him to be valued by his peers and his profession was the most profound, and the most appropriate honour. Thanks to him, the PRS and the Royal Opera House had emerged as strong institutions in an increasingly hostile environment, while under his wise Chairmanship, Boosey & Hawkes had enjoyed decades of profitable and high-profile business. He lived another two years and died in 1979, aged 92.

In a memorial address Sir Thomas Armstrong described LAB's long, private search for meaning in a life shattered by the First World War, and identified the strong Christian principles behind his devoted work in the field of music: 'This was the light that guided him, placing him sometimes at a temporary disadvantage when he assumed that others would behave as well as he behaved himself.'

A farmboy in New York

Vocal score of Copland's
The Tender Land

Meanwhile, in 1976 a farm boy with a pony-tail and thick boots stepped into the New York offices of Boosey & Hawkes. It was the year of the American bicentennial, and the staff of B&H Inc on 57th Street were working at full tilt. The anniversary had brought a shower of commissions, including those for their composers David Del Tredici, Dominick Argento, Ginastera and Ned Rorem. Negotiations had already started with Bernstein, who would go on to form a significant relationship with B&H Inc. Stuart Pope was actively involved on the boards of ASCAP and the MPA, lobbying for the extension of copyrights. Since taking over from David Adams, he had already established himself as the English gentleman abroad and was greatly respected in New York music circles. That year, 1976, the good news arrived: after decades of wrangling, the American copyright laws had been changed, extending the copyright period to 75 years from the date of publication. This would significantly extend the revenues for B&H Inc which had been operating at a disadvantage for years. (A combination of Russia finally joining the Berne Convention in the 1990s, an amendment to the US copyright law related to the GATT trade treaty restoring copyright in some older Russian works that had long been unprotected in the US, and a further 20-year copyright term extension late in 1998, brought additional revenues from works by Rachmaninoff, Prokofieff and Stravinsky.)

Stuart Pope enjoyed close relations with his house composers, particularly Argento, Ned Rorem, Carlisle Floyd, Ginastera and the father of them all, Copland. Then in his late seventies, Copland requested that the full score of his opera *The Tender Land* be engraved and published, as it was only available in a photostat rental form. Fell delayed a decision, while David Drew in London favoured bringing out a vocal score of his youthful work *The Second Hurricane*. Pope felt responsible for his most senior composer's contentment and wrote to the London office in dismay, 'I find it somewhat embarrassing that Aaron should hint as strongly as he has ... that he would seriously consider subsidizing the publication himself, Copland being so clearly one of the people that our Chairman [Hugh Barker] loves to describe as "bonanza" composers.' He points out that as Copland was writing so little, it would seem 'mean' not to do as he asked, especially, Pope pointed out rather acidly, given that all the recent von Einem operas have received full scores 'without apparent question'. It was a typical example of the familiar tug of priorities between the two offices. But Pope had a point: it was Copland's royalties that had played a major part in keeping the New York company going through the vicissitudes of the past four decades. Of all composers, he should not have been subsidising publications, and the story ended well. Another

Ned Rorem (1977)
(Photo: Joseph Adorniak)

composer who enjoyed the devoted service of B&H Inc staff was Copland's protégé, the composer and writer Ned Rorem. Sylvia Goldstein, still there since the days of Ralph Hawkes, had long ago taken him under her wing and they were close, personal friends. A 1986 diary entry says it all: 'Sylvia's just left, after 96 hours of relaxed hard work, mostly (I'm embarrassed to say, but not terribly) on setting my affairs in order – a half-dozen commissions, plus contracts for tiny choral pieces etc. She and JH treat me like a bright nine year-old ...' He memorialised her in his essay, 'Who is Sylvia?'.

To return to the young farm hand, the man who had stepped into the office that day in 1976 was in fact a music post-graduate from

Bloomington, Indiana, if anything over-qualified for a junior assistant's job, but some of the staff were not so sure he would fit in. Pope's first impression of this 'unsophisticated, gangling son of the land' was that he 'didn't look like someone to promote contemporary music'. But Jean Golden, Pope's secretary, and Sylvia Goldstein sensed someone special.

And as Pope listened to him, he discovered a broad knowledge of contemporary composers and mature insights into the direction music was going. He decided to give the young stranger a chance, so David Huntley spent his first months working his way painstakingly through the composer files. Within a few months he would know more about Boosey & Hawkes's American composer list than anyone alive. And within a few years he would be effecting the biggest shake up of the catalogue the office had seen in decades.

164

Score of Steve Reich's
Drumming (1970-71)
© Copyright 1973 by Hendon
Music, Inc

The performance begins with two three or four drummers playing in unison at measure ①. When one drummer moves to the second measure and adds the second drum beat the other drummer(s) may either join him immediately or remain at bar ① for several repeats. This process of gradually substituting beats for rests within the pattern is continued with at least 6 or 8 repeats for each measure until all drummers have reached the fully constructed pattern at measure ⑧. At ⑨ only drummers one and two continue, and after several seconds of getting comfortable in close unison, drummer two begins to slightly increase his tempo so that after 20 or 30 seconds he has finally moved one quarter note ahead of drummer one, as shown at ⑩. The dotted lines indicate this gradual shift in phase relation between the two drummers. Throughout the piece the alternation of stems up and stems down indicate the alternation of right + left hands. The choice as to which hand is indicated by stems up or down is left to the performers.

The man from Yves Saint-Laurent

The year 1980 proved to be a critical one for Boosey & Hawkes. Although the company ranked as number three in the world league of instrument companies, behind Yahama and the American Selmer company, its profit had all but disappeared. From a high in 1976 when sales of roughly £17m resulted in a profit of £2m, in 1980 a similar sales figure produced a pre-tax loss of £146,000. (Someone should have smelt a rat long before, since 1976 was the most profitable year partly because of the insurance money from a fire at the Edgware plant.) Something was very wrong. Competition from Japan and America was intensifying, and any fluctuation in currency to B&H's disadvantage proved devastating. A turnaround king was needed, and in September 1980 a new Chief Executive arrived.

Michael Boxford (1984)

Tony Pool has a vivid memory of his first meeting with Michael Boxford. The Board still had not recovered from the Connor-Pool debacle. Sir Richard Young had taken over from Hugh Barker as Chairman of the Board. He tried hard to engineer a rapprochement between the younger generation of the two sides – now that Frank Connor was dead and Kenneth Pool had retired – without success. Pool and his father were still significant shareholders and so were called in on a regular basis to meet the Chairman after the accounts were published. Following one such meeting, Young invited the soon-to-be appointed new Chief Executive, Michael Boxford, to meet the Pools. All they knew was that he had been the international marketing manager for Parfums Yves Saint-Laurent. Pool takes up the story: 'My father and even I were somewhat surprised to see our potential new Group Chief Executive arrive dressed in *leather trousers* – this did *not* create a favourable impression. He looked for all the world as if he had just come off a motorbike.'

There was no doubt that Boxford came from a very different business world. Tall, glamorous, with a sweep of silken, greying hair, he had successfully developed Yves Saint-Laurent into a global brand in an impressively short space of time. He had worked for the pharmaceuticals giant Squibb, so had experience of multinational companies. Furthermore, he was a competent pianist and had a genuine interest in the music business. He was impressive with a balance sheet, had a grasp of modern marketing techniques that was certainly new to the company, and proven commercial acumen. Walter Connor was keen for him to develop the instrument business, but he faced a steep learning-curve. Says Boxford, looking back, 'I was very ambitious for the company, perhaps over-ambitious. I had been given the clear remit of growing the instrument business. And at Yves Saint-Laurent I had been growing sales by 50% per year, that was my context.' What he did not know at the beginning was how costly his strategy for the instrument business would be, and what a severe financial impact it would have on the publishing business.

As well as Michael Boxford, a new Managing Director was brought in to run the instrument-making operation, Peter Ashcroft. His aim was to improve communication between the marketing people and the factory, and to put 'an engineering discipline on what is basically a craft industry'. The old conflict between the cottage craft industry and a mass-production business would not go away. B&H had succeeded with the high-end, professional instruments, but had always struggled with the cheaper student models. As one retailer remarked at the time, 'When you took a Japanese instrument out of its case you could be 99% sure that it would work. With a B&H instrument, that figure dropped to 80%, and when changes or spare parts were needed you could be waiting months not weeks.' Fell showed the then new student Emperor flute to star player James Galway. He played it, squinted down the barrel and said, 'It's in tune but it's a bit of a blow-torch job.'

Boxford wasted no time in trying to overhaul the whole business: 'I commissioned a strategy research review from Professor Dean Berry. I redefined job descriptions, set new objectives, and appointed an international marketing manager for printed music.' There were two big ideas. The first was to expand the instrument company by extending the range of instruments. He recognised that while the wide-bore clarinet – the famous Boosey & Hawkes 1010 – was popular in Britain and Northern Europe, French, German and American players favoured the narrow-bore instruments, which were easier to control and therefore better for beginners. The famous clarinet maker Buffet Crampon was near bankruptcy and Boxford decided to acquire it, with its Buffet and Schreiber wind instruments, its Paesold stringed instruments and Winter instrument cases. But the price was high: he was forced to sell the long lease on the Margaret Street premises (adjacent to 295 Regent St) for £4.6m to buy it. (Eventually, none of the freeholds in the upper Regent Street area, originally owned by the Boosey & Co, would belong to B&H.) Boxford was a big spender, and he raided the company's remaining assets to invest in further instrument acquisitions and in marketing and retail franchises, putting an emphasis on specialist dealers who would offer good service. 'My aim was to get the top brands for each instrument, and to develop student ranges. It was essential that we bring volume to the business, which meant being strong in the US and Japan, which then made up 60% of the market. We needed to force retailers to distribute our whole line from the first student instrument to the top professional model.'

It was a sound strategy in theory: to buy up all the best instrument brands and to market them internationally. But was it affordable? 'Sales did grow very quickly,' explains Boxford. 'We even developed a nucleus in Japan. But what I had not predicted was the way the instrument business consumed cash: you'd have six months of stock in transit or in the warehouse and the US retailers demanded 12 months credit. You needed at least 18 months worth of capital in the bank to sustain it.' Only two or three years elapsed before it became clear how much money had been spent and what sort of a state the company's finances were in.

His second key strategy was to make the staff think more internationally. This was long overdue, as Fell admits: 'Everyone was doing their own thing in the different territories. There was little sense of group responsibility.' Stuart Pope in New York was able to pursue a fairly independent publishing policy which no longer chimed with the new direction in London. The Swiss Gunther Mott ran the German office in Bonn in his own inimitable style: 'Ernst Roth had ruled the German office with a rod of iron. Mott was similarly autocratic: the staff were terrified of him, and there was no tradition of taking any initiative,' explains Fell. Didier Duclos in the French office was charming and eccentric. Says Fell, 'the chief accountant came to me one day and said "I think this man is money laundering". I knew that couldn't be true, but I saw there were two million francs credited in one column and debited in another, which seemed unbelievable. I rang him and he said "Oh! that was just some yen that came in and I didn't think they were worth converting!"'

Boxford's strategy for Music Publishing was never fully realised: 'I felt that we needed to be publishing only the sheet music that sold on a worldwide basis. But I got so caught up in the instrument side of things that I never followed that plan through. The important thing was to make Tony Fell totally responsible for Music Publishing internationally – it was crazy to have all these satellites.'

By the time of Boxford's first international conference in May 1981, it was clear that Tony Fell was now at the heart of the publishing concern, and that the US and other European branches were to report to him, if only by a dotted line. It was a start, and some important relationships were the result.

Their loss is our gain

All was not well at the old music publishing rival in New York, G Schirmer, to which Heinsheimer had fled in the late forties. Schirmer owned the valuable copyrights of Leonard Bernstein, Samuel Barber, Gian Carlo Menotti's operas (all thanks to Heinsheimer), and, via its subsidiary Associated Music Publishers, Elliott Carter and works by a young 'minimalist', John Adams. In the late seventies Schirmer had been bought by the giant book publisher Macmillan, and its composers were beginning to feel disaffected with the direction of the company. They had the impression that the senior executives liked their box at The Met but did not have much interest in nurturing living composers. This was all good news for B&H. When word reached them that Carter wanted out, the joint forces of New York and London worked promptly to make him an offer appropriate to his standing in modern American music. Carter admired Stuart Pope's commitment and commented over lunch with Fell, 'I see him everywhere – even at concerts featuring non-B&H composers'. But he went on to say 'Oh, I don't know if it's worth your while. I'm 73 and you might not get many pieces.' (Generally, existing copyrights remain with a composer's previous publisher if the composer moves.) Astonishingly, since 1982 when Carter signed the new contract, he has written a stream of masterpieces and is still at work today. In January 2006, aged 97, he crossed the Atlantic to take an active part in the BBC's 'Get Carter' weekend and was hailed with standing ovations. Few could have predicted this Indian summer of creativity, nor that the works would have been of so new and luminous a beauty. He has said himself that he began to compose in a simpler, less time-consuming way, and the results shimmer with invention and precision. There was his first opera *What Next?*, which Daniel Barenboim persuaded Carter to tackle when he was pushing 90, a range of chamber works and the 50-minute orchestral triptych *Symphonia: sum fluxae pretium spei*. A critic wrote of its first complete performance in 1998 by the BBC Symphony Orchestra under Oliver Knussen, '*Symphonia* sounds like nothing so much as a magisterial summation of the millennium.' His first work for B&H was the Robert Lowell setting *In Sleep, in Thunder*, and Carter expressed himself 'clearly delighted' with the turn of events which had led him to another publisher, whose staff included friends, notably David Drew.

Deutsche Grammophon recording of Carter's *Symphonia*

Also in 1982, negotiations started in earnest with another composer who was unhappy at G Schirmer, Leonard Bernstein. One of the few mistakes Ralph Hawkes ever made was in not signing Bernstein when he had the chance in the late forties. Hawkes is reported to have said to Bernstein when they were introduced by Copland, 'When you've made up your mind whether you are going to be a composer or a conductor, come and see me again.' Hawkes was influenced by Koussevitzky, who never came to terms with Bernstein's genius as a Broadway composer, considering the idiom 'trashy'. Hawkes waited for Bernstein to evolve into the next Copland, and by the time of Ralph's death the young composer was already being published elsewhere.

As previously noted, an agreement had been reached in 1975 with Bernstein's company Amberson Enterprises Inc, for B&H to act as sole worldwide agent for the suites to his music for *The Dybbuk* and for Bernstein's future works. But in 1982 talks began on moving the entire Bernstein catalogue over to B&H. By the following year, Amberson had started a legal action against Schirmer for various alleged shortcomings, and Stuart Pope, Sylvia Goldstein and Tony Fell began to work on the negotiations with Bernstein's manager, Harry Kraut, and Paul Epstein and Jim Kendrick, attorneys from Amberson's lawyers. It was a long and tortuous process, but by 1986 Schirmer had returned nearly all of Bernstein's concert works to him, and the deal was done. B&H Inc at last had a contract with one of the country's most successful composers with

Bernstein signing his publishing contract, with Ronald Asserson, Jim Kendrick and Tony Fell (1986)

works including the *Symphonic Dances from West Side Story*, *Candide*, *Trouble in Tahiti*, *The Age of Anxiety*, *Chichester Psalms*, *On the Waterfront* and *Prelude, Fugue and Riffs*. Dramatic rights to the two musicals *On the Town* and *Wonderful Town* were subsequently added outside North America, and in 1997 individual numbers from *West Side Story*.

The composer who did not need a publisher

Bernstein and Carter were indisputably grand old men of American music, and there was no controversy regarding their signing beyond the industry gossip about the flight from Schirmer. But in 1983 talks also began with a younger composer, who, at the time, only allowed one group, his own ensemble, to perform his music. With the potential for performing royalties therefore so limited, what interest could a publisher have in him? Yet his music was achieving wide recognition and excited, particularly, a young audience. As Tony Fell was to write to the parent Board in 1986, 'Steve Reich is unquestionably one of the hottest properties in contemporary music, crossing as he does the borders of "serious" music and pop.'

It was at a time when new computer note-setting programs were beginning to be adopted and there was a general feeling that the music publishing role would soon be redundant, as composers such as Philip Glass and Reich had almost proved with their self-publishing set-ups. Reich himself remembers his change of heart: 'In the late sixties, most people weren't interested in my music, they didn't have a grasp of the concepts and there were hardly any recordings of my ensemble, so there wasn't a guide to how to

Steve Reich drumming (early 1970s)

perform it. Gavin Bryars, Michael Nyman and Cornelius Cardew had all played with us, so there began to be a handful of people who were qualified to pass on performing techniques. In the seventies I played frequently in London, and by about 1979 I was becoming aware that there were people out there who could perform my music.'

During the seventies, Annette Morreau, who founded the Contemporary Music Network, organised several ground-breaking British tours of Steve Reich and Musicians, and Bill Colleran, the perceptive promoter for

Universal Edition in London, had persuaded head office in Vienna to take on several of Reich's early pieces, including *Piano Phase*, *Violin Phase*, *Four Organs* and *Clapping Music*. So, although Reich created the masters of his own scores and controlled the use of them rigorously, he did have a publisher. And yet he did not feel that UE Vienna, the epicentre of the post-war avant-garde, was sympathetic to his pulse-driven, essentially tonal, percussion-rich music. He remembers some murky family conflicts in UE at the time, but appreciated Colleran's support. Nevertheless, it would make a great deal of sense to have a publisher with an American base.

Reich began discussing the situation with members of his group, and then with David Huntley (who was already known to him and, always one step ahead, had been a passionate advocate of Reich's music since the sixties), David Drew, Stuart Pope and Tony Fell: 'They were people I could relate to. And I was approaching fifty. It became crystal clear in my mind that I must have everything published.' After Reich had spoken to David Huntley, negotiations began between Stuart Pope and Ellis Freedman, attorney to several major composers, and an agency deal was signed for all the non-UE works. The following year Reich met David Drew in Cologne at the premiere of *The Desert Music*, and remembers 'going through the whole score with him'. (Despite the Darmstadt-heavy scene in Germany, Reich has always been generously supported in the territory, and several of his biggest commissions originated there). He had written *Tehillim* a few years before. 'These were very large pieces. My ensemble was obviously not going to be touring with them, and their only future lay in being available to other groups.'

David Huntley (1987)

Four years later, Reich agreed to sell his copyrights to B&H and enter into a full publishing agreement: 'The first agreement was for distribution only and I did camera-ready art work. But in 1987, I went the whole way. At first my income went right down, but by the third year it went up and then it grew way beyond anything that I could have imagined. While my ensemble was doing five or six performances of a piece per year, there are now 200 taking place.' He was also proud to be associated with the publishing house of Bartók and Stravinsky. 'I grew up

on the Boosey & Hawkes pocket scores, I held them in high regard.' He
has not been disappointed in the arrangement, despite relinquishing some
of his control over the production and use of his scores: 'To my
knowledge, B&H are the only company who publish in a timely fashion,
promote and distribute. I have an ideal relationship with everyone in the
company. I work in Sibelius notation, send a disc and it's farmed out to
copyists to make the spacing right and make it practical for performing.
They print it up and send it to me for corrections. I've realised that it's a
better use of my time than slaving over the spacing!'

David Huntley, who had played a critical behind-the-scenes role in the
process by inspiring Reich's confidence in B&H, was keen that the
composer's music should be promoted for its own, unique qualities and
without the use of easy, inaccurate labels: at the start of the new
publishing relationship, he wrote to his fellow promotion teams across the
world: 'Reich is not happy about the term "trance music" … we might do
well to ponder, during spare moments in elevators and buses, the term
"minimal". My first response is to avoid it with a bit of disdain.'

'You've been disloyal – I'm coming over on Concorde …'

So, by 1987 Carter, Reich and Bernstein had joined Copland in the B&H
Inc stable and the American list had moved to a new level of prestige and
earning power. But three years earlier a series of corporate events had
occurred that looked set to derail the signing of both Bernstein and Reich.
Michael Boxford, who was continuing to struggle with the modernisation
of the UK instrument business, started to reorganise the New York
company, without any serious discussion with the publishing staff.

B&H Inc had had little involvement with the instrument business until
the acquisition of Buffet Crampon. Boxford put John Crist, an ex-Buffet
Crampon manager, in charge of both the publishing and instruments
divisions, much to the discomfort of Stuart Pope, who remained
President of the music business. It was no secret in the industry that
Pope was very unhappy with the restructuring, while Pope's son, who
was also in the firm, was openly hostile to the changes. Stuart Pope was
a loved as well as respected figure in both serious music and choral and
band publishing, and though his tastes were generally conservative, he
supported the Carter and Reich negotiations: he did not need a new line
manager with no experience of his business. He sat it out until Crist was
fired in the summer of 1983, replaced by a former Magnavox executive

named Ken Ingram, who had had a successful career with Selmer, the woodwind manufacturers.

Then came the second blow: Boxford and Ingram thought Pope was insufficiently commercial, so they insisted on appointing a Buffet session clarinettist called Jerome Bunke as the President of music publishing, making Stuart Pope Chairman. It was actually a demotion, and the composers knew it.

Tony Pool remembers Boxford bringing Bunke over to London, ostensibly so that the London directors could meet him. He took him out to lunch and asked him various questions about the business and about how he would handle the very awkward situation with Pope, who was highly respected in the musical community. Bunke had no answers. 'He won't do,' Pool reported back to his colleagues, only to discover he had already been appointed, and the 'discussions' were a mere formality.

It was an impossible situation for Pope, and he resigned in November 1984 after 47 years' service and went to work for an educational publisher and owner of the lucrative (though difficult to police!) copyright to 'Happy Birthday to You'. The New York music world erupted in outrage at Pope's departure. Bunke was up against a barrage of disapproval and barely stood a chance. (In his innocence, he wrote to Bernstein asking him to write piano music which 'would range from a person's introduction to the instrument to gradually include more difficult material'. Fortunately it never reached the eyes of the perennially over-committed Bernstein.) 'It was a mistake,' admits Boxford, 'Jerome did have flair and came highly recommended, but his people management was not good, and the fact that he was imposed meant he didn't stand a chance.' Back in London, Fell, who was getting increasingly alarmed by the parlous financial state of the group, felt the aftershocks of the New York situation. He took the next plane over to see Walter Connor, the most senior member of Carl Fischer Inc and therefore the major shareholder. 'I said to him "the situation is serious, the company is in disarray, there is no confidence, morale is at an all-time low, we see money being thrown around in the most prodigal way, while we are working to the tightest possible budgets". The preservation of the publishing company was my sole concern. I suggested that we sell off Instruments, create the greatest international music publishing company in the world, make media acquisitions – TV, book publishing, whatever – and eliminate head office with just a small staff and Board, with Walter Connor as Chairman and a high powered, music-related non-executive director for prestige. Carl Fischer would be seen as saviour of the group, which would be a highly profitable concern rather than the current fiasco. I said that I was not lobbying, had consulted no-one and didn't expect him to comment. He thanked me, said he didn't want to ditch Instruments but would take some action. The next thing I knew I had a call from Boxford saying, "You have been disloyal. I'm coming over on Concorde today".'

Fell expected to be fired but thought on his feet. It was November 1984, and negotiations with both Bernstein and Reich were at a delicate, early stage. Events in the New York office had knocked both composers' confidence in the company, and Fell needed Boxford to realise the gravity of the situation. He rapidly briefed Bernstein's manager Harry Kraut and Reich's lawyer Ellis Freedman, who was also lawyer to the B&H composers Copland, Carter, Del Tredici and Jacob Druckman. When Boxford arrived, recalls Fell, 'We stood on a fire escape in the sunshine and he said, "What is going on?" and I said, "I'm sorry I've been disloyal, but this town is up in arms about Stuart Pope leaving." So I took him to see Kraut and Freedman, who expressed grave concern about the state of the company and in particular dissatisfaction with the recent changes in the New York office. They made it clear that neither of these composers would sign if the New York office wasn't sorted out. I showed Boxford it was no secret: everyone was talking about it.'

Elliott Carter with Janis
Susskind (1987)

Boxford, to his credit, stopped attacking Fell, and said, 'This is very serious'. He insisted however that Bunke should be given a chance with a more limited brief, and that someone from London should go over and work in the New York office for a while until things had settled down and possibly a new President found. Nothing more was said by either Boxford or Connor about the broader corporate concerns which Fell had expressed.

So, in December 1984, a young American woman from the London promotion department was selected to go over and care-take the Manhattan office. Her name was Janis Susskind, and one day she would be Publishing Director of the company.

Transatlantic harmony

Janis Susskind had come to work for B&H London in 1980 as a promotion assistant ('I spent a year typing index cards'). At the time the department was led by Bernard Jacobson, who spoke several languages and did a great deal to further the international network for promotion. He was offered a management position at the Philadelphia Orchestra and left early in 1984, when Susskind took over as Head of Promotion. (Sally Cavender, who was impressively efficient and passionately loyal to composers, had resigned in 1981 after disagreements over Nicholas Maw and others. She went to work for Faber Music, where she is now Director of Performance and Vice-Chairman.) Boxford had early on sensed that there were structural problems, which had been identified by the management consultants. It was an uncomfortable time, but by 1984, David Drew was Director, New Music, Susskind was Head of Promotion and Paul Meecham (later to move into senior positions in orchestral management in the US) was Head of Publicity.

Susskind was born in Houston, Texas and studied English and Music at Princeton. She had married the Czech-born conductor Walter Susskind in 1973, but was widowed after seven years and decided to settle in London. Having served an apprenticeship in the Regent Street office, she found the chance to be thrown in at the deep end in New York was one she grasped eagerly. 'I hardly slept, I lost ten pounds, but it was just what I needed. The composers were very upfront, very demanding there. They were always on the phone saying "What is going on?" She worked closely with David Huntley, 'a wise man in our tribe', and took note of the younger composers he was currently interested in. Susskind wrote of Huntley, 'In a

subtle, original way, David was a born mover and shaker. His natural
reserve was balanced by an extraordinary inquisitiveness, and he was
both generous and persuasive in sharing his discoveries. I, like many
others, came to count on him to broaden our musical and cultural
horizons and to coax us into new directions.' The signing of Steve Reich,
the 21-year-old Michael Torke, then John Adams signalled a totally new
direction for B&H, whose American list then featured Ned Rorem, Alberto
Ginastera and Dominick Argento, all mainstream rather than radical
figures in contemporary music. Jacob Druckman and David Del Tredici
were the exceptions, since the former was gaining acceptance in
European new music circles and the latter was seen as revolutionary, if
controversial, in having moved from serialism to neo-tonality.

It soon became clear that Bunke could not stay the course, and Susskind
had her eyes out for a replacement. During the negotiations for the
Bernstein catalogue, Sylvia Goldstein had noticed the young attorney
working for Amberson, the composer's company, who seemed an
interesting candidate. He was an oboist, with degrees from Manhattan
College of Music and Juilliard; he was a trained lawyer; and he had
worked for EAM, the US branch of Schott and UE. Susskind took him out
to lunch and came back excited: 'This is the man, we have to have him!'
Fell, Boxford and Ingram interviewed him and by the time Susskind
returned to London in March 1985, Jim Kendrick had been appointed
President of B&H Inc. Like Bunke he was a President chosen from
'outside' the company: times were changing and a new professionalism
had entered the business. Key skills such as high-level legal and copyright
knowledge could now be identified and required, instead of choosing staff
on the basis of their experience with the company (Stuart Pope, for
example, had worked for the firm since he left school at 16).

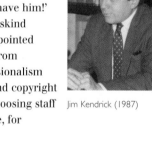

Jim Kendrick (1987)

Kendrick's time as President saw the clinching of important new
relationships with Adams and Torke. Huntley knew Adams and persuaded
staff to listen to his music. Not all of them were convinced. David Drew
remembers listening to Adams's *Grand Pianola Music*, recognising the
talent, but 'missing the point'. Huntley knew that Adams, like many others,
was unhappy with his current publisher G Schirmer and had in fact
decided not to renew his contract but to self-publish. B&H signed an
agency agreement with Adams's company, Red Dawn Music, in 1987. With
the world-wide attention and acclaim that greeted Houston Grand Opera's
premiere of *Nixon in China* that year, it was clear that Adams was likely to
become an important opera composer, as indeed he has. The paucity of

Michael Torke (late 1980s)

operas entering the repertoire post-Benjamin Britten made the arrival of *Nixon* all the more significant. It was not until 1992 that a full publishing agreement was to be reached with Adams, by which time he had written *The Death of Klinghoffer* and a collection of highly successful orchestral works.

Michael Torke, at 21, was perhaps the youngest-ever signing. *Ecstatic Orange* was one of the first of his pieces to make an impact, with its direct but exuberant pulses and textures. Susskind remembers, 'It was fun to break him in the UK and Europe, because we could do a lot for him, introduce him to people and really make a difference.' Andrew Cornall at Decca Records was responsible for reviving the Argo label at the time and took an active interest in this bright American spark. A whole disc devoted to Torke's music was issued in 1991, which rapidly raised his international standing. It was the beginning of the CD boom and much of the promotion team's time was spent with record companies.

John Adams in his studio, early 1990s
(Photo: Nonesuch/Richard Morganstein)

Kendrick recalls those years with fondness. He was able to promote Huntley to Vice President. 'We would go on the road together and he would eat, drink, sleep, breathe music. Not for one moment would he be reading about or listening to anything else. He was a stealth promoter. He would never make you feel ignorant, he just loved to discuss music and had such catholic tastes. I never met anyone who didn't love him.'

Although relations with London had always been cordial, Stuart Pope had tended to keep his cards close to his chest and liked to work independently. When Jim Kendrick arrived, a spirit of intense collaboration between New York and London was established, both at the senior management level and between Huntley and Susskind and their teams. The reporting lines were restructured so that Kendrick was no longer reporting to the manager of the instrument company, but directly to Fell. They worked hard on communicating regularly, but Kendrick remembers getting the first fax machine: 'That changed the dynamic. Suddenly responses could be instantaneous. I think that helped.' The acquisition of the important American composers also helped the London office go into Europe again: 'Once we had Elliott Carter and Steve Reich in our portfolio, we had

Nixon in China by John
Adams, first staged by Peter
Sellars at Houston Grand
Opera in 1987
(Photo: ENO/Bill Rafferty)

something to shout about in places like Germany. Maxwell Davies had
always been important, but he was on his own. We were beginning to
build a heavy-weight catalogue again after the gap of Roth's late years,'
explains Susskind.

Reviving a lost career: Berthold Goldschmidt

One area Boxford left to others was the small matter of 'composers', a
business which occasionally left him floundering: 'I had huge respect for
David Drew and Tony Fell and always left artistic evaluation to them.
I know the rights business is very complex and long-term, but I did
struggle with the idea of taking a composer on if it was not an obviously
good investment decision. What was the economic benefit of investing
£30k in a score when it might only be played once? This did not seem to
trouble anyone: the culture was composer-centred. I always felt they could
have been more commercial.'

Drew, however, knew that to make commercial gains you need to spend
time on R&D. During the mid-eighties, he was as active as ever in
gathering information about new musical developments, whether or not
they seemed directly relevant to the B&H catalogue. One evening in 1983,
he happened to meet his friend the composer David Matthews on Regent
Street, who said, 'Do come and hear Bernard Keeffe's Trinity College
students doing Goldschmidt's *Hahnrei* opera for his 80th birthday.' Drew
was then on the Board of the New Opera Company, and felt he should go,

though the opera in question, *Der gewaltige Hahnrei* (*The Mighty Cuckold*), had not made a great impression on him when he had read the vocal score some years before. The piece had been published by UE but had not been heard since its successful premiere in 1932, a year before Hitler came to power. Dutifully, Drew turned up at the church: 'I took a file of B&H correspondence with me, and settled down in a remote corner of the gallery, thinking I could get on with my work while listening with one ear. Not a bit of it. From the first bar I was absolutely gripped by the piece. It reeked of theatre – and of talent. At the end, I introduced myself to the composer, and suggested we talked about finding a way to stage it, perhaps with help from his friend and admirer Simon Rattle.'

Goldschmidt was already 80, but this was an irrelevance to Drew. He recognised in him an important composer, whose essentially tonal music had been rejected by the British music establishment for decades. (Moreover, many of his early works had been left in Germany and lost during the war, while others, like his 1950 opera *Beatrice Cenci*, had never received a performance.) He tried to persuade Rattle to conduct *Der gewaltige Hahnrei* with the New Opera Company. Few would listen, but Rattle went on to become an important advocate of Goldschmidt. Drew conferred with Paul Meecham, who wholeheartedly supported his opinion. Composers Colin and David Matthews were also crucial in ensuring Goldschmidt's name emerged again – they had met when they collaborated with him on the preparation of Deryck Cooke's completion of Mahler's Tenth Symphony.

David Drew with Berthold Goldschmidt (early 1990s)
(Photo: courtesy David Drew)

Plans for a British premiere of Goldschmidt's *Der gewaltige Hahnrei* came to nothing. But Goldschmidt appreciated the interest Drew had shown in a work belonging to a rival publisher, and appeared one day in his office with an envelope containing the manuscript of an unpublished piece from his Berlin years – two settings of poems by Erich Kästner (the celebrated author of *Emil and the Detectives*). Drew was preoccupied at the time with the newly-appointed Head of Promotion of Boosey & Hawkes GmbH, Winfried Jacobs, who was endeavouring to establish a real publishing base in Bonn. Here, perhaps was the German composeer they had been looking for. When Drew recommended that B&H publish the Kästner

settings and the String Quartet No. 2 of 1935, one or two colleagues were
heard to say 'Aha, another of Drew's exhumations'. But much was to grow
from that modest start. Stimulated by commissions from Austria and then
from Germany, Goldschmidt began composing again after a break of
nearly 25 years. 'It was the rejuvenation of Berthold himself that illumined
the whole adventure,' recalls Drew.

He was determined to take the composer back to German-speaking
territories, where he sensed there would be receptive audiences for him
and his music. Their first port of call was the Austrian Mürz Valley
Workshop in October 1984, a contemporary arts festival founded by Henze
and local musicians. As guest of honour, Goldschmidt attended the
premiere of his Erich Kästner settings, and was interviewed about life and
music in the Germany of his day in the presence of a large audience that
had come to hear a concert of avant-garde music. 'The effect of that
occasion on Berthold and on his audience was
electrifying,' recalls Drew, 'and it was to be the
same in Germany whenever people from the post-
war generations encountered the man and his
music – sparks flew, connections were made, and
history came alive.' In 1987, Rattle performed his
Ciaconna Sinfonica (1936) at the Berlin Festival,
where Goldschmidt finally experienced the level
of public acclaim that the march of history had
denied him. The following year, he returned to
his home town of Hamburg to conduct the NDR in
the same piece. There was a large audience,
mainly of young people, and a standing ovation
after the performance. In time, *Der gewaltige
Hahnrei* was performed again in Germany at the
Komische Oper in Berlin and recorded for Decca's
'Entartete Musik' ('degenerate music') series. It
was a true homecoming, aided and abetted by David Drew in cahoots with
Michael Haas and Didier de Cottignies at Decca. Proms performances in
the nineties by Rattle and Yakov Kreizberg further put the stamp of
success on Goldschmidt's 'rehabilitation'. Goldschmidt, in a letter of
thanks, refers to Drew's 'truly magnificent energy' in reviving his career
and a mutual friend at the time commented wryly, 'I am happy to hear that
publishers can now do double duty as fountains of youth. I had always
heard they took years off a man's life.' Goldschmidt had suffered as an
'unfashionable' composer, but he never lost a sense of his own worth.

Letter from Berthold
Goldschmidt to David Drew
(1983)

Drew says of his reinstatement: 'It was a real blow for justice, not a sentimental thing. He was tough enough to have preserved his sense of self, he was damn well going to hang on until he was recognised – something instinctive within told him he would be.'

The banks are on our backs

By 1985, as Fell had warned Walter Connor, B&H was in a precarious financial state. The instrument company had expanded, but was still not making projected profits and continued to drain the publishing company of money. When Macmillan finally decided to divest itself of the important G Schirmer catalogue, which Simon Boosey had wanted to buy twenty years earlier, Tony Fell made enquiries. But the price tag, at $6m, was too high; the company reserves were running dry, and with further borrowing impossible, such a substantial acquisition was out of the question. Bob Wise of Music Sales snapped Schirmer up. It was extremely frustrating for the music publishing management to have had to stand by and watch the acquisition of many smaller instrument companies, without being able to acquire anything themselves. It frustrated Boxford too: 'If we'd had the resources, of course we would have bought Schirmer. I had looked

The print bindery at Hendon (c1980)

seriously at Chappells too. I went to Walter and asked him to do a rights issue but he refused: he was too concerned about the share-holders. So I suggested that we create a new company that merged Selmer and B&H instruments, and float it off. I have since been proved right when Selmer merged successfully with Steinway. But, again, Walter refused – he wanted to keep B&H.' Just how critical the situation was became clear to all at an international conference held at a grand country hotel in 1985, when the new Chairman Ashley Raeburn (successor to Richard Young), Boxford and the group secretary had to keep disappearing to London to face the banks, who were threatening to foreclose on the business. It later emerged that the end of year loss for 1985 was £5m, all of it due to the instrument company, since the music publishing profits were marginally up that year. Later in the year there was a vote of no confidence in Michael Boxford and he left.

Warehouse racking at Hendon (c1980)

The Board badly needed someone with an impeccable track record to chair it and act as CEO, in order that trust could be once more restored. They were fortunate in finding the semi-retired Ronald Asserson, who had been a senior director of the large metal company Delta, and who was prepared to face down the banks and take the hard decisions needed to get the business back on track. Says Fell, 'Asserson clearly had such a standing in industry that he could go to the banks and persuade them to give us time. He didn't pretend to be a music person: I remember he used to say "sheet metal" instead of "sheet music" by mistake!' He set about cutting costs, laying off staff, moving the headquarters out to Edgware, and, at the bank's insistence, had the company independently audited at vast cost. He said in an interview at the time, 'Every time I turn over a stone there is something dreadful underneath'. The first day he came in he stumbled on 3,000 unsold metronomes, a stock that could take 15 years to shift.

But no remedial action could be taken before the annual figures were announced in April 1986, making the £5m loss public. It had been a disastrous two years. In 1984, for the first time in its history, the company was unable to pay any dividend to the ordinary shareholders, a situation repeated in 1985 and 1986. The share price had collapsed. The Pools had had enough. They had obligations to Ralph Hawkes's widow, Clare, who was living off the dividend of the Hawkeses' shares. The Pools now wanted to get out at any reasonable price, and Tony even formally offered his shares to Walter Connor, but they were not actually sold until the late eighties.

Bob Wise of Music Sales
(Photo: Music Sales)

As far as Boxford was concerned, the game was not over yet: with support from Candover, he got together with Bob Wise at Music Sales and Bankers Trust and made an informal bid for the company of £9.8m. The plan, again, was to buy the lot and sell on the instrument company, a proposal that had been on the agenda since the days of Ralph Hawkes, and one which would be achieved fifteen years later. Carl Fischer blocked the bid, increasing its share from 48.9% to 50.1% in a move to support Asserson. Fell appreciated the Connors' belief and back-up: 'However difficult the relationship was, they stood by us at this point when it would have been very easy to lose us to Music Sales.' Boxford would go on to make three more attempts to buy the company, none successful: 'I felt entirely at ease in that business' he says 20 years on. 'I felt I understood it, and I wanted to own it. It was a very stressful time, though. My wife tells me I used to wake up screaming in the night while I was working there!' Asserson and the team braved it out and, by 1987, when the exclusive Reich signing took place, they were back on track, and the company was in profit.

Elliott Carter and Steve Reich attend BBC Proms performances in London, conducted by Pierre Boulez (1985)
(Photo: The Times/Jonathan Player)

184

A Polish voice reaches the West

In 1985 David Drew was in Warsaw for the first time since the end of martial law. Sitting in the crowded bar of the Europeiski Hotel after a concert, he was surprised to hear a native German and a German-speaking Pole at the same table having a lively and outspoken discussion about the political state of the country. As his ear was drawn into the conversation he heard the Pole declaring that Solidarity had scored moral and political victories from which the Soviet Union – despite appearances – would never recover. Towards the end of the discussion, Drew was introduced to this formidable Polish figure who turned out to be the composer Henryk Mikołaj Górecki. Though honoured in Poland, Górecki was virtually ignored in Western Europe, where he had once enjoyed high favour until his scores no longer chimed with the aesthetics of the avant-

garde. (On a later occasion in the traditionally new music stronghold of the Donaueschingen festival he was cold-shouldered by former admirers, one of whom said to Drew, 'He is no longer one of us.') Górecki had a reputation for speaking out against the regime and had been under police surveillance since the imposition of martial law. Drew returned to London with a pile of scores from his publishers PWM.

'At first I hardly dared look at them,' remembers Drew. 'I couldn't believe that the conflict between that enormously powerful personality and a repressive culture was not reflected somewhere in the music.' But when he first opened the score to the Third Symphony it looked bafflingly simple

Henryk Mikołaj Górecki at home in Katowice (1990)
(Photo: Malcolm Crowthers)

and unsophisticated. Five months later he steeled himself to listen to a recording without the distraction of the score, 'and then I felt the composer's unmistakable and formidable presence'.

He discussed Górecki in New York with David Huntley and Huntley's close friend the WNYC broadcaster Ruth Dreier, who had started playing the recording on the strength of its use in the French film *Police*, and won the biggest audience response her programme had ever had. By that time, Drew and his colleagues in London – notably Fell, Susskind, and Meecham – had assured themselves that Górecki would not need to be revived as a one-work composer. To begin with, the Symphony had an

obvious companion-piece in *Beatus Vir*. It had been commissioned for the
Pope's return visit to Poland, which had hardly endeared the composer to
the authorities, who saw him as a considerable threat to the status quo –
an outspoken right-wing, anti-communist nationalist, who expressed
himself with peasant-like bluntness. Drew remembers him in a State-
owned office leaping to his feet and slamming his fist on the desk at some
polite reference to a prominent government spokesman, and at the top of
his voice, with the windows open, declaring him to be 'a lying scoundrel'.
Needless to say, his phone-line was tapped: 'During the first year or two I
doubt if I had a single conversation with him that wasn't broken off,'
recalls Drew. 'The repression got harder as things fell apart. After all, he
was a symbol of resistance for many people. But he disliked being called a
religious composer: in a sense politics and religion were still indivisible in
1985.'

The following year Fell approached PWM and proposed to represent
Górecki's music outside the Eastern bloc. A ten-year deal was signed and
a promotion strategy began to emerge. Drew knew it was important that
Górecki should come to Western Europe if they were to promote his work,
but he was only willing to travel to Germany and Austria, where he could
speak the language, and even then was highly reluctant. Drew contacted
Michael Vyner, the influential director of the London Sinfonietta, and sent
him some tapes and an objective assessment. 'I had a huge letter back
from Vyner and I remember it chiefly for being the response of someone
who was already personally and deeply committed.' David Atherton
proved a fellow enthusiast and in December 1987 gave the British
premiere of the Third Symphony with the BBC Symphony Orchestra
before an invited audience in Maida Vale Studios. He then, with Vyner,
began plans for a London Sinfonietta Górecki/Schnittke weekend. In May
1988, Górecki finally met with Fell and Drew in Warsaw and in November
signed a full publishing agreement for his future works in all territories
except the 'socialist countries'. Górecki was now a fully-fledged B&H
composer.

Nonesuch recording of
Górecki's *Symphony No. 3*
(1992)

Meanwhile, in New York, David Huntley had interested both the Kronos
Quartet and Bob Hurwitz of Nonesuch Records in Górecki. Drew
suggested a fragment of a string quartet as a starting point for a new
piece, and Górecki transformed it into his sixteen-minute quartet *Already
it is Dusk*. He met the quartet on tour in Bremen and, with Drew as
interpreter, joined in with their rehearsal. They went on to record it: the
links in the chain were forming.

Górecki with Kronos
Quartet, David Drew, and
Bob Hurwitz of Nonesuch
(second right) in New
York (1992)
(Photo: Martha Swope)

The London Sinfonietta's Górecki/Schnittke weekend was booked for early
April 1989, and Drew and Vyner were determined to get Górecki over to
London for it. 'It was fiendishly difficult,' recalls Drew. 'There were
changes of mind and cancellations, and there was great resistance from
the Foreign Office. Thatcher had been in Poland spreading the message of
free-market capitalism, and declaring, "our doors are open to you". So the
Visa Offices in Poland were besieged and Whitehall was aghast.' Górecki's
confiscated passport had now been returned to him, but it was not until
representations had been made in London at the highest levels that he
obtained a British visa.

Schnittke was by this time well-known in Britain, so audiences were large
for the London Sinfonietta concerts, but the music of the unknown Górecki
made its impact. Bob Hurwitz, who flew over from New York, remembers
the experience as 'an amazing weekend – I heard Górecki's *Lerchenmusik*
which we ended up recording, some terrific pieces of Schnittke's and then
heard the Third Symphony live for the first time. I found it overwhelming.
The Woytowicz recording I had heard was more operatic; but Margaret
Field, who performed it in London that night, sang in a style with much
less vibrato and a tone that seemed to fit the music in a more organic way.
Minutes into the performance, I thought: this would be perfect for Dawn
Upshaw.' The recording was made with Dawn Upshaw and David Zinman
in London in May 1991 and, as Hurwitz describes, 'went on to become the
most successful recording of a new composition in the history of the record
business. It was released a year later, went to number 3 on the British pop
charts, sold over a million copies around the world.' This would turn
Górecki's fortunes and prove a boon for B&H.

1989 was an auspicious year: by December, 'Velvet' popular revolutions had swept across Eastern Europe, and the Communist governments in the GDR, Poland and Czechoslovakia had collapsed. Górecki was freer to travel, and did so in Western Europe and even went to New York for the launch of the Nonesuch disc in 1992. The simplicity, serenity and centred tonality of this symphony 'of sorrowful songs' gave it its powerful emotional appeal, but it caused huge resentment in the contemporary music firmament. Górecki's earlier compositional style had been markedly more radical, but, like Arvo Pärt, he had arrived at another language in later life. There was a time, Drew recalls, when the very mention of Górecki or the Symphony in musical company was enough to provoke guffaws and sniggers. But B&H had picked a winner, and Drew had particular reason to be pleased that the composer had bought himself the Mercedes they had often talked about, and a new cottage in his beloved Tatra Mountains.

But the happy story of Górecki and Boosey & Hawkes took a sour turn. In 1993, Tony Fell discovered that the composer's Polish publishers, PWM, had sold the world sub-edition rights to most of his pre-1987 works to Chester Music, owned by Bob Wise's Music Sales, for the life of the copyrights. B&H would retain rights in the Third Symphony, for example, until 1998, but they would then revert to Chester. This occurred just at the height of Górecki's success and was a major blow to the publisher who had worked so hard to bring him to the world's attention. Fell and Kendrick discovered that the US copyright renewal rights and world-wide synchronisation rights had not been included in the Chester deal, and Susskind was rapidly despatched to Katowice to secure the required signatures of the entire Górecki family. 'Score wars have broken out in the usually quiet cloisters of classical music publishing' trumpeted the *Daily Telegraph*. The composer himself regretted the situation and immediately renewed his B&H publishing agreement covering his new works from 1993 onwards. It was a bitter twist to a story of promotional triumph, but underlined the competitive commercial realities behind every publishing deal.

A strategy for the end of the century

An article by Andrew Clements published in *The Guardian* in September 1994 gives a snapshot of the bewildering number of different composing styles that could be identified as the century neared its close. Gone were the days of 'neo-classical' or 'high-modernist/serial', when Roth could be sure that he was for Stravinsky and Britten and against Stockhausen and Boulez. Clements came up with no fewer than ten categories of modern serious music: Neo-classicism (into which category Carter now fitted, alongside Tippett), Total Serialism (Boulez, Nono), New Complexity (an extension of the former: Brian Ferneyhough and James Dillon), Indeterminacy/Experimental (Cage, Feldman), Minimalism (Reich, Terry Riley, Philip Glass), Post-minimalism (Andriessen, Adams, Nyman and increasingly Reich), Polystylisticism (Schnittke, Ligeti, Robin Holloway – sometimes), Neo-romanticism (Górecki, Kancheli), Holy Simplicity (Tavener, Pärt), Eclecticism (Turnage, Henze).

Of course, looking back at this now, it is clear that some of these composers were heading out of their categories even at that time, and the whole exercise was tongue-in-cheek (to give an idea of the tone, he wrote of New Complexity, 'too hard to see or hear the wood for the trees'; of Indeterminacy, 'anything you like' and of Post-minimalism, 'a recipe for indulgence'). But it gives a good idea of the issues that the publishing team was wrestling with in the 1980s, as it attempted to understand the future direction of music and public taste.

In 1988 a review was held of the copyright situation in Europe. At the time, copyrights in most countries including the UK lasted until 50 years after the composer's death. Delius and Elgar copyrights had already ceased in the early 1980s, while the end of Rachmaninoff, Bartók, Strauss and Prokofieff loomed large. The works of these composers did not go into the public domain in all territories at the same time, so there was never a sudden plunge in royalties, rather a slow decrease over several years. Still, a reprieve was needed, since by 2010 there would be a heavy dependence on Britten, Copland and Stravinsky.

A few years earlier, in 1984, the B&H Board had demanded a strategic review of publishing policy. Roth's conservative policy after Hawkes died had resulted in a 20-year gap in potential royalties. Von Einem, Barraud and Jolivet may have had a decade or two of activity but were producing no significant royalties for B&H by the late eighties. The major figures of the generation, Lutoslawski, Penderecki, Ligeti, Berio and Henze, were all with other publishers. The economic picture of the post-war music industry had been painfully distorted in France, Germany and to some extent Britain by the high modernist agenda with its cloistered and subsidised world of new music specialists. This had led European publishers to pursue publishing policy along musico-political lines 'rather than follow their instincts and judgements about what would be likely in the long-term to succeed with a wider public', commented Fell in his strategy paper. While the establishment's espousal of modernism had sustained pioneering music publishers such as UE, B&H had to face up to the commercial realities: it could not solely invest in music that lacked a significant audience and had to look to the next generation of composers.

The conclusion of Fell and Drew's 1984 publishing presentation to the Board was that B&H should sift through the surfeit of highly qualified composers, identifying the individual voices that would stand out from the crowd and pass the test of time. There was no place for aesthetic ideology in this new world: 'Mastery of a "central, dominant, or leading style" is acquired with such speed and efficiency by today's more gifted and well-placed composition students that the very concept of mastery has lost its post-Beethoven connotations … A style's attraction for publishers in an uncertain world is self-evident: without any need for real discrimination, a catalogue of more-or-less impeccably qualified and intelligent young composers could be assembled overnight with built-in guarantees of commissions, first performances and laudatory press … But the fact remains that the enduring quality of a composition is in the last resort determined solely by the quality of its composer; his or her relationship to any "central, dominant, or leading style" is essentially an academic question, and one to which the public for such works as *The Rite of Spring*, the *Concerto for Orchestra*, *Eight Songs for a Mad King* or *Frankenstein!!*, will remain supremely indifferent.'

The publishing strategy endorsed by the Board in 1984 was essentially a formal validation of Drew's policy in the mid-seventies when he had pursued both distinctive modernist experimenters and the composers who had forsaken the New Music fraternity and were returning to tonality: Gruber, Schwertsik and Holloway. With David Huntley's guidance, B&H had similarly been tapping into the American phenomenon, with composers such as Reich, Adams and Torke who had liberated themselves from European modernist constraints and forged a new path between popular and serious camps.

This period saw a number of high-profile premieres, including John Adams's operas *Nixon in China* (1987) and *The Death of Klinghoffer* (1991). These were both the result of a collaboration between the director Peter Sellars, who was determined to create operas that engaged with contemporary events, the poet Alice Goodman, choreographer Mark

Morris and Adams himself. Houston Grand Opera commissioned the first, but by *The Death of Klinghoffer*, no fewer than six opera houses were involved, giving the work the sort of rapid international exposure not seen since the days of Britten. Indeed, there is another parallel. In both cases, particularly *Klinghoffer*, the critics flocked but in many cases dismissed his music. Adams had become something of a punchbag for the European modernist fraternity, as witnessed at the Huddersfield Contemporary Music Festival in 1987, where he was featured composer alongside Brian Ferneyhough. *The Observer*'s elder statesman Peter Heyworth was incensed by *Harmonielehre*, now recognised as a repertoire classic, and stormed out muttering, 'Utter forgery!'. Another distinguished critic, Michael Kennedy, had a longer memory: 'It is easy to accuse him of eclecticism and of trying to be all things to all men by drawing on elements of popular music as well as on minimalism, Stravinskian rhythms and Delian harmonies ... but I remember the same sort of thing being said 40 years ago about Britten and Mahler. The score of *Klinghoffer* contains much impressive, dramatic and beautiful music.' Here, at last, was a dramatic composer whose works were accessible without being an 'aural jacuzzi' and who could deal with serious subjects without being grimly earnest.

While *Nixon* focused on a period in the recent past, characterising iconic figures with a blend of affection and wry, black humour, *Klinghoffer*

The Death of Klinghoffer by John Adams, in the premiere production by Peter Sellars (1991)
(Photo: Clärchen Baus-Mattar)

provoked outrage by dealing with the current Middle East crisis via the hijacking of the Achille Lauro cruise liner, allowing both the terrorists and the hostages to reveal their inner turmoil in melismatic ariosa. It was a high-risk project. Many American critics loathed it on moral grounds, Edward Rothstein complaining in the *New York Times* of the 'evenhandedness that holds sympathy and horror at bay'. For better or worse, it has become the most controversial opera of the last fifty years: there were protests and picket lines when it was staged in New York and San Francisco, and both Glyndebourne and Los Angeles Music Center Opera, two of its commissioners, cancelled their productions. With world events, it has become if anything even more topical with recent stagings in Helsinki, Rotterdam, Prague and at the Edinburgh Festival. Since then Adams has written a 'songplay' about the 1994 Los Angeles earthquake, *I was looking at the ceiling and then I saw the sky*; a mesmerising Christmas oratorio, *El Niño*; the story of the creator of the atom bomb, Robert Oppenheimer, in *Doctor Atomic*; and most recently *A Flowering Tree*, based on an Indian folk tale – all collaborations with Peter Sellars. When Adams was asked to compose a work to commemorate the events of 11 September 2001, the haunting *On the Transmigration of Souls*, it was clear he had become America's unofficial composer laureate.

The *Cave* by Steve Reich and Beryl Korot (1993)
(Photo: Andrew Pothecary)

Steve Reich, too, had for even longer been grappling with the moral issues of the 20th century in his works. His seminal *Different Trains* (1988), for taped quartet, tape and live quartet, deftly and movingly dramatises the fate of Jews in the forties in wartime Europe in contrast to those safely in America. Almost at the same time as Adams, he began work on an opera that also examined the Middle East question, a documentary-style video work *The Cave*. Premiered at the Vienna Festival in 1993, the work centres on the story of Abraham as it is understood by Arabs, Israelis and Americans today. *The Cave* was a highly complex and sophisticated technical enterprise, using video created by his wife Beryl Korot, computers, live electronics and performers. Criticised by some as an 'MTV' opera, others, like Andrew Porter in the *Observer* and John Rockwell in the *New York*

Times, deemed it a work of high seriousness and a glimpse of what opera could become in the 21st century. His *Three Tales* (2001), a further collaboration with Korot dealing with the Hindenburg disaster, the atomic trials at Bikini, and Dolly the cloned sheep, was critically acclaimed as a powerful, provocative audio-visual statement. Reich's style has expanded and relaxed in many of his concert works, but the rigour controlling his operas, their technical and intellectual ambition, and his intense focus on the texture and rhythmic patterning of the human voice, an obsession since the 1960s, set them apart.

Back in Europe, several composers signed in the early eighties came into their own as the decade reached its close. At the suggestion of Michael Vyner, the quirky, highly individual tonal composer Jonathan Lloyd had been signed in 1984. Both his Second Symphony and Mass for solo voices were performed in Germany as well as the UK, and Simon Rattle premiered his First Symphony in 1989. An important German signing by Drew in 1983 was York Höller, who had worked at IRCAM with Boulez and whose spiritual home was Paris. He explored the fusion between live and electronic music and his work was praised for its 'notable finesse and delicacy' and the 'absolute mastery' of his scoring. He succeeded Stockhausen as director of the WDR electronic studio in Cologne, but the forms in which he chose to write were far removed from Stockhausen's own. His Bulgakov opera *The Master and Margarita* was a great success in Paris in 1989, as was his entirely acoustic Piano Concerto No. 1, premiered with Boulez conducting the BBC Symphony Orchestra in 1986 and later championed by Daniel Barenboim as soloist. Höller received a key opera commission in the late eighties but after starting to write it discovered, tragically, that he was going blind. His doctor recommended that he drop the opera project since his intense focus on such an activity would only hasten the loss of his sight. It was an agonising situation, and the opera was never written, though he has continued to compose using an extra-large computer screen.

The conclusion to Fell's 1988 strategy paper expressed some caution: 'The current publishing strategy or any other policy related to serious music is unlikely to produce significant growth over the next 20 years'. But in the following five years there were several further signings. The young British composer Andrew Toovey and the sparky, Scottish piano prodigy and composer David Horne joined in 1989, while the much-performed Christopher Rouse, already a Pulitzer Prize-winning composer, was signed to B&H Inc in 1993.

What happened next could not have been predicted: the arrival of important, established composers from another publisher. Once again, as half a century before, it was Universal Edition who provided the talent. After the great, pioneering Alfred Schlee retired in 1985, UE adopted a more cautious approach to the economics of publishing and in the early 1990s decided to make a considerable reduction in its UK catalogue. (This was partly the result of Bob Wise of Music Sales buying a large stake in the firm when a member of the Kalmus family sold out. He put considerable pressure on the Board not to tolerate unprofitable composers, though he eventually tired of fighting and sold out.) It was not a repeat of the Schirmer situation in the early 1980s by any means, but the outcome was rather similar. In 1991 a tip-off from Bill Colleran at UE's London office suggested that James MacMillan was unhappy with his situation and put him in touch with Tony Fell. That year a deal was done with UE to buy his complete works, including *The Confession of Isobel Gowdie*, which had received such a striking premiere at the 1990 BBC Proms, and MacMillan signed an exclusive deal with B&H. The popular Scot was already enjoying enthusiastic support among musicians and conductors. Almost immediately, several of his works such as the percussion concerto espoused by Evelyn Glennie, *Veni, Veni, Emmanuel*, were taken up internationally and recorded, and before the end of the decade he had become one of B&H's most performed living composers.

James MacMillan with Evelyn Glennie at rehearsals for *Veni, Veni, Emmanuel* (1992)
(Photo: Malcolm Crowthers)

For similar reasons Harrison Birtwistle became disaffected with UE and his agent, Andrew Rosner, led B&H to believe he would be interested. He signed in 1995, though his earlier works remained with UE: in terms of prestige, Birtwistle was a prize indeed. Caricatured as a gritty modernist, the absolute quality of Birtwistle's music was now recognised, even among most sceptics or anti-modernists. His operas – from the grave, stylised grandeur of *The Mask of Orpheus*, to the mythic power of *Gawain*, through to the arch and fantastical comic delights of *The Second Mrs Kong* – had placed him firmly on the map as an artist of enduring stature. Since joining B&H, Birtwistle has written more than 40 works, including the notorious *Panic*, which caused an uproar at the Last Night of the Proms in

1995, two operas *The Last Supper* and *The Io Passion*, and the orchestral pieces *Exody*, *Theseus Game* and *The Shadow of Night*.

The signing of Birtwistle reflected a welcome trend during the 1990s, as B&H again became the publisher of choice for many European composers of international renown. In 1992 Louis Andriessen, hitherto happy with his Dutch publisher, opted to come over with his major works, which he termed 'my skyscrapers', drawing them on a napkin in the restaurant where he met Janis Susskind. 'I wanted to explain to Janis', he recalls, 'that I consider the large pieces as the core of my work. Not the nice and practical chamber music. I think I wanted to warn Boosey of my non-practical, non-commercial thinking, which they accepted gladly.' Having fulfilled a boyhood fantasy 'to have my printed score look like the cover of a score of Stravinsky', Andriessen is now very much part of the family: 'I once said to Janis, "What is so amazing in your contacts with me is that I always have the feeling that I am the sole composer in the catalogue of Boosey & Hawkes".' The decade saw the creation of his two important stageworks in collaboration with Peter Greenaway, *ROSA: The Death of a Composer* (1994) and *Writing to Vermeer* (1998), which pushed forward the fusion of music theatre and cinematic techniques. By 1997 the gifted Finn Magnus Lindberg had also approached B&H and come under Susskind's wing, going on to write hyperactive and richly coloured scores for leading orchestras, including a clarinet concerto (2002) that has travelled the world.

The expert editing team was a tremendous bonus for the incoming composers of the 1990s. Sally Cox, who had been editing for B&H since 1977, began to find her job involved a closer working relationship with them: 'In the days of David Drew, we were very much the workers in the background, and he looked after the relationships, but gradually I began to be relied upon to be more involved. It is fascinating to discover what it is a composer needs from you, what you must ask, what you must never do. As I'm a harpist, many have relied on me over the years to sort out the complexities of harp notation. With most composers we only change what is grammatically incorrect in notational terms, but even these changes sometimes generate debate. When I have clarified or standardised Robin Holloway's rhythms he has said to me: "But I do like my double dots!" Kurt Schwertsik is bright and breezy, saying "Oh dear, that's missing!" when you point out an omission. My relationship with Mark-Anthony Turnage is continuous as he expects to be revising the score several times and working with me in detail. I've edited Max for close on 30 years:

I remember having lunch with him once and telling him I had thought of becoming a nurse when younger. Quick as a flash he said "Oh, you nurse me!". Working with Harrison Birtwistle has been extremely rewarding: I feel, in a small way, he relies on me. You have to go through the scores note by note. He has a liking for writing in flats, so he asks me to try to make the notation friendly for the instrument. And as I work through the staves I trace how he is picking up notes in other parts and begin to see how his mind is working. When I am editing music which excites me in this way, trawling though a score to spot the occasional inaccuracy is not tedious, it's a privilege. I couldn't be happier.'

After 1992, when David Drew left the company, Janis Susskind took on an increasingly active role in searching for new composers. She was still titled Head of Promotion, but began to direct the serious music strategy. One of her first signings was the Korean composer Unsuk Chin, in 1994. The story is revealing of Susskind's open-minded, inquisitive stance: 'In 1993 I read a review by David Murray of a concert conducted by George Benjamin, and was intrigued by his description of her music. I rang George to find out more about her. He was surprised, but very pleased and sent me a tape.' Eventually Winfried Jacobs in the German office arranged to meet the Berlin-based composer, who had moved there following studies with Ligeti in Hamburg. Susskind played one of her pieces to key staff at an international promotion conference: 'Everyone said this was fresh, unusual, something special and accomplished. There was a unanimous feeling that here was a leader not a follower, someone with her own voice.' Their positive response was borne out as Chin blossomed, following her much-performed *Acrostic-Wordplay* with a piano concerto for Rolf Hind and the Grawemeyer Award-winning Violin Concerto.

Harrison Birtwistle (1995)
(Photo: Malcolm Crowthers)

Chin was a 'complete start-up' in Susskind's words, joining the small, very select group of composers with whom B&H has been involved right at the beginning of their careers. Before taking on such unknown voices, there are several considerations. Says Susskind, 'Of course, if you are bowled over by the music, that is the most important thing. But we also need to know that the composer has potential to be promotable in all three main territories, UK, Germany and America. Lastly, if a young composer hasn't got to grips with one of the computer note-setting programmes, and they are unproven, that can be a problem because production costs will be very high.' With this blend of leading figures and new voices B&H had within a decade gone a long way towards fulfilling the publishing strategy outlined in 1984, pursuing the creative quality of individualistic composers rather than the former notions of style and school. The contemporary catalogue was truly refreshed.

Routes to the young: a renaissance in educational publishing

With the two great cornerstones of 20th-century educational music in the catalogue, Bartók's *Mikrokosmos* and Kodály's *Bicinia Hungarica* choral series, B&H always had a high reputation as an educational publisher. The firm had printed instrumental methods since the *Simplicity Tutors* of the early 1900s, but by the mid-seventies the market began to demand a new approach. Three figures emerged during this period who were pioneering educational literature in a fresh way. The first was Peter Wastall, whose *Learn As You Play* books for wind and brass were the result of in-depth research into how children actually learned to play. He had done a masters degree in the psychology of teaching music, and his books are informed by his findings. His inclusion of popular and ethnic music in his choice of repertoire was significant, says Stephen Richards, who in 1986 became Publishing Manager with responsibility for the educational department of the London company: 'Much of the educational music being sold at that time did not reflect the needs or interests of young people. We, as publishers, had a duty to respond to current trends, to introduce new ideas to music teachers and to stretch them in their teaching. If we could make the exercise of learning an instrument more enjoyable to more children, then we were helping make the teacher's job easier. Also, the whole issue of multi-culturalism was raising its head, while pop music was all-pervasive. Somehow we had to bring the musical worlds together.'

Stephen Richards (1991)
(Photo: John Greenwood)

While Peter Wastall's books grew in popularity throughout the eighties and became best-sellers, another very special teacher had already attracted attention in the early seventies in Tower Hamlets, one of the poorest boroughs of London. Sheila Nelson had taken some elements of the Suzuki method (also published by B&H during the days of David Adams) and other approaches to musicianship, and created an effective system of group violin teaching with ordinary school children. The results of the Tower Hamlets String Project were impressive, and spawned a host of such projects worldwide. Nelson became the doyenne of British group string teaching, partly due to the promotional workshops funded by B&H. Says Richards, 'At first we simply published the material she used. But we soon developed a relationship whereby she would be going on promotional tours and giving training sessions. Our staff would accompany her into workshops with teachers and develop ideas from them. We were in the business of influencing the whole teaching profession, of bringing about change.' Nelson herself was resolutely against developing a personality cult, as many in her position would have done. She refused to put her name to an actual 'method' book, but in 2000 was persuaded to create the *Essential String Method* with the Guildhall School of Music and Drama, to whose faculty she belonged. It became a top-selling series and won a Millennium Award for Innovation.

Peter Wastall's
Learn As You Play

If Nelson's forte was the development of violin technique and musicianship, Christopher Norton's was in composing contemporary, popular and jazz-style music for piano that reinforced a classical keyboard technique. Norton's *Microjazz* series broke new ground in giving children and teenagers access to the popular music they desperately wanted to play without compromising the piano technique their teachers were trying to instil. '*Microjazz* was a phenomenon. It opened a gateway for teachers into the musical world espoused by their pupils: they could facilitate technique and develop talent with the enthusiastic support of the children. Even the teachers themselves would say that they didn't know they could play this kind of music until they tried Chris's pieces – they were so cleverly written.' The full potential of Norton's concept to fill a gap in the market was recognised by Rex Billingham, the sales manager at B&H, who coined the name *Microjazz*. Since the mid-eighties, 30 or 40 Norton books have been published, adapted for all instruments including a version for MIDI-file developed with Roland and useful in piano-lab and studio teaching and, most recently, Norton has created a step-by-step *Easiest Way to Improvise*. Norton, like Nelson, has travelled extensively, devising workshops and is still in demand as a teacher-clinician.

Christopher Norton's
Microjazz

With these three teacher-writers working closely with the B&H editors in research and development, educational publishing began to earn income on a new scale. 'Traditionally our educational composers hadn't made much money, but we proved it was a viable and valuable form of publishing. By 1990 the sales of new educational materials had risen from 10% to 25% of our total printed music sales,' says Richards.

Sheila Nelson taking a workshop on the *Essential String Method* at the Hendon office (1994)

Doreen Rao's *Choral Music Experience*

But it was labour-intensive and required constant updating. 'The UK music education system underwent various upheavals. In 2003/4 our research revealed that many children were starting to learn earlier, at primary school, so they needed a different kind of language, different music and music of other cultures had to be part of the fabric, not just a token feature. They are also expected now to be able to improvise and ensemble music is needed from the start. So we commissioned suitable teachers to develop the *Boosey Woodwind Method* and the *Boosey Brass Method.*' Another success story was Edward Huws-Jones's *Fiddler* series, which explores styles of violin playing from around the world, such as Celtic, gypsy, Eastern European, South American, tango and the like. 'We've put in piano, guitar chords and accompanying fiddle parts so they can get a band together in no time,' explains Richards.

During this period, the new management at B&H Inc had been similarly assessing the crowded US market for sheet music and had decided to focus on band, choral and string music. Boosey had previously published largely for the more advanced, high-grade wind bands, but now moved into the education market with a popular series for the early grades – as Max Winkler had done in the forties. The choral publishing had mostly been provided by the concert composers under general contract, but soon Mary Goetze created a series for treble and women's voices, Betty Berteaux introduced the *Betty Berteaux Choral Series* for children and Doreen Rao, then Head of the Glen Ellyn Children's Chorus, developed the *Choral Music Experience* series for children's choirs. Rao, like Goetze and Berteaux, was renowned for her inspiring workshops and clinics, and this series still ranks among the bestsellers in the highly competitive American market. For adult choirs, Philip Brunelle developed a wide and successful range of sacred and secular choral music. The violinist and teacher Sheila Johnson had taken up the teaching principles of Paul Rolland, whose work at the University of Illinois at Champagne-Urbana was legendary. She fashioned them into the acclaimed series for group string teaching, *Young Strings in Action.*

Money, management and maximising resources

The late eighties and early nineties represented a switchback ride in the fortunes of B&H, though, as ever, the music publishing company managed to protect its composers from any ill-effects of the commercial maelstrom. In 1988, for the first and last time, the Connors of Carl Fischer Inc pulled rank on B&H Inc and insisted that they put all their sheet music distribution through Carl Fischer's New York operation. The B&H warehouse at Farmingdale, Long Island, had to be closed at some considerable cost, while the new premises were not nearly large enough, the stock got damaged and the losses stacked up. There was disorganisation on Carl Fischer's side and, it soon came to light, problems with the printed music department on the B&H side too. An unholy mess resulted, and Jim Kendrick was up at all hours of the night trying to restore order. The situation impacted on the sales figures for at least a couple of years, ironically just as the American performing royalties hit an all-time record. Jim Kendrick resigned in 1990, in order to return to legal practice. Fortunately, he stayed as the attorney for B&H and, as will be seen, has continued to play a key role in many important cases and deals. He was replaced by Linda Golding, so with Susskind in charge of publishing policy in London, women were finally in influential positions at Boosey & Hawkes, after decades of working behind the scenes.

The refurbished Regent Street shop in 1991, following the fire in 1990

Following the financial drain of the Boxford years, there was a large amount of cost-cutting to be done. After Asserson's initial streamlining measures, Richard Holland, recruited by Asserson as Group Finance

Director and appointed CEO in 1989, proceeded to shut two of the foreign offices. The Paris company was closed and the B&H agency moved to Alphonse Leduc along with Madeleine Albert, who had been with B&H since 1965. Described by François Leduc on Albert's retirement as 'très discrète, très efficace', she had always worked in assistant roles before, but had in Fell's words 'blossomed' with her increased responsibilities. The South African office was sold to a management partnership in 1989. The sale was done for commercial reasons but Fell also did not feel comfortable maintaining an office in the apartheid-riven country.

Disaster struck in October 1990 when the Regent Street showroom went up in smoke. Fortunately the blaze, which broke out after hours and was spotted by staff working late, was contained on the ground floor and did not destroy the Victorian ballad archive, or the important manuscripts and hire library music. But the cost of the damage to all the sheet music stocked in the shop was estimated at £0.5m, including the destruction of the famous 1930s panels and designs by Anna Zinkeisen, which had been commissioned all those years ago by LAB and Ralph Hawkes. Eventually a competition was held to choose a young artist to replace the panels, and the shop was restored.

This period represented the end of an era in terms of staff. Martin Hall, who had been there since the days of Ernst Roth and had been instrumental in showing Fell 'the ropes', left in 1986. David Drew resigned in 1992, after 17 years at B&H, to work more full-time on the Largo record label and fulfil other freelance projects, and the Promotion department was

Tony Fell, arts minister Tim Renton, Sir Peter Maxwell Davies and Richard Holland at the reopening of the shop (1991)

(Photo: John Greenwood)

restructured. Paul Meecham had left to run the London Sinfonietta, and Susan Bamert had arrived from Novello and would become Senior Promotion Executive. (B&H had considered buying Novello when it came up for sale, but had decided that with the imminent expiry of the Elgar copyrights and without Lloyd Webber's *Joseph and the Amazing Technicolour Dreamcoat*, the catalogue was not worth its price. Music Sales eventually acquired it and benefited from the 1995 copyright extension.) Malcolm Smith, widely known through his almost nightly attendance at concerts, had for years been a respected advisor to conductors, orchestral managers, soloists and record companies, on repertoire and the back catalogue. He had managed the hire library but was, in 1992, given the title of Repertoire Manager and moved into the promotion department following Susskind's reorganisation. This was an important gesture of recognition for a man who had done so much, so lovingly, to enlighten the profession and the public, and had ensured that B&H's back catalogue was alive and out there, and not gathering dust on the shelves.

The untimely death of David Huntley in 1994, at the age of 46, brought together composers and publishers from all over the world, who gathered in New York to share grief and pay tribute. Elliott Carter, Steve Mackey, James MacMillan, Kurt Schwertsik, Christopher Rouse, Aaron Jay Kernis, Tod Machover, Michael Torke, Robin Holloway, Louis Andriessen, Barbara Kolb, Ned Rorem and several others composed pieces in tribute that were played at the memorial service, and John Adams, who had dedicated his Violin Concerto to Huntley, wrote *The Wound-Dresser* in his memory. As so many keenly felt, the world of new music would be an infinitely poorer place without Huntley.

Could we be on the up?

If the eighties had been characterised by financial instability and near bankruptcy, during the early nineties a rosier picture emerged. First of all came the Górecki phenomenon, which had an immediate effect on the share price of B&H. Then came a pending $200m law suit against Disney in America for their use of *The Rite of Spring* in the video release of *Fantasia* without payment or permission, a case that *The Times* was to describe as a 'David and Goliath tussle' from which 'the tiny UK group' was to 'emerge triumphant'. With heated speculation in the media over the case's potential outcome, shares rose to £11.75 from £2 a year before. Then came the welcome news in 1993 that, from 1995, the copyright period was to be extended from 50 to 70 years. This brought Bartók, Prokofieff and

Stravinsky's *The Rite of Spring*, the first in the Masterworks series of full scores, launched in 1997

Rachmaninoff back out of danger. Of course, it was not a gift out of the blue, but the result of strong lobbying from the MCPS, MPA and PRS, all bodies with whom Tony Pool had been an active and leading member.

The publishing side of the company was still in the original building in Hendon, until in 1992 Sainsbury's bought the site and agreed to the construction of new, purpose-built premises nearby, which would house the production, marketing, sales, royalties, IT, copyright licensing and distribution departments, while the hire library and promotion department remained in central London. The Hendon premises also boasted 15,000 square feet of warehouse space with a racking system specially designed for B&H. Back in Regent Street new technology was beginning to come on stream and a Notestation computer was installed in the shop, which offered 3,000 songs, a transposing service and an instant print-out. It was a rather pale shadow of Robert Cowan's Professional Management service, which provided a warm welcome to artists and singers who wanted music that was out of print, together with a cup of tea, a photocopy and a chat with the passionately knowledgeable Cowan.

At the opening of the new Hendon premises in 1992, Sally Cox explains note-setting to the Duchess of Kent

By April 1993 the financial pages of the press were proclaiming relatively high profits once again. Despite currency turbulence at the time, it was cheering to see pre-tax Group profits rising 5.4% to £4.23m. And this was really a reflection of the success of the publishing business. Although the instrument division was slowly recovering from reorganisation, its profit was down in that year. The Pool family had, by this time, chosen to sell their shares. Bob Wise of Music Sales was offered them, but in the end they were bought by the American investment banker Herb Allen. It was the end of an era: the last Hawkes family holding had been sold. But it was a relief to Tony Pool, who had never been allowed to sit on the Board himself yet had contributed so much to the publishing effort over three decades.

With its gleaming new building in Hendon and a hot list of new composers, the publishing company was straining at the bit once again to be independent from its instrument-making big brother. The next decade would bring liberation, but at a critically heavy price.

Offenbach's *Orphée aux Enfers* (1858) at the Oper Düsseldorf in 1999, the first German production to adopt the Offenbach Edition Keck, published by Boosey & Hawkes/Bote & Bock in Berlin.
(Photo: Eduard Straub)

Striking the right note

The years 1996 and 1997 saw seismic changes at Boosey and Hawkes. Tony Fell was due to retire as Managing Director of the publishing company after more than twenty years at the helm. He had modernised the division, had kept it on an even keel during the tumultuous Boxford period, had cemented relations with the American company and been responsible for a period of dynamic publishing matched only by the Hawkes era. Few would have had the mettle, the vision or the *sang-froid* to have survived, let alone thrived during this era of change, boom and bust. One of his key strengths had been appointing the right people to fulfil his long-term vision. But he could be ruthless, and was known as 'Machiafelli' in some quarters: Ralph Hawkes would have approved.

Trevor Glover with Tony Pool (2000)

Finding his replacement was never going to be easy. Just how difficult it would be became clear when the chosen new MD arrived, an experienced manager with a background in the pharmaceutical industry. Alas, he never quite made the switch into music publishing and its idiosyncratic economic planning and balance of revenue streams. Fell remained Managing Director Group Publishing and was needed once again six months later when feelers were put out to find a second replacement. Trevor Glover, the Managing Director of Penguin Books (UK), was asked if he could recommend any candidates and surprised everyone by saying he might be interested himself.

Glover's experience in the publishing business and his lively interest in music were to prove invaluable. Starting the job at 56, he was never going to stay for very long, but the list of achievements and battles fought in those five years is impressive. On his arrival he reassured the staff in a statesman-like speech, declaring that he was here to oversee a great brand name and an ethical, principled company. 'He struck the right note', says Susskind, 'He was warm, funny, committed and well-liked.'

On the music side, his signing of Karl Jenkins made an impact in the media and on the bottom line. The Welsh composer had enjoyed remarkable success with his scores *Adiemus: Songs of Sanctuary* and *Palladio,* the former topping one million CD sales at the beginning of

1997. In the same year B&H published his *Adiemus II: Cantata Mundi,* another haunting combination of classical and ethnic sounds with true popular appeal, and Jenkins' music was increasingly aired on the UK's new commercial radio station Classic FM. Hardline critics had their knives out for Jenkins, and a debate raged about the classification of his music in the record charts: was this truly classical music? There was no such debate from B&H's perspective, as its publishing of Jenkins was only the latest example in a long tradition embracing popular music for the masses, from Boosey ballads in the Victorian age to light music classics in the 1930s and 1940s. The music of Jenkins was also highly attractive to the media industry and could be heard frequently on TV adverts and documentary films. Most prominently, *Palladio* was used by De Beers to sell diamonds on TV and *Adiemus* to convert investors to the Cheltenham and Gloucester Building Society. In recent years Jenkins has composed two large-scale choral works that have topped the CD charts and have been rapidly taken up by amateur choirs around the world. *The Armed Man (A Mass for Peace)* (1999) and *Requiem* (2004) furnished B&H with a pair of high-selling scores.

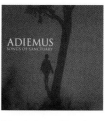

Adiemus: Songs of Sanctuary by Karl Jenkins

Glover's other significant musical achievement was the acquisition, signed in 1998, of 40 of Rachmaninoff's late works, including the *Rhapsody on a theme of Paganini*, the Fourth Piano Concerto and *Symphonic Dances*, allowing B&H to promote across virtually his entire output. This involved a long and tortuous negotiation with the Rachmaninoff family, including Alexandre Rachmaninoff, the composer's grandson. Prior to this the copyrights had been recovered by the family from their previous publisher, who they felt had not been exploiting them with sufficient energy. Glover became close to the family and on his retirement from B&H continued to run the Serge Rachmaninoff Foundation. The catalogue was an expensive but very valuable acquisition: in 1998, a new law was passed in the United States increasing the period of copyright by 20 years to 95 years from date of publication for all works written between 1923-77. For the late works, including the *Rhapsody on a theme of Paganini*, this meant an additional 20 years of earning potential in the US.

At the time, Rachmaninoff's music was not only ubiquitous in concert and on CD, but was also reaching a new peak in the critical firmament. The hit film *Shine*, a biopic of pianist David Helfgott, had featured the Third Piano Concerto, while pop singers of every ilk continued to borrow the Russian's melodies whenever a love song was needed. Now it was the Canadian chanteuse Celine Dion who had recorded versions of *All by myself*, which quotes directly from the Piano Concerto No. 2, and *Never gonna fall in love again*, which took its melody from his Symphony No. 2.

Another initiative during Glover's tenure was B&H's relaunch of its media music department, building on the Cavendish Production Music Library – the renamed, modernised version of the 'mood music library' founded by Ralph Hawkes in 1937. Rebranded as BooseyMedia and acquiring a fully-equipped production studio in London's Soho district, this division was able to offer film and television producers 'a complete range of musical genres to meet the needs of the media industry', and soon became an important generator of revenue. Music by Terry Devine-King was successfully placed in an award-winning series of television advertisements for Orange and in a worldwide Adidas campaign. And an innovative new product, the Editor's Construction Kit, provided TV editors with a toolbox of sound design elements to construct their own atmospheric soundtracks. It continues to generate royalties a decade after its launch.

The happy story of copyright extension in the US had a negative counterpart back in the UK. The PRS, the institution LAB had helped to build and strengthen, made the decision to cut its classical composers subsidy of long standing. In the ocean of royalties collected every year for all music, this concession to creators of intricate art works was a very small drop. But it made all the difference to the classical composers and

Karl Jenkins conducting at a recording session

prevented their income from live performances plunging down to ludicrously low levels. The management of the PRS argued that an Office of Fair Trading investigation demanded more transparency, and that the subsidy was a blatant example of hidden accounting. Tony Pool, a member of the PRS board at the time, argued vociferously that the subsidy was transparent as it was overt and known to all parties. But the pop composers' and publishers' lobby was powerful and had been pushing to remove this resented 'charitable gift' to classical composers for years. It suited the PRS to bow to this pressure, though they claimed their newly created charitable PRS Foundation was a generous gesture to the affected composers.

Glover led the charge against the PRS, establishing an alliance with his fellow publishers including Faber, Music Sales, Peters, UE and Schott. In the end the campaign was not successful, and over the next two years it made a sizeable dent both in B&H's income and that of many of its composers. This was particularly stressful when, as a public company, the dividend was being examined every six months, and the need to please shareholders threatened to distort long-term planning.

Glover also made changes to the way the publishing company was structured, which can now be seen as the beginning of a ten-year streamlining process. Despite the opening of the brand new purpose-built premises in North London in 1993, Glover had experience of outsourcing and decided that B&H should pull out of non-core activities such as warehousing and distribution. The Hendon base was abandoned in 1998 and Grantham Book Services took over the distribution. There was now no reason to have two sites, and all staff moved back to Regent Street, sharing the same roof for the first time in the firm's history: promotion, sales and marketing, business affairs, hire library and editorial ('thank goodness', said Roger Brison, after years of cycling up to Hendon in all weathers). It was not always easy to accommodate everyone in the old building, but, explains Susskind, 'being together did lead to better communication and put a stop to the divisiveness that had existed for years between departments'. In 2000

The South Bank Centre's exploration of Rachmaninoff in 1999 helped prompt a reappraisal of his wider œuvre

Tempo, the venerable contemporary music journal, still being edited by Calum MacDonald, successor to David Drew in the mid-seventies, was transferred to Cambridge University Press, where it could better thrive within a stable of other academic journals.

With Trevor Glover now confidently in control, Tony Fell was able officially to retire as Managing Director Group Publishing at the end of 1996, but retained his place on the Board. Dick Holland, the chief executive, demanded that a new Director of Serious Music be found and a search was officially initiated. But, once again, everyone knew that the obvious candidate was right under Holland's nose – Janis Susskind. She had been doing the job since 1992 in all but name, but sensitivities over the presence of Fell – now her partner – in his role of Managing Director, had stalled her promotion. With Fell's retirement, Glover fought hard to have Susskind properly promoted and remunerated.

Janis Susskind (2005)
(Photo: Fergus Wilkie)

Susskind was already held in high esteem in the musical community and by the composers. Says HK Gruber of her: 'Janis is charming, very precise and a violin player. When Janis makes a decision it is with the ear and not just the brain. She always considers everyone on their own, individual merits; she has a wonderful way of understanding people. I had been writing an opera, *Der Herr Nordwind* (2005), which was running over schedule: nobody from the office phoned me to ask what was happening. The people who work on the scores are amazing: I call it the 'stress bunker' because they are always up against such tight deadlines for performances, schedules that don't look humanly possible. I had such a bad conscience that I was too afraid to call. I later discovered that she had advised everyone *not* to phone me, saying "Nali is nervous enough, don't push him – he will be working as fast as he can, he will be trying!" Ah – that's the best champion a composer could have in the publishing world!'

In the mid-eighties, Susskind had brought the music of Gruber's *Frankenstein!!* to the attention of choreographer Jiří Kylián through a piece in the newsletter *Quarternotes*, and a new dancework was born. This provided the model when, in 1995, she and Promotion Executive Emma Kerr decided to launch a special project specifically aimed at the dance community, trying actively to bring composers and choreographers together. The initiative was rapidly adopted by the offices worldwide. Sampler CDs featuring all kinds of 20th-century music, dance listings and choreographic histories were circulated to choreographers and dance organisations. Kerr worked with choreographers who wanted to commission completely new pieces from living composers and with those who needed to find existing music to choreograph. The results were surprising and successful. William Tuckett,who was creating a dance for the Royal Ballet based on the story of *The Turn of the Screw*, chose Panufnik's *Arbor Cosmica*, a work he might never have encountered. Johann Inger from the Nederlands Dans Theater and Nacho Duato in Madrid created ballets around Jenkins' *Palladio*, and Philip Taylor's exploration of B&H repertoire led to new danceworks for the Ballett Theater in Munich employing Reich's *The Four Sections* and *City Life* and Adams's *Fearful Symmetries* – a score that received 15 new choreographies

Fearful Symmetries by John Adams, choreographed by Ashley Page for the Royal Ballet Covent Garden (1994)
(Photo: Catherine Ashmore)

during this period. A collaboration between composer Elena Kats-Chernin and Meryl Tankard was launched with an aerial ballet for the Sydney Olympics opening ceremony in 2000 and developed into a full-evening Hans Christian Andersen ballet, *Wild Swans*, premiered by Australian Ballet in 2003. Jenny Bilfield, who headed the promotion team at B&H Inc following the death of David Huntley, becoming President from 2002 until 2006, actively promoted similar connections in America, such as those between Steve Mackey and Donald Byrd, and Kats-Chernin and Hernando Cortez. When Cortez adopted the music of Kats-Chernin, as Bilfield notes, 'Hernando felt he had discovered this composer for his community.' The project is still on-going and active, with over 80 new ballets created to date.

During the last years of the millennium the publishing team was managing an increasingly lively diary of performances: the return of new orchestral music to mainstream programming was a key phenomenon of the 1990s, making a sizeable contribution to royalty income. Spearheading this development was Michael Torke's *Javelin*, written for the Atlanta Olympics in 1996, and soon selling 100,000 CDs and clocking up over 100 performances. Yet, most significant was the number of new concertos actively toured by major soloists. James MacMillan's percussion concerto *Veni, Veni, Emmanuel* has received over 350 performances since its premiere in 1992, largely thanks to the advocacy of Evelyn Glennie and Colin Currie, while John Adams's Violin Concerto has been championed by the likes of Gidon Kremer, Midori and Leila Josefowicz, and *Century Rolls* by Emanuel Ax, Joanna MacGregor and Garrick Ohlsson. Other much-travelled concertos from this period include Christopher Rouse's *Der gerettete Alberich*, again thanks to Glennie and Currie, Adams's *Gnarly Buttons* and HK Gruber's trumpet concerto *Aerial*, toured widely by Håkan Hardenberger.

Premiere recording of Elgar-Payne: *Symphony No. 3*

Anthony Payne's extraordinary realisation of Elgar's abandoned Third Symphony also made a huge impact on audiences. Payne had for many years been fascinated by the sketches dating from the early 1930s, but it was only when he received permission from the estate to issue an authorised performing version that he engrossed himself afresh and found a convincing way to complete the score. The four movement symphony finally received a momentous premiere in 1998 and was an immediate hit: it proved to be much more than an analytical working out – this was a musical haunting. The symphony has received over 130 performances to date and is already available in three recordings.

A new German hub

Perhaps the most significant event of the mid-nineties was the acquisition of the German publishing house Bote & Bock. While the instrument company had frequently acquired other brands, the publishing company had been thwarted in its attempts to expand ever since the days of Simon Boosey and his stillborn plan to buy G Schirmer. Bote & Bock GmbH was a distinguished, family-run business with a rich European heritage, and Tony Pool shared a long-standing friendship with its proprietor Hans-Jürgen Radecke. Founded in 1838, the Berlin-based company had a wide catalogue, including works by Reger, Mahler's Seventh Symphony, Strauss's *Symphonia Domestica*, Offenbach's operettas, d'Albert's *Tiefland* and von Einem's *Der Prozess*. It also represented three Czech 'Terezín' composers, Pavel Haas, Gideon Klein and Hans Krása, whose children's opera *Brundibár* had received numerous performances and two recordings since its rediscovery in the early nineties. Bote & Bock had an important contemporary catalogue, including Henze's student Detlev Glanert, Helmut Oehring and the highly original Korean Isang Yun, who died in 1995 and several of whose elegant yet powerful works appear on the ECM New Series label.

Winfried Jacobs (2003)

The acquisition of Bote & Bock in 1996 revolutionised the German office and gave B&H the prominent foothold in Germany it had struggled to establish since the war. With reunification, Bonn had begun to feel like a musical backwater and, like the German government, the new combined company transferred to the real hub, Berlin. Winfried Jacobs headed up the new team, many of whom were staff from Bote & Bock. The latter had also owned the most famous music shop in Berlin, the only one to survive the war in the West of the city, and it was with sadness that B&H was eventually forced to close it down. But this was one of the very few casualties of the buyout.

Detlev Glanert (2006)
(Photo: Iko Freese)

Berlin-based composer Detlev Glanert, who joined B&H from Bote & Bock, recalls the changeover: 'My first major opera, *Der Spiegel des großen Kaisers*, was being performed in 1995 in Mannheim. There was talk of Bote & Bock being sold, and there were several publishers present at the opera's first night. But a friend said to me conspiratorially, "Don't move! You will be moved". Sure enough, I had a phone call from Tony Fell, who came to Berlin and took me out to dinner and assured me that I would have a good life with Boosey & Hawkes. All I knew of the firm at the time was that they had published Strauss, Stravinsky and Prokofieff, and I loved their study scores, but I wasn't well informed – London seemed a long way off. I appreciated what Bote & Bock had done for me: they were a small, family firm and they took a huge risk in taking on that opera. But it was the right time for me to move: B&H brought international connections, in London and at the BBC, also in America. I was offered a general contract which gave me room to breathe, time to develop, and I became friends with Winfried Jacobs, Reinhold Dusella and Frank Harders in the Berlin office. So much depends on trust, it is like a marriage. I am now an opera composer in Germany and a concert composer in the UK and the USA.'

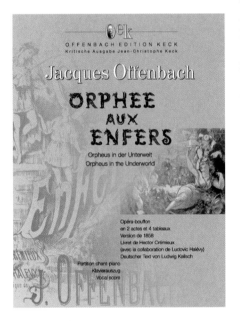

Vocal score of *Orphée aux Enfers* in the Offenbach Edition Keck, winner of the German MPA's Best Music Edition Prize in 2001

One of the first projects for the new Boosey & Hawkes / Bote & Bock was to launch a critical edition of Offenbach's operettas, which for years had been performed using materials riddled with unsanctioned changes – even to the plots – editing errors, and even the lack of full scores. The French conductor Jean-Christophe Keck, president of the French Offenbach Research Center, joined the team in Berlin to produce the new Offenbach Edition Keck (OEK). *Orphée aux Enfers* was the first operetta to receive the full OEK treatment, winning awards and sparking off renewed critical interest in the composer. Next came editions of *La Grande-Duchesse de Gérolstein, La Vie parisienne, La Périchole* and *Les Brigands* which all received performances in the opera houses of Europe. EMI recorded the new editions of *Les Brigands, La Vie parisienne* and *Grande-Duchesse*, Offenbach's Romantic opera *Les Fées du Rhin* was revived on stage and disc, and the OEK soon attracted committed advocates including conductor Marc Minkowski and director Laurent Pelly.

The second important step in the creation of a significant German publishing centre was the acquisition in 2002 of Richard Schauer Music Publishers, owners of the famous Benjamin/Simrock catalogue. Discussions had begun during Trevor Glover's time, but continued under his successor John Minch, who joined in 2001. Winfried Jacobs was involved at every stage and now manages the catalogue from Berlin. The German émigré, London-based owner Irene Retford had for many years been on friendly terms with Tony Pool, and this was an important factor in her decision not to sell to Bob Wise of Music Sales, who was wooing her energetically, but to B&H. The catalogue was a prize indeed, containing not only the famous Simrock editions of Dvořák, Tchaikovsky and Beethoven, but also works by Rachmaninoff, Prokofieff and Zemlinsky. Yet the Board decision to proceed with the purchase hung on a single vote, yet another indication of the reluctance of the instrument-focussed Board to value and invest in publishing.

Brahms chamber music in the Simrock edition

The 200-year-old German company held authoritative editions of the 19th-century symphonic repertoire, including 300 pieces by Nicholas Simrock's friend Beethoven and a pioneering edition of Bach's *Well-tempered Clavier*. Following the economic crisis of the First World War, the Simrock catalogue had been sold to Anton J Benjamin in the 1920s, a firm which owned the original Jurgenson editions of Tchaikovsky. With his nephew Richard Schauer, Benjamin was forced out during the Aryanisation of German businesses in the 1930s, and the final straw came when the Leipzig offices were bombed in 1943, destroying practically all its plates, manuscripts and archive. Schauer regained ownership after the war and, based on his retained rights in Dvořák, Bruch, Dohnányi and Zemlinsky, started to rebuild the company into a thriving business. The addition of these catalogues has made a greater contribution to B&H's figures than expected since, to the surprise of many, orchestras do still hire the parts for standard symphonies by composers such as Dvořák and Tchaikovsky, even though other editions are available for sale.

The company's range of repertoire was further extended at this time through its representation in a number of major territories of the Warner-Chappell-Scandinavia catalogue. This included music by Einojuhani Rautavaara, Kalevi Aho and Veljo Tormis and early works by Magnus Lindberg, all Finnish and Estonian composers who had come to the fore internationally during the 1990s, via the world-class group of conductors and musicians emerging from the region and the backing of Nordic record companies such as BIS and Ondine. In 2003 when the head office at Warner decreed the end of investment in publishing serious composers, the distinguished, meditative composer Rautavaara joined the B&H stable, and has since embarked on a new opera based on Lorca.

Carl Fischer quits

The events related above all took place in the shadow of doubts about the future of the company sparked off by the sudden death of Walter Connor in 1996. It was not immediately clear what the implications of his death would mean for B&H – the American firm still held tightly to its majority shareholding. The share price in 1996 was on a high, with the instrument company making profits again at last, and the bold new acquisition of the Rico clarinet and saxophone reed business for £17m. But as time went on it emerged that the Connor family wanted to sell out. Who would buy?

Despite the difficult relationship between the two companies over the years, Carl Fischer Inc and Boosey & Hawkes had essentially remained two medium-sized music companies pursuing similar aims, and, crucially, the Connors had always supported the overall publishing strategy of the London office. If Carl Fischer sold out now, as the family intended to do, B&H's music publishing division faced the prospect of being taken over by a multinational: Warner, Sony, Polygram, BMG and EMI were cited. 'It was a very uncomfortable time,' remembers Fell, 'We were horrified to see the major pop publishers coming in to look over our books.' When Fischer finally announced it was putting itself (together with its controlling stake in B&H) up for sale in April 1997, speculation drove the B&H share price up sharply reaching a high of 1,063p.

The B&H group was an attractive prospect for many: a thriving $300 million business with 1,200 employees, and factories across Europe and the United States. But insiders knew the risk of potential neglect if their valuable rights were absorbed into a conglomerate. As Sally Groves of Schott once said, publishing is rather like forestry: you cannot simply chop down trees, you must always be planting and nurturing new ones. One of B&H's house composers in America, Carlisle Floyd, knew just what could go wrong. Creator of the popular John Steinbeck opera *Of Mice and Men*, his copyrights were held by Belwin Mills (the firm connected to B&H back in the thirties). But when, in 1985 this was bought by Columbia Pictures, part of the Coca Cola Corporation, he saw the opera disappear from the stage: there was not a single performance between 1986 and 1990. Floyd wrested his copyrights from Belwin, took them to B&H in 1990, and in the subsequent fifteen years the opera has received over 100 performances.

Another vocal critic of the attitude of large media corporations was Bartók's son, Peter. Interviewed by the *Wall Street Journal*, he praised the care taken by B&H over his father's scores, recalling that one orchestral piece had needed 1800 corrections. With Bartók royalties bringing in a large sum each year, his father's catalogue was a tempting investment prospect, but who would take the trouble to correct scores?

By 1998, Glover had ignited a full-scale campaign in the musical community to 'save' B&H from being swallowed up into a faceless media organisation. Donald Mitchell, by this time chairman of the Britten Estate, spearheaded the lobby. Despite his own brief and turbulent experience all those years ago, he had since gone on to establish excellent relations with the firm and recognised that keeping B&H intact was a matter of national importance, as his letter to *The Times* set out: 'Boosey & Hawkes may shortly fall victim to what is essentially a hostile takeover bid. It seems most unlikely that the bidder would be competent, or would wish, to operate both the musical instrument and publishing arms. Therefore a takeover would inevitably lead to the break up of the company. We believe that this would cause irremediable damage to the British musical heritage. Boosey & Hawkes is an independent publisher with a genuine and vital interest in serious music. Unlike the large multinational 'pop' publishing companies, it is able to provide a close and sensitive service both to contemporary composers and the estates of those deceased.' He goes on to praise their record in music education, and the 'dedication and commitment' of their staff, and concludes that it must be in the nation's interest to preserve the firm as it now stands. The letter was signed by John Stravinsky, Robert Montgomery (for the Elgar estate), Oleg Prokofiev, Rosamund Strode (Holst Estate), Martin Williams (Delius Trust) and two of the firm's most prominent composers, James MacMillan and Harrison Birtwistle.

The Times, 30 July 1997

LETTERS TO THE EDITOR
1 Pennington Street, London E1 9XN   Telephone 0171-782 5000

Threat to Britain's musical heritage

From Dr Donald Mitchell and others

Sir, We write to raise concerns we have over the future of the music publishing and musical instrument manufacturing company, Boosey & Hawkes plc.

Boosey & Hawkes is the major publisher for the works of British composers such as Britten, Elgar, Holst and Delius, and has a unique international catalogue including, among others, Bartok, Copland, Prokofiev, Strauss and Stravinsky. John Adams, Sir Peter Maxwell Davies, Steve Reich and two of the undersigned are among those in its contemporary catalogue.

Due to circumstances beyond its control relating to events at Carl Fischer Inc, the company's major shareholder, and despite a healthy financial track record, Boosey & Hawkes may shortly fall victim to what is essentially a hostile takeover bid. It seems most unlikely that a bidder would be competent, or would wish, to operate both the musical instrument and publishing arms. Therefore a takeover would inevitably lead to the break-up of the company.

We believe that this would cause irremediable damage to the British musical heritage. Boosey & Hawkes is an independent publisher with a genuine and vital interest in serious music.

Unlike the larger multinational "pop" publishing companies, it is able to provide a close and sensitive service both to contemporary composers and the estates of those deceased.

Boosey & Hawkes has been a household name in this country for over a century and is synonymous in Britain and, indeed, internationally with musical education. Virtually every child in Britain will have used Boosey & Hawkes instruments or materials at some stage in their education. Should the company lose its independence, we have no doubt that there would be a major loss in dedication and commitment to those involved in serious and educational music, with adverse consequences for future generations of composers, performers, and audiences in this country.

We firmly believe it to be in the national interest that Boosey & Hawkes remains a single and independent firm.

Yours faithfully,
DONALD MITCHELL
(Britten Estate Limited),
HARRISON BIRTWISTLE,
JAMES MacMILLAN,
ROBERT MONTGOMERY
(Estate of Edward Elgar),
OLEG PROKOFIEV
(Estate of Sergei Prokofiev),
JOHN STRAVINSKY
(Estate of Igor Stravinsky),
ROSAMUND STRODE
(G. & I. Holst Limited),
MARTIN WILLIAMS
(The Frederick Delius Trust).
The Britten Estate Limited,
The Red House,
Aldeburgh, Suffolk.
July 28.

These two spoke out publicly in support of their publisher in another *Times* article, Birtwistle praising a 'thoroughly professional organisation' and MacMillan explaining that 'I chose them, ironically, because the name is synonymous with security. They take personal care of their composers. They discuss my work and what I'd like to do, advise me on performances and commissions, produce marvellous scores, turn out orchestral parts with amazing speed – a pop publisher would have no idea what is involved.'

This was really the main concern of the composers and the staff at B&H. External commentators made much of the need to keep the company as it had been established by Ralph Hawkes and LAB in one piece, rather than allow the instrument side to be bought by Selmer or Yamaha. The truth was, those in the music publishing division would not have been sorry to be released from what had often been a burdensome relationship with their instrumental partners. However, a united front was imperative at this delicate stage. If the two parts of the company had been sold off, the music publishing business could have been particularly vulnerable to unwelcome take-over.

Eventually, in May 1998, the crisis was resolved. B&H raised a staggering £33m by offering stock to 964,000 new and existing shareholders and bought out Carl Fischer Inc. Colleagues from all over the world sent messages of congratulations, including staff from Ricordi, UE and all B&H's old rivals, proving how tight and supportive the publishing fraternity really was. The ingenious solution was seen as a coup for chief executive Dick Holland. Despite the events of 1997/8, the company had performed remarkably well during his eight-year tenure: the share price had grown 20-fold and pre-tax profits were £7.7m in 1997. But the elation was short-lived. Within three years disaster struck in an unexpected quarter: Chicago.

The Libertyville Fraud

Since he took over in 1989 Dick Holland had been a high-profile and apparently successful CEO. The US instrument distribution company was now in Libertyville, near Chicago and appeared to be performing spectacularly well. Had Holland had his ear closer to the ground he might have got wind of the accounting irregularities. There were those like Richard Mackie and Michael Winter who had suspected the Chicago team of sharp practice for some time.

Indeed, when the extent of the deceptions was uncovered in 2000, it became clear that there had been fraudulent accounting for several years. And the sums involved were terrifying: in November a statement was issued declaring that an £11.9m write-down had to be made following the Chicago audit. By May 2001 the write-down had risen to £15m; in the end it was £20m. The directors responsible were dismissed but by the time they came to investigate the other members of staff, office records had been destroyed and computer disks wiped. The music publishing staff stood by, aghast, as their business was threatened once again by its own sister company. Fell felt that they should have gone to the banks as Asserson had done in the mid-eighties and faced them down, but the break-up of the company now seemed inevitable. 'The financial basis of the company had been irreparably weakened by the Carl Fischer buy-out, and when this debt hit us, we could not absorb it unharmed,' he admits. He is referring to the thirteen institutions that supported the 1998 buy-out, who were now getting distinctly cold feet, pushing for a quick sale and their assets back. The extent of the loss put B&H in breach of all its financial covenants, and all long-term debt could now be called in. Its share price had plummeted from 200p to 80p. From 2001 onwards, for over two years, a vote had to be taken at every board meeting to agree on whether B&H could continue trading.

It was perhaps the biggest wobble the company had ever faced. To the great credit of the music publishing staff, not a single composer was lost at this time: Susskind, Bilfield, Jacobs and their teams managed to instil a sense of calm confidence to the outside world. In fact, the publishing record during the early years of the millennium is extraordinary.

A millennium blossoming

The perception of Boosey & Hawkes as a publisher to which established composers aspired was reinforced when Mark-Anthony Turnage chose to leave Schott and come to B&H in 2003. It was a blow to Schott's London company, whose list was small and whose central composer, Michael Tippett, was now dead; but it was a huge boost to B&H to have yet another prestigious and highly productive British composer on their books, despite the fact that his earlier compositions remained with Schott. B&H Inc was also active during this troubled period, signing in 2000 the 'downtown' art composer Meredith Monk, and in 2001 the folk double bassist Edgar Meyer, who had worked extensively with Yo-Yo Ma and Joshua Bell. The following years saw new contracts with Aaron Jay Kernis, who had just won the

Mark-Anthony Turnage
(2002)
(Photo: Hanya Chlala/ArenaPAL)

Grawemeyer Award for his *Colored Field*, Tod Machover, the experimental musician who had produced the first 'computer' opera and created a new generation of computer 'super' instruments, and the much-performed Michael Daugherty. The Berlin office signed three very different voices: the radical Austrian composer Olga Neuwirth, whose work Boulez chose to perform in his major millennium world tour with the London Symphony Orchestra; the Australian Brett Dean, then a violist in the Berlin Philharmonic, whose full-length ballet *One of a Kind* for Jirí Kylián had caused a stir and whose work *Carlo*, inspired by Gesualdo, was espoused by Simon Rattle and has received over 60 performances since its premiere; and the young Dutch rising star Michel van der Aa, exploring the interface between music theatre and film.

BOOSEY & HAWKES

COPLAND 2000

Copland 2000 campaign design by Al Hirschfeld (1997)

But not all the promotion work centred on living composers. Staff met the challenge of two important anniversaries in 2000 and 2001 head on. The first was Copland's centenary, and the huge, 15-month-long multimedia retrospective became a model for all future such centennials. Jenny Bilfield, then heading the promotion team in New York, was a key player in galvanising the American performing world. Mayor Giuliani opened events by proclaiming 1 June 1999 as Aaron Copland Day, so launching the three-week 'Completely Copland' festival by the New York Philharmonic, followed by the Eos Ensemble's 'Celluloid Copland', an examination of his music for film. There were more than 600 concerts all over the world, from performances of the new edition of *The Tender Land* on farms in Minnesota to a Copland weekend from the BBC Symphony Orchestra at the Barbican. The net spread wider than the concert stage: American Airlines provided a two-hour Copland programme in their in-flight entertainment channel and Sony and BMG issued boxed sets of his complete works. Howard Pollack's new biography published by Henry Holt in the USA and Faber and Faber in Europe was just one of several publications, including the reissuing of Copland's autobiography with Vivian Perlis.

Aaron Copland was already a national institution, but the second centenary concerned a less well-known and sometimes neglected English composer, Gerald Finzi. He had been published by B&H since the early 1930s, but had perhaps always felt overshadowed by giants like Britten. In the late nineties Robert Gower of the Finzi Trust felt that the relationship with B&H had got into the doldrums and more could be done with active promotion. This was not merely special pleading: the Trust meant business, and brought in Henry Brown, an arbitration lawyer, to chair meetings between the two parties. The result was the rekindling of a lively collaboration in the three years leading up to the Finzi Centenary, which exceeded all expectations.

The figures speak for themselves: there were 450 performances of Finzi's works in 2001. Most were in the UK, but international highlights included the Japanese premiere of *Intimations of Immortality*, a Finzi Festival in Philadelphia and a documentary *With heart and voice* aired on 100 US radio stations. A B&H CD sampler, a centenary website and personal promotion brought about a year-on-year overall royalty growth of 125%, with sheet music sales growing by 40% and record sales, including new Finzi recordings by Naxos and Chandos, increasing by 57%. Most significantly, perhaps, the Wigmore Hall ran a series of five recitals, confirming Finzi's rightful place in the song repertoire, and involving some of the finest singers of our time, Bryn Terfel, Philip Langridge, Ian Bostridge, Mark Padmore, Christopher Maltman, Jonathan Lemalu, Gerald Finley and Thomas Allen. Living British composers, including Judith Weir and Colin Matthews, reached back to their forebear to orchestrate some of his songs, one of the most creative projects of the year.

Such promotional work is painstaking, requiring specialist knowledge, energy and powers of persuasion. Treading with confidence in the shoes of their predecessors, the staff of B&H once again quietly went about the business of making a big noise.

From public to private

After the events of 2001, Dick Holland was on his way out, though he oversaw the break-up and sale of the company over the next two years and retired in 2003. Fell had stepped down from the Board in 2001, and John Minch, who had run the directories division of Reed Business Information, was brought in to succeed Trevor Glover as the Managing Director of Music Publishing. Minch had been successful in transforming trade magazine brands and directories into effective on-line products, and the Board was convinced that it needed a 'dot.com' wizard in music publishing. In fact, Minch tried to persuade them it was not the obvious opportunity they had envisaged. But he was intrigued by the business and, provided he was given a place on the Board, agreed to take the job.

Arriving in the midst of the crisis in February 2001, Minch could not have started at a more 'interesting' point in the company's history. The full extent of the Chicago fraud had just been uncovered, and with the B&H share price having plummeted, the Group was vulnerable to takeover. That summer, Bob Wise of Music Sales, armed with capital from Fidelity, reappeared to make an offer for the music publishing business. He was in a strong position to deliver cost-savings, and many staff would have lost their jobs, including the management. At the same time, and in tandem, Graphite Capital, whose advisor was none other than Michael Boxford, bid for the instrument business. Boxford now worked for a venture capital firm but had never lost his sense of unfinished business at B&H. He still believed he could make the instrument companies work. When news of a bid reached the Stock Exchange, the ailing share price rose 50%.

John Minch (2003)
(Photo: Hilary Schedel/ArenaPAL)

Given the financial position of the Group, something had to be done, but the Board faced a dilemma. It could pursue exclusive discussions with the Music Sales/Graphite consortium or it could initiate a fully-fledged sale process, inviting in all suitors. It took the momentous decision to do the latter and put the whole group up for sale. The professional advisers recommended the sale of the instruments and publishing divisions separately, but no one predicted that the process would take over two years and would turn into one of the longest negotiations in corporate history.

Another period of nail-biting uncertainty gripped the offices worldwide. Minch remembers: 'I had to try to hold the publishing company together, to keep morale up and persuade senior people not to leave, that it *was* worth staying. I couldn't properly recruit anyone – we went through four finance directors between 2001 and 2003, but somehow we had to keep faith. It wasn't easy.'

After a 16-month-long series of negotiations which ended in February 2003, the private equity investors Rutland Fund Management bought the instrument business for £33.2m, renaming it The Music Group. Michael Winter, who had been head of the instrument division, stayed on with the new group and bought a stake in the company with two colleagues. The historic collection of brass and wind instruments was sold to the

Horniman Museum in London, where it still resides in gleaming splendour, taking centre-stage in an exhibition in 2006. But the instrument business was to be beset by challenges once again. Says Minch, 'The sale couldn't have happened at a worse time: with the instrument factories located in France and Germany, all their costs were in Euros, while their revenues were in, then weak, dollars. One year the group made an £8m loss; it's still a struggle.' The instrument group was subsequently broken up further, with the Rico reeds business sold and Buffet Crampon spun off to a management buy-out. The troubled UK brass instrument factory was ultimately closed in 2005.

Nevertheless, the Rutland buy-out did 'clear the way' at long last for the sale of the publishing division. As Minch said publicly at the time, from out of the wreckage of the instrument company, here was 'an absolute diamond of a publishing company'. He had already found an interested investor in Hg Capital, who had agreed in principle to back a management buy-out with him. But first of all there had to be an auction and many formal hoops to jump through, as required of public companies under Stock Exchange rules. Out of a field that included BMG, the Sanctuary Group, Music Sales, and two financial investors, Stirling Square, a new venture capital company, out-bid all suitors, including Hg Capital, and was given exclusivity to do due diligence. They brought in EMI as an 'invisible' partner in their bid. However, when it became clear that workable 'back-office' synergies did not really exist between the two companies – one pop, one classical – and that there were divergent views about the merger within EMI senior management, EMI was gradually 'eased out'.

While Stirling Square was grappling to make their financial model work without EMI, Hg Capital came back in October 2003 with an increased bid, heightening the competitive tension. As Dick Holland wrote to staff, 'All this feverish bid activity is obviously good for shareholders but is testing the patience of everybody who works here! I am hopeful that this process can be completed quickly and once again I would like to thank you all for your continued patience and loyalty.' Hg Capital had been observing the company closely for two and a half years and was confident that it was stable and profitable and that John Minch was the man to back. Finally, more than two long years after the group first went up for sale, the deal was done, with Minch leading a £74m management buy-out of the publishing division, financed to the tune of £45m by Hg Capital and two banks. There were six manager shareholders – Minch, Susskind, Jacobs, Bilfield, Andrew Gummer (a new business affairs director appointed by

Minch following Tony Pool's retirement) and Greg Smith, the finance director recruited by Hg Capital – and a share-holding established in trust for the staff. What had been a public limited company since the days of Geoffrey Hawkes and LAB was made private once more, to the relief of many. In a note to staff, Minch wrote: 'From any perspective, this must be the best possible ending to a very drawn out affair. B&H will remain independent and committed to publishing the very best in new music and to the imaginative and active promotion of our wonderful music catalogue. We could not and would not have fought to maintain our independence without the great support we have had from our composers, estates, partners and, above all, our exceptional and dedicated staff.'

By the beginning of 2004, John Minch was CEO of the newly private publishing company, and had his sights firmly set on growing the company's rights list and restructuring and streamlining its internal workings. Though at first he had been 'bewildered by this secret world with its foreign language', he soon found colleagues eager to coach him and initiate him in the ways of grand rights, mechanicals, hire libraries, and copyright assignments. With the focus now fixed on publishing and rights exploitation, Minch set out to divest the firm of all its non-core activities and develop a strategy for growth.

During the 'phoney war' years of the extended sale process, Minch had developed a relationship with Peter Hanser-Strecker, owner of the Schott publishing group with headquarters in Mainz, and they had hatched ideas about a number of initiatives. The world was shrinking: music publishers were under pressure and needed each other to keep afloat. The buzz words were 'outsourcing' and 'exploiting synergies'. Here was a partner who could help provide efficiencies and cost-savings without demanding equity in the company. Minch presented the plan to the Board in August 2001. 'It was going to save us £1.5m in costs. But everything had to be put on hold while the instrument company was sold.' Now in charge, Minch could finally implement all of the strands of his strategic plan.

First, the well-known Boosey & Hawkes Music Shop in Regent Street was sublicensed to Brittens Music, an established music retailer who soon moved the shop and staff to new premises in Wigmore Street. Having got out of 'bricks and mortar' retailing, B&H nonetheless retained control of its successful online music shop at www.boosey.com, forming a partnership with Music Exchange, a Manchester-based wholesaler who would manage stock, fill mail orders and provide customer service.

In June 2004, the strategic partnership with Schott was finally announced. Each company would provide certain services to the other, with both maintaining their creative independence and publishing programmes. Schott would be responsible for distributing, selling and marketing B&H sheet music everywhere except the Americas, Australia and New Zealand (territories covered under a parallel new deal between B&H Inc and Hal Leonard) while B&H would provide royalty accounting and copyright control services to Schott via their unique software programme. Having begun development during the mid-1980s, B&H had been in the vanguard of royalty processing software tailored for the complexities of classical music. Tony Fell had believed that because classical music publishing was such a 'penny packet' business, it was essential to automate and make failsafe the system by which income was traced, calculated and distributed. Sarah Davidson, then Finance Director, had headed up a review of the IT needs of the publishing group and had identified an established software package that could be adapted to deal with the specific needs of their business. It provides special reports, in-depth income analyses for composer estates, 'real-time' accounting and clear on-line records. By the late nineties all royalties were being processed centrally through the team in London, with dedicated 'royalty trackers' chasing missing income from myriad sources.

The final plank in the Schott/B&H alliance caused initial consternation in the music world and even prompted some press comment. B&H's mammoth London hire library, long ensconced in the basement of Regent Street and a magnet for conductors and musicians over the years, would be moved to Schott's new warehouse in Mainz. A small staff would remain in London to take orders and continue to provide familiar voices on the end of the phone to countless British performing groups, but no longer would casual visitors be able to wander in and browse through scores in the basement at will. The banks of heavy, rolling music shelves in the basement were emptied. They had seen many a secret assignation or a private tear shed over the years.

The new Boosey & Hawkes offices at Aldwych House, following the move from Regent Street in 2005.

Of course, it was a traumatic couple of years. Staff worldwide were reduced from 160 to 100, with many of these transferring to become employees of Schott and Brittens Music under the new agreements. The Australian office, which had previously handled musical instruments as well as publishing, was no longer economically viable after the sale of the instruments group and was closed in 2004. The biggest upheaval of all occurred in the spring of 2005 when the entire London staff moved out of 295 Regent Street and into new, open-plan offices in Aldwych. The new office was opened by Sir Peter Maxwell Davies in May 2005, who had recently become Master of the Queen's Music.

Epilogue

The 'keyboard' design can no longer be seen at the entrance to 295 Regent Street, but you can still observe people searching in vain for the shop that had stood there for more than 75 years. Decades of paper work and correspondence, old scores and recorded music tapes were dredged up out of the basement and put into new storage or removed. It is a brave and sometimes bracing new world at B&H, but there is no sense of shrinking or turning inwards. Growth of the business and catalogue is now the aim, with £10m earmarked for the acquisition of new lists and composers. In 2005 alone, B&H bought the French Jaune Citron catalogue, featuring popular pieces by Astor Piazzolla; the complete works of the late French-Canadian composer Claude Vivier; and the Czech catalogue, Tempo Prague. New-found confidence in promoting its classical music for use in TV, film and advertising has produced one of the fastest growing areas of the business, with extra staff recruited in London, New York and Berlin, engaged in making a persuasive case for the usage of classical music in the media. The 'mood music' library started by Ralph Hawkes in the 1930s continues to expand, with B&H's own Cavendish brand joined by Abaco, a newly-purchased American production library catalogue, and a state-of-the-art mixing studio constructed in Aldwych House. B&H Inc, honouring its American roots, is embarking on a new jazz adventure, signing Chick Corea and David Benoit and taking on representation of Second Floor Music, a historic jazz standards catalogue.

Hg Capital will eventually sell its stake in B&H. Having tested the market for a sale at the end of 2005, it found lively interest from many of the earlier suitors, including Music Sales and BMG, plus some new buyers backed by private equity. 'Rock meets Rachmaninov as Bono firm eyes Boosey & Hawkes' screamed the headline in *The Times*, referring to one of the private equity bidders whose backers included the Irish pop icon.

What *is* a publisher today? Autumn 2005 saw the launch of Booseytones, the new mobile phone ringtone website with several hundred downloadable melodies from the B&H catalogue, from John Adams to *The Archers'* theme tune. Ernst Roth might be turning in his grave, but the initiative fits the unchanged core strategy of disseminating music to as wide as possible an audience. In a hugely expanded music world, with a thousand-year repertoire available, the publisher's role is increasingly that of an expert adviser. 'We serve in a sort of artistic consulting role' Jenny Bilfield once explained. 'Sort of' speaks volumes: the music publisher is essentially back stage, a modest inspirator, a silent star. No artistic director or conductor would want to admit that a music publisher had devised their programme: but listen and look, the imprint can be felt, the reach, as Hawkes wanted it to be, *is* global.

Mozart with Bluetooth: image for Booseytones, launched in 2005

In the Depression and during the War, when commercial success was the only guarantor of survival, the artistic vision and brazen opportunism of Ralph Hawkes, Leslie Boosey and Ernst Roth ensured that the greatest composers were supported. In a post-War world where ideologically-driven subsidy threatened to distort and even block the path of serious music, the vision of a David Drew or a David Huntley helped bring the art form back to the people once again. In a brave new era where composers thought their computers could do it all for them, the sheer imagination, drive, expertise and dedication of the Boosey & Hawkes staff worldwide have been enough to persuade them otherwise. The most recent struggle to survive at the top is nothing short of heroic.

B&H may have historically followed in the wake of pioneers like Universal Edition, picking up talent from Schott, Chester, G Schirmer and UE itself, but it has usually had the money and the quality of staff to retain and nurture the very best composers with an unequalled level of care. Today the firm can be seen as a 'graduate school' for composers, somewhere to aspire to: once a house composer at B&H you know you have arrived, and there is a good chance your music will survive. As Steve Reich commented amidst his 70th birthday celebrations, 'I have been fortunate in so many ways. The bottom line is that I see the music existing, with or without me. That is the most a composer can hope for.'

But this nurturing relies on a staff with a sense of vocation, devoted to assisting composers and the promulgation of their music despite modest pay and little or no limelight. Ultimately, it is the music that drives them on, as they walk that tightrope between the profit and the prophets, guardians of the old, midwives of the new.

228

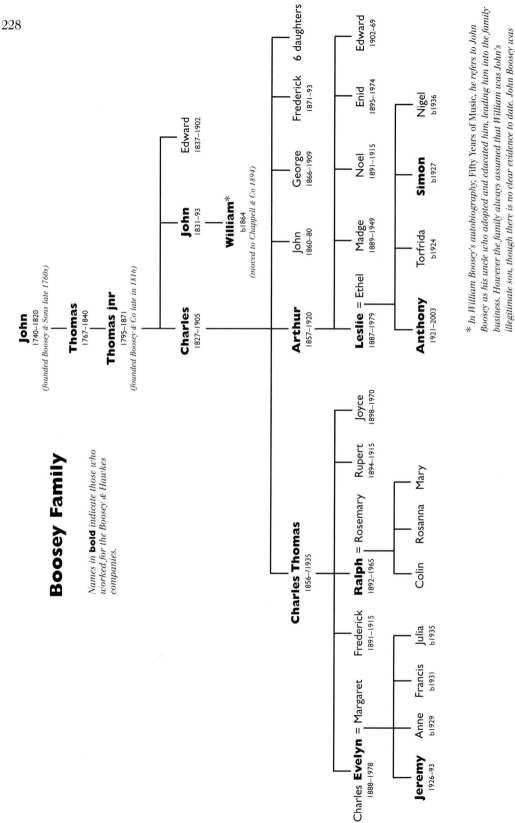

Boosey Family

*Names in **bold** indicate those who worked for the Boosey & Hawkes companies.*

John
1740–1820
(founded Boosey & Sons late 1760s)

Thomas
1767–1840

Thomas jnr
1795–1871
(founded Boosey & Co late in 1816)

Edward
1837–1902

Charles
1827–1905

John
1831–93

6 daughters

Frederick
1871–93

George
1866–1909

William*
b1864
(moved to Chappell & Co 1894)

John
1860–80

Edward
1902–69

Enid
1895–1974

Noel
1891–1915

Madge
1889–1949

Arthur
1857–1920

Leslie = Ethel
1887–1979

Nigel
b1936

Simon
b1927

Torfrida
b1924

Anthony
1921–2003

Charles Thomas
1856–1935

Joyce
1898–1970

Rupert
1894–1915

Ralph
1892–1965

= Rosemary

Mary

Rosanna

Colin

Frederick
1891–1915

Charles **Evelyn**
1888–1978

= Margaret

Julia
b1935

Francis
b1931

Anne
b1929

Jeremy
1926–93

* In William Boosey's autobiography, Fifty Years of Music, he refers to John Boosey as his uncle who adopted and educated him, leading him into the family business. However the family always assumed that William was John's illegitimate son, though there is no clear evidence to date. John Boosey was unmarried and a staunch member of the Sandemanians, a Christian sect founded by John Glas in 1730.

Hawkes Family

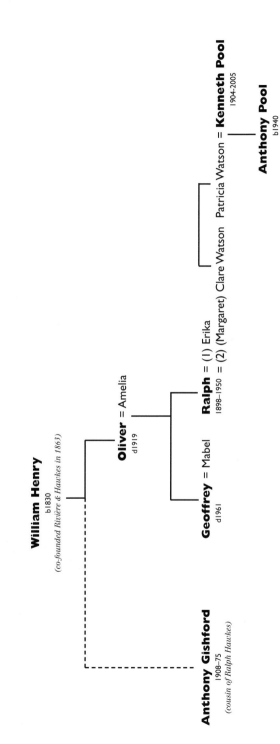

William Henry
b1830
(co-founded Rivière & Hawkes in 1863)

Oliver = Amelia
d1919

Geoffrey = Mabel
d1961

Ralph = (1) Erika
1898–1950
= (2) (Margaret) Clare Watson   Patricia Watson = **Kenneth Pool**
1904-2005

Anthony Pool
b1940

Anthony Gishford
1908–75
(cousin of Ralph Hawkes)

Blom, Eric. *Music in England* (London: Pelican, 1942)

Boosey, William. *Fifty Years of Music* (London: Ernest Benn Ltd, 1931)

Britten, Benjamin, ed Donald Mitchell, Phillip Reed and Mervyn Cooke. *Letters from a Life: Selected Letters and Diaries Vols. 1, 2 & 3* (London: Faber & Faber, 1991/2004)

Burton, Humphrey. *Leonard Bernstein* (London: Faber & Faber, 1994)

Carpenter, Humphrey. *Benjamin Britten* (London: Faber & Faber, 1992)

Carpenter, Humphrey. *The Envy of the World: Fifty Years of the BBC Third Programme and Radio 3* (London: Weidenfeld & Nicolson, 1996)

Ehrlich, Cyril. *Harmonious Alliance: A History of the Performing Right Society* (Oxford: Oxford University Press, 1989)

Ehrlich, Cyril. *The Music Profession in Britain since the Eighteenth Century: A Social History* (Oxford: Oxford University Press, 1985)

Eősze, László. *Zoltán Kodály: His Life in Pictures and Documents* (Budapest: Kossuth Printing House, 1982)

Ferguson, Howard and Hurd, Michael (ed). *Letters of Gerald Finzi and Howard Ferguson* (Woodbridge, Suffolk: Boydell Press, 2001)

Gillies, Malcolm. *Bartók Remembered* (London: Faber & Faber, 1990)

Hayes, Malcolm (ed). *The Selected Letters of William Walton* (London: Faber & Faber, 2002)

Heinsheimer, Hans. *Best Regards to Aida*, (New York: Alfred A Knopf, 1968)

Heinsheimer, Hans. *Fanfare for Two Pigeons* (New York: Doubleday & Co, 1952)

Heinsheimer, Hans. *Menagerie in F sharp* (New York: Doubleday & Co, 1947)

Hewett, Ivan. *Healing the Rift* (London: Continuum, 2003)

Keller, Hans. *Criticism* (London: Faber & Faber, 1987)

Kennedy, Michael. *Richard Strauss: Man, Musician, Enigma* (Cambridge: Cambridge University Press, 1999)

Kildea, Paul. *Selling Britten: Music and the Market Place* (Oxford: Oxford University Press, 2002)

Kostelanetz, Richard (ed). *Aaron Copland: A Reader: Selected Writings, 1923–1972* (New York: Routledge, 2003)

Lambert, Constant. *Music Ho!* (London: Hogarth Press, 1934)

Lebrecht, Norman. *Covent Garden: The Untold Story* (London: Simon & Schuster, 2000)

May, Thomas (ed). *The John Adams Reader* (Pompton Plains, NJ: Amadeus Press, 2006)

Mellers, Wilfrid. *Music and Society* (London: Dobson, 1946)

Mihule, Jaroslav. *Bohuslav Martinů* (London: Phaidon Press, 2000)

Mitchell, Donald. *Britten and Auden in the Thirties: The Year 1936* (London: Faber & Faber, 1981)

Mitchell, Donald. *Cradles of the New: Writings on Music 1951–91* (London: Faber & Faber, 1995)

Pollack, Howard. *Aaron Copland: The Life and Work of an Uncommon Man* (London: Faber & Faber, 2000)

Rorem, Ned. *Other Entertainment: Collected Pieces*
(New York: Simon and Schuster, 1996)

Roth, Ernst. *The Business of Music: Reflections of a Music Publisher*
(London: Cassell, 1969)

Schiff, David. *The Music of Elliott Carter*
(London: Eulenburg Books, 1983; rev. ed London: Faber & Faber, 1998)

Seabrook, Mike. *The Life and Music of Peter Maxwell Davies*
(London: Victor Gollancz, 1994)

Slezkine, Yuri. *The Jewish Century* (Princeton: Princeton University Press, 2004)

Snowman, Daniel. *The Hitler Emigrés* (London: Chatto & Windus, 2002)

Stein, Erwin. *Orpheus in New Guises* (London: Rockliff, 1953)

Stevens, Halsey. *The Life and Music of Béla Bartók*
(New York: Oxford University Press, 1953)

Stravinsky, Igor. Craft, Robert (ed). *Memories and Commentaries*
(New York: Doubleday & Co, 1960)

Stravinsky, Igor. Craft, Robert (ed). *Selected Correspondence Vols. 1, 2 & 3*
(London: Faber & Faber, 1982/1984/1985)

Walsh, Stephen. *Stravinsky: The Second Exile, France and America, 1934–1971*
(London: Jonathan Cape, 2006)

Articles & Sources

Boosey, Jeremy. *Beethoven, Bellini, Ballads and Bands*
(Boosey & Hawkes 150th Anniversary Supplement, 1966)

Boosey, Simon. *An appreciation of L.A.B.* (unpublished)

Cowan, Robert. *The London Ballet Concerts*
(Theatrephile Vol. 1 No. 4, September 1984)

Cowan, Robert. *The Sight of Music* (The Ephemera Society, *c*1980))

Articles in issues of *Tempo* 1940–2005 including:

Earl of Harewood. *Erwin Stein: 1885–1958* (Tempo No. 49, Autumn 1958)

Newman, George. *Ernst Roth: A Personal Recollection*
(Tempo No. 165, June 1988)

Roth, Ernst. *The Vision of Ralph Hawkes*
(Boosey & Hawkes 150th Anniversary Supplement, 1966)

Spinner, Leopold. *The Boosey & Hawkes production diaries*
(Royal College of Music)

Boosey & Hawkes Hire Library performance records (Royal College of Music)

Boosey & Hawkes Edgware newsletter 1950–1969

Boosey & Hawkes press review archive 1955–2005

Index

Page references in bold type indicate appearances only as illustrations

The abbreviation LAB is used for Leslie Boosey